Writing Across Worlds

Writing has always been a means of making crossings and forging connections between different worlds. However, some writers have found it hard to reach an international audience; for decades the Western literary establishment has been all too ready to sideline writers with mixed cultural or migrant backgrounds as 'marginal', 'multicultural' or simply 'other'. Since its foundation in 1984 the literary magazine *Wasafiri* has focused on the idea of the writer as someone who transports the imagination beyond the maps of narrowly defined borders, and has promoted a range of new and established voices as well as signposting new waves in contemporary literature worldwide.

To celebrate *Wasafiri*'s twentieth anniversary, *Writing Across Worlds* brings together a selection of interviews with major international writers previously featured in the pages of the magazine. Conducted by a wide constituency of distinguished critics, writers and journalists, the interviews offer a unique insight into the views and work of a remarkable array of acclaimed authors. They also chart a slow but certain cultural shift: those once seen as 'other' have not only won many of the Establishment's most revered literary prizes but have also become central figures in contemporary literature, writing across and into all of our real and imagined worlds.

With an introductory comment by Susheila Nasta, editor of *Wasafiri*, this collection is essential reading for all those interested in contemporary literature.

Susheila Nasta is a critic and broadcaster, the founding editor of *Wasafiri* and a distinguished academic. Currently Reader in Literature at the UK's Open University, she has published widely in the field of twentieth-century writing.

Writing Across Worlds

Contemporary writers talk

Edited by Susheila Nasta

Routledge
Taylor & Francis Group

LONDON AND NEW YORK

First published 2004
by Routledge
2 Park Square, Milton Park, Abingdon, Oxfordshire OX14 4RN

Simultaneously published in the USA and Canada
by Routledge
29 West 35th Street, New York, NY 10001

Routledge is an imprint of the Taylor & Francis Group

Editorial material and selection © 2004 Susheila Nasta

Interviews with Caryl Phillips, Kazuo Ishiguro, Michael Ondaatje,
Maggie Gee © Maya Jaggi

All other interviews © *Wasafiri*

Typeset in DIN and Minion by RefineCatch Limited
Printed and bound in Great Britain by
MPG Books Ltd, Bodmin

British Library Cataloguing in Publication Data
A catalogue record for this book is available from the British Library

Library of Congress Cataloging in Publication Data
Writing across worlds: contemporary writers talk/edited by Susheila Nasta.
    p. cm.
Includes bibliographical references.
1. Authors–Interviews.   I. Nasta, Susheila.
PN452. W75 2004
809–dc22   2004002923

ISBN 0-415-34566-9 (hbk)
ISBN 0-415-34567-7 (pbk)

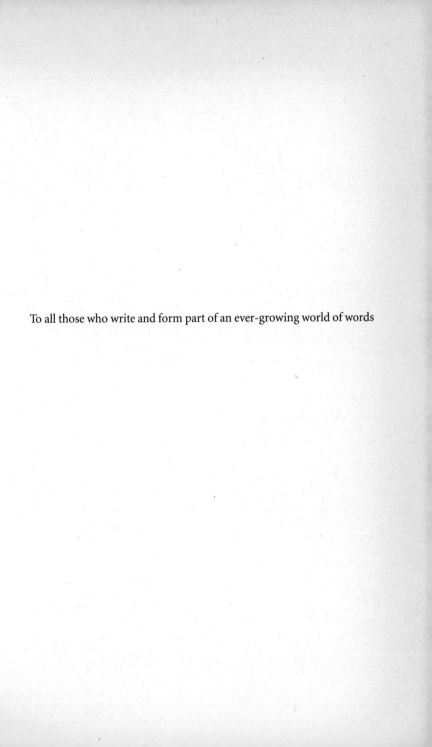

To all those who write and form part of an ever-growing world of words

Contents

Acknowledgements

This book celebrates twenty years in the history of *Wasafiri*. The magazine's survival since 1984 has been dependent on the generous support of a number of different institutions and funding bodies including, first of all, the University of Kent, and more recently the Arts Council of England, London Arts, the School of English and Drama, Queen Mary College (where it has been housed since 1992) and the Open University. My thanks go to all of these different bodies, which have enabled the financial and material survival of the magazine in different ways. Publication could not have been sustained, however, without the hard work of the many people who have been connected with the magazine for the past twenty years. Day-to-day editorial tasks and subscription management have worked only because of the labour and dedication of the editorial staff, who have struggled, often against the odds, to ensure publication, distribution and sales.

Invaluable advice has also always been provided by a committed editorial board of internationally distinguished writers and critics. Many have guest-edited special issues, read copy, introduced new writers and are also amongst the contributors to this book. I am particularly grateful as far as this celebratory birthday volume is concerned to all the writers interviewed, for their generous help with reviewing, editing and updating some of the material, as well as to those who revised material or provided new interviews at short notice. My thanks also go to all who have provided *Wasafiri* with interviews which took place live at conferences, cultural events or radio broadcasts, or were commissioned for special issues of the magazine. I am particularly grateful to Maya Jaggi for licensing us to print edited transcriptions of her well-known discussions with award-winning writers, the Arts Council for the interview with V. S. Naipaul at the time of the award of the first David Cohen Prize and for Naipaul's acceptance speech and Gretchen Holbrook Gerzina, host of the *Book Show* (a US radio programme recorded at WAMC, New York) for the interview with Zadie Smith. The AHRB Centre for African and Asian Literatures at SOAS, University of London has also been very generous in the past few years in working collaboratively with us.

Many individuals on our editorial board have given up valuable time to assist with the selection process for this book, particularly Lyn Innes, Louis James, Bernardine Evaristo, Robert Fraser and Laura Chrisman. Its publication would not have been possible at all however without the assistance of Fiona Cairns and Liz Thompson at Routledge, who enabled the transcription of much of the new material and generally speeded up the editorial process. And many many thanks are also due to Glenda Pattenden and Nisha Jones, who worked well beyond the bounds of duty in the *Wasafiri* office, as well as Richard Dyer, Managing Editor, who enabled us to carry on.

The publishers would like to thank Lyn Innes and Rod Edmond, editors of *Postcolonial Literatures*, for bringing this volume to their attention. The *Postcolonial Literatures* series is published by Routledge, in collaboration with the Centre for Colonial and Postcolonial Studies at the University of Kent at Canterbury.

Introduction

Is only those who take chance with land and water, who go far from home and roam world views, who stretch distance with foot, who for ever making home out of homelessness and drift, no matter what, that can see what Anancy seeing, here, right now.

(Andrew Salkey, from *Anancy Traveller*)

When we speak of the best contemporary writing in English today, we must inevitably refer to a diverse body of literature deriving from all over the globe and written in different forms of the English tongue. As with Anancy, the familiar trickster figure who frequently leaps across the Middle Passage, the language has shifted its shapes whilst simultaneously becoming a mouth for many worlds. This is not to suggest that we now exist contentedly in some form of a literary McDonald's, a global village where despite the fact that cultures jangle, everyone tastes the same food and enjoys the same palatably bland, if 'exotic', menu. Any serious discussion of the internationalization of English as a literary language in the past century would need to show that whilst a long history of empire successfully took that language elsewhere, ownership of it has long ceased to reside in the 'sceptred isle'. And although it cannot be disputed that much writing in English today derives from histories linked, at least in part, to Britain's colonial past, the plural nature of its voices and imaginative range are not contained by that past. Such observations may be obvious to readers familiar with the work of some of the distinguished international writers interviewed in this book. Nevertheless, despite the wide-ranging and often cross-cultural concerns of many of these writers, the literary establishment in Britain has persistently tended either to package those from mixed cultural or migrant postcolonial backgrounds into the convenient pockets of separate national traditions or alternatively to stitch them together according to racial derivation or country of origin, regardless of specific histories or individual preoccupations. Consequently the so-called 'colonial', 'Commonwealth' or 'postcolonial' links of these writers are heightened and the often significant differences between them subsumed by a reviewing practice that misleadingly levels out important contextual issues of history, politics, generation or location.

A similar picture emerges if one looks at the history of the reception of literary works by African, Caribbean or South Asian writers within Britain. These writers have for many years formed part of Britain's large and heterogeneous multicultural population, but are too frequently sidelined as figures who speak only to minority ethnic interests. Hence, aesthetics always play second fiddle to politics as such writers are seen to be driven primarily by questions of cultural identity, race or class. Although much lip service has recently been paid to Britain as model of a post-imperial plural society, a society in which cultural differences can co-exist and transform the dominant status quo, it is clear that writers who are assumed not to form a natural part of the mainstream remain in a peripheral position, designated as ambassadors not of the whole story, but of another story, tellers of tales which belong elsewhere. As Caryl Phillips notes in *The European Tribe* (1987), describing his own schooling in 1970s' Britain: 'I was never offered a text that had been penned by a black person, or that concerned the lives of black people. . . . If the teaching of English literature can feed a sense of identity then I, like many of my . . . contemporaries . . . was starving.'

This is of course not just a British story, as is obvious if one examines the history of African-American or Chicano writing in the United States or the ways in which Aboriginal, Maori or so-called 'multicultural' writers are so often separated off from the mainstream in Australia, New Zealand or Canada. It has always been difficult in any context to be comfortable with the creation of literary canons which, by their very nature, attempt to define and locate, include or exclude. Such 'pigeon-holing' prevents the development of an open literary community which can move beyond the perpetuation of the narrow stereotypes by which most modern nations have attempted to protect their borders in opposition to an imagined 'other', however that 'other' has been variously defined. This experience was also combined for many with the experience of growing up under the still lingering influence of a British colonial system, a system which had transported its invented national canon all over the globe. As many writers featured in this volume have frequently noted, William Wordsworth's poem 'Daffodils' or Charles Dickens's London were more familiar to them than the landscapes outside their own windows.

There is of course a long history behind this marginalization of writers from mixed cultural backgrounds, that is not possible to detail here. Perhaps the main point that should be made if we take the case of Britain is that most writers who arrived in the post-war period differed little in their expectations from earlier generations of white immigrant writers such as American-born T. S. Eliot or Polish-born Joseph Conrad. Many came, often from middle-class and partially Westernized cultural backgrounds, with the same aspirations: to expand the horizons of their work in what they imagined to be a larger cosmopolitan literary world. Yet the new forms and languages they brought with them and the innovative modernity of their work was seldom recognized. Instead, their writing was either seen by metropolitan critics to be derivative (due to borrowings from their colonial pasts), or alternatively regarded as over -concerned with cultural experiences that had no place within the European canon.

There are of course exceptions to this rule, as was apparent in 1981 when previously little-known writer Salman Rushdie won the Booker Prize for his novel *Midnight's Children*. This moment in the history of the prize began to make more visible vibrant writing from 'outsiders' or migrants *within* Britain such as Kazuo Ishiguro, Timothy Mo, Caryl Phillips, Ben Okri, Abdulrazak Gurnah and Romesh Gunesekera (all shortlisted authors or winners of the prize in later years) as well as many others who preceded or have followed them. A similar impact was made in a different way with the publication in 1990 of Hanif Kureishi's *The Buddha of Suburbia*, the first novel to supposedly herald diversity and create the possibility of imagining a different kind of mixed-race Englishman, half-Pakistani, half-white, 'born and bred' in this country, 'almost'. This desire to valorize works by Britain's apparently 'new' breed of black and Asian writers is a trend which has continued, with influential first novels like Ravinder Randhawa's *A Wicked Old Woman* (1987), Diran Adebayo's *Some Kind of Black* (1996), Meera Syal's *Anita and Me* (1996, now a film), Zadie Smith's *White Teeth* (2001) and Monica Ali's *Brick Lane* (2003). Some have optimistically seen such shifts as evidence that perceptions of what constitutes contemporary British writing has finally begun to change. After all, this new generation has clearly moved centre stage, reinvented 'Englishness' and eroded what seemed previously to be the impassable boundaries of culture, race and class.

However, the fashionable media visibility of such works only teases the edges of a much bigger story. It is a story that goes back several centuries. In fact the so-called national canon has always been built from the influence of 'outsiders', even if they have at times been seamlessly co-opted into it. If we go back only as far as the 1950s, we can find the 'mother-country' being colonized in reverse by the experimentations of a number of talented West Indian writers who represented Britain through different eyes. Included amongst them were V. S. Naipaul, Sam Selvon, George Lamming, Wilson Harris, Beryl Gilroy and Andrew Salkey, now all major award-winning international figures. Looking further back, well before the 1950s, Britain was already 'home' to a number of other influential literary migrants such as Mulk Raj Anand, C. L. R. James, Jean Rhys, Tambimuttu, Una Marson, Raja Rao, Aubrey Menen, G. V. Desani and Attia Hosain. Interestingly, however, only a handful of indigenous white writers have addressed issues of migrancy and cross-culturalism within Britain, including Colin MacInnes, in his 1957 novel about West Indian immigration, *City of Spades*, and more recently Marina Warner's *Indigo* (1992) or Maggie Gee's *The White Family* (2001). As Marina Warner intimates in her interview with Robert Fraser in this book, certain histories were always hidden from her. Her own family's denial of aspects of its West Indian planter past was one of the things that provoked her to examine the nature of what she likens in *Signs and Wonders* (2003) to a 'theft', a 'foundation act of empire', and to explore her resulting cultural inheritance.

In his interview with poet Fred D'Aguiar, Wilson Harris discusses the vital significance of a cross-cultural perspective, which he sees as crucial to the modern world as well as the latent source of all imaginative truths. Similarly Warner reveals her view that the illuminations provided by such cultural crossings have always been the food of literary and mythical transformations, now or in the ancient world. This is a theme also taken up in the conversation published here with Nobel-winning Nigerian writer Wole Soyinka, who has drawn on the myths and religions of several different cultures in his work, discovering links and parallels between them.

Most readers will be familiar with the names of some of the writers who are in dialogue in this book. Fewer may be familiar with the literary magazine, *Wasafiri*, in which many of these conversations were first published. In bringing together some of the contemporary world's most exciting and distinctive literary voices, this book celebrates twenty years of *Wasafiri*, a magazine which has focused, since its inception, on the figure of the writer as cultural traveller, moving words/worlds across cultures and transporting the imagination beyond the maps of narrowly defined borders. The name of the magazine derives from 'traveller' in the East African language Kiswhahili. As a hybrid offshoot itself from the Arabic 'safari', it was originally chosen to draw attention to the way in which writing has always been a form of cultural travelling, a means of transporting words into other worlds, of making crossings and forging connections between apparently conflicting worlds. Such literary crossings are not new, though perhaps in the context of the mass migrations of the late twentieth century – whether enforced or voluntary – the nature and perspectives of the voyages are. It has perhaps always been accepted that literature provides a passport to imaginary worlds previously unseen, that it can unlock doors and ask questions which sometimes undermine official histories. As such, creative works can not only alter lives but perhaps provide both readers and writers with a bigger window on the world, a wider-angled lens which can shift perceptions as well as the shapes and contours of that world in the process.

Since it was founded in 1984 in Britain, *Wasafiri* has given particular prominence to the work of writers whose literary and historical preoccupations do not necessarily fit within the confining national rubrics of any particular movement, tradition or culture, and whose perspectives have been cross-cultural. As one of the few publications to have provided sustained and serious exposure to several generations of African, Caribbean, South Asian and black British writers in Britain, it has not only charted an important cultural and literary history but has also effected curriculum change, signposting new waves and connections in the related literary community worldwide. The journey of this magazine is inevitably only a small one within the wider context of the worlds of some of the writers published within its pages, but its long-standing commitment to making the work of all these writers more visible and creating a forum for an ongoing discussion between them has been extremely important.

The magazine's task has not always been an easy one, however. Despite the fact that *Wasafiri*'s aim has always been to position the work of its often distinguished contributors as part of the mainstream, as crucial makers and shifters in the world of contemporary writing today, it has often, like some of the writers themselves, been marginalized. As one reviewer sarcastically put it in a 1990 *Times Literary*

Supplement review of an exhibition of small-circulation arts magazines then running at London's South Bank Centre:

> The old style aesthetic challenges to the accepted order (*vers libre*, stream of consciousness, graphic description of sexual acts) are being replaced by political ones. The style revolutionaries of today are the feminist artists, the black artists . . . demanding attention as much by their political condition as by their works.

The point being made here is that in contrast to the traditional role that literary magazines such as the *Transatlantic Review* (quoted by the *TLS* reviewer as an example) played in the past, as vital organs spearheading new artistic movements (such as modernism in the early twentieth century), the role of publications like *Wasafiri* is to be deemed less significant, since they are concerned with issues of race and culture, rather than those of 'pure' literary aesthetics. *Wasafiri* was then further condemned in the same article for depriving other 'more serious' literary causes of mainstream public funding from the Arts Council coffers. This was somewhat ironic, given the fact that two weeks previously the *TLS* had devoted an entire issue to 'Commonwealth' writing as an important new wave in contemporary world literature and had featured many of the same writers that *Wasafiri* had published over the years. This kind of double-think and double-speak represents the nature of the literary culture in Britain with which *Wasafiri* has had to contend. And although in the past few years a popular interest in literary prizes combined with the globalization of the publishing industry have drawn the diversity of contemporary writing to the attention of a much wider international readership, many unanswered questions still linger, questions that remain indissolubly linked to the perpetuation of stark global inequalities, old and new imperial histories, as well as the ever-present realities of race and class.

The interviews selected for publication in this volume represent a number of different literary voices, genres and cultural contexts. As such they move words not only across worlds but across generations and different histories. They have been arranged chronologically in order to create the sense of what is still an ongoing dialogue, a dialogue which in fact (as we learn from the writers' frequent cross-references) moves backwards and forwards in time and also maps the process of a history in the making. Within this framework, discussions about individual books are located within their appropriate contexts but also have wider reverberations. Often such conversations occurred soon after the award of a literary prize, the publication of a book, or following a specific cultural event or anniversary, such as the celebrations in 1998 marking fifty years since the docking of *SS Windrush* in Tilbury, a moment which, for many, signalled the beginning of the mass migrations which were to transform the face of post-imperial Britain. In these cases the material focuses particularly on the relevance or significance of that prize or event, as is the case in the interview between Alastair Niven, then director of the Arts Council, and V. S. Naipaul, just before Naipaul was awarded the David Cohen Prize for a life's work as a 'British' writer. Others reveal illuminating affinities between the writers themselves and illustrate the ways in which many of them already know each other through a sea of stories which they share. In some cases, chains of influence are made explicit, as is apparent in David Dabydeen's namings of his literary 'fathers' Sam Selvon, V. S. Naipaul and Wilson Harris. In other instances, readers will be able to trace their own patterns of development or affiliation – whether it is the recognition of a tradition of South Asian diasporic writing, or a link between Sam Selvon's London as a black city of words and the contemporary postcolonial cities of Monica Ali and Zadie Smith. The conversation between Caryl Phillips and George Lamming reveals how both writers are concerned with the retrieval of unspoken histories and the crossings of the black Atlantic, an issue explored from a different historical and cultural perspective by both Michael Ondaatje and Abdulrazak Gurnah.

The intention behind this selection has not been to provide a comprehensive coverage. In fact these interviews represent less than half of all the conversations that have been published in *Wasafiri* since it first appeared in 1984. In addition, due to the magazine's strategic agenda within the political context of Britain in the 1980s and 1990s, more emphasis has perhaps been given to writers with links to Africa, the Caribbean and South Asia, although this has certainly not been the only focus, as is apparent from the dialogues with Keri Hulme, Kazuo Ishiguro, Maxine Hong Kingston, Maggie Gee and Marina Warner.

There are many points of convergence and disagreement. Some writers discuss the value of transnationalism; others stress the importance of the local. For some, like Amit Chaudhuri, a migration from Bengal to Bombay has been as complicated in cultural terms as any larger journey. Many focus on the need to combat oppressive political regimes, others emphasize the experience of exile and the need to constantly create new landscapes and literary terrains which give voice to previously silenced histories. What is clear, however, from all of the interviews is the eclectic and international range of the material that writers have drawn on in creating their works. Very important too is the observation that Michael Ondaatje makes when talking with *Guardian* journalist Maya Jaggi, quoting John Berger, 'never again will a single story be told as if it were the only one'. For as the majority of the writers in this book make plain, modernity has never been written only from within the European body. Although all may, metaphorically speaking, be 'immigrants' in that 'every time you write a new novel you're coming to another place' (Ondaatje), the literary journeys that have been made are often very different ones. Whilst many have been subject to the realities of moving from one continent to another, others, like Ngugi wa Thiong'o, have had to tackle head on the complex politics of living in a global world caught between languages that are often unequal. As George Lamming puts it in his interview with Caryl Phillips:

> there is no part of the planet that can now escape the triumph of modernity. What each culture has to try and do is to find how it incorporates modernity into whatever it imagines its specific destiny to be . . . modernity and modernization can be seen as a

metaphorical extension of Prospero ... this simply cannot be killed off. The great challenge is how that is to be incorporated in what you conceive to be your specific and special cultural space. So Prospero is not simply the old imperialist. In fact, he comes up now, if you take the technological society, in new and more sinister forms ... [as] the most absolute of all the dictatorships we have known.

It might seem, in the new millennium, that we live in an increasingly frontierless world: a world made smaller and more accessible by the aeroplane, global communications and new technologies. However, it is also increasingly a world, as the events of September 11 and their aftermath have made plain, where the aeroplane, once a symbol of freedom for writers like Virginia Woolf, has become an icon of fear, a world where the borders of nations are shutting down, restricting freedoms of movement and blocking access to those new 'barbarians' deemed unsuitable for entry at their doors. In such a world, the role of the writer in writing across worlds, of asking questions and creating affinities across often impassable barriers of prejudice and thought, is not only vital but urgent. Yet as many of the experiences of writers in this book testify, the right to freedom of speech often puts them on dangerous ground. When Salman Rushdie participated in the interview published here, he was still under the fatwa of the Ayatollah Khomeini issued against him in 1988 with a charge of 'blasphemy' for his novel *The Satanic Verses*. Wole Soyinka and Ngugi wa Thiong'o, both of whom were denied the right of freedom of speech and detained at different times in their own countries (Nigeria and Kenya respectively), also discuss the difficulties facing writers who speak out against the grain. Nadine Gordimer elaborates further on the question of politics and the difficulties confronting the creative writer when commenting here on her experience of staying on in South Africa during the harsh years of the apartheid regime. And as Maxine Hong Kingston tells us, it is only recently that she was imprisoned for reciting her 'Woman Warrior' poem at a rally in Washington DC against the Iraq War.

It has often been said that the world of the writer is a private one and that the act of writing is a solitary activity which takes place between one person and the words they write on the page. Yet, as Salman Rushdie once put it, the world of literature is also the one place 'in any society where, within the secrecy of our own heads, we can hear *voices talking about everything in* every *possible way'*. The complexity, vitality and new horizons offered by these voices are revealed in this collection of conversations, which took place between a wide constituency of writers, critics and journalists published in the pages of *Wasafiri* over the past twenty years.

Susheila Nasta

Sam Selvon

with

Susheila Nasta

Sam Selvon's fiction, published between 1950 and the mid-1980s when he left Britain to live in Canada, was a milestone in the history and development of Caribbean and black British literature. Frequently described as the father of 'black writing' in Britain, a 'natural philosopher' and 'alchemist of language', Selvon was one of a group of now-distinguished writers who arrived in Britain from the Caribbean during the 1950s. Whilst in Britain, Selvon wrote ten novels set both in Trinidad and London, and was a frequent contributor to BBC Radio, author of several radio plays as well as co-author of the screenplay for Pressure, *directed by Horace Ove in 1975.*

Selvon's London works, which include the collection of short stories Ways of Sunlight *(1957),* The Housing Lark *(1965) and the 'Moses' novels* The Lonely Londoners *(1956),* Moses Ascending *(1975) and* Moses Migrating *(1983), span a crucial period in the literary and cultural history of black Britain. His experimentations with language and form in his London works were to be a major influence on a later generation of writers as he lifted his immigrant characters out of the stereotypical strait-jackets imposed on them and created an alternative way of seeing and reading that world. Selvon's city is a mongrel city, a mishmash of languages, people and identities jangling with each other and vying for a place. It is a world which anticipated by many years the literary visions of a multicultural and postcolonial London created in works such as Salman Rushdie's* The Satanic Verses, *Diran Adebayo's* Some Kind of Black *or Monica Ali's* Brick Lane.

The interview was first broadcast on BBC Radio 3 following the publication of Moses Migrating.

Susheila Nasta The central figure in this group of novels, which spans about thirty years, is called Moses and we first meet him in *The Lonely Londoners*. How did you come to create Moses?

Sam Selvon Well, I think I wanted to have a voice belonging to the old generation, the first immigrants who came to this country [in the 1950s] and Moses is representative I think. He came as an immigrant, he went through all the experiences that he relates, he typifies to my mind all that happened among that older generation and he also spoke in the voice, in the idiom of the people. I think that in spite of all his presumptions to be English, that he still remains basically a man from the Caribbean, and that this comes out in the way he relates all the experiences that happen to him and through using this identical voice which is so much a part of the West Indian immigrant.

But he also seems, despite the fact that he's part of this group, almost as his name suggests, like a prophet; he's looking forward, into the future, he's looking in from the outside at the community he's describing and in *Moses Ascending* he's trying to be a writer. Do you identify with Moses at all yourself as a writer?

Well, I have had very many similar experiences as Moses describes. I have been around with the boys. I have 'limed' with them, I have had experiences that are very comparable, I have heard stories from them, and the creation of this character is really and truly based on a true-life man from Trinidad. And as I say, it seemed to me that the only way to give expression to what happened to the original immigrant was by using this idiom, this language form that he brought with him. There was no other way. I tried to write *The Lonely Londoners* in Standard English and it just would not work, and when I got into the Trinidad way of speaking the whole thing seemed to flow so easily and everything seemed to come to life. This idiom is so much a part of the people, so much a part of the characteristics of the people, that you cannot separate a language from the experiences.

In *The Lonely Londoners* we have all these people in Moses' room and they all keep talking to him. I think you say at one point that they are like voices in the wilderness crying out to him for guidance. Who are all these people, who are all these characters that Moses knows and why are they together?

Well, these are all people from the various West Indian islands. You see when this immigration happened, for the first time the Trinidadian got to know the Jamaican or the Barbadian, because in the islands themselves the communications were so bad that they never really got in touch with one another, they never got to know what happened in other islands. And it was only when they all came to London that this turned out to be a kind of meeting place where the Jamaican met the Trinidadian and the Barbadian and they got to know one another, they got to identify in a way as a people coming from a certain part of the world. Not so much as islanders, no, but as black immigrants living in the city of London. And so they got together, and it's a very strange thing that they had to move out of their own part of the world, and it was only when they came to London that this kind of identity happened to them.

What effect did this have on the West Indies?

Well, in a way this kind of unity of the islanders that happened in London reflected back to the Caribbean to some extent I think. And even people down there in that part of the world began to think of, at least of the immigrants who had travelled all this way into London, that they had all come from one part of the world. I think in this way it helped to make all the islanders feel as if they all belonged to one region of the world.

There's even a Nigerian character, isn't there, in *The Lonely Londoners* who gets drawn into this general sort of West Indian world that you've created?

Yes, yes, all the blacks living in London were thrown together. For the first time West Indians were in contact with people from Africa who were black like themselves, and it was a strange kind of experience because they were all away from their homeland and this thing was happening to them way up in London so far away from their own homes. But it helped in a way to form a kind of feeling of community and this is why they always tended to get together and talk about their troubles and relate incidents that happened to them.

So were they brought together in a sense by their own exile, their own isolation?

I think this is what basically caused the whole thing, yes.

Towards the end of *The Lonely Londoners* we have a very powerful image of Moses sitting in his basement room and all the voices of the 'boys' ringing out and he is listening to their stories about this and that, the 'ballad of the episode'. They have these get-togethers every Sunday morning but nothing really seems to be happening; the characters keep saying, 'What happening, what happening?' but there's no direction, and Moses himself seems to see this gap and to reflect on it. So what happens to Moses in his basement?

Well, eventually Moses does manage to save up enough money so that he buys a house. It is a dilapidated house, it's one of those houses that is almost collapsing, which is really the only kind of property that black immigrants were allowed to buy. And Moses manages to get one of these and he's feeling pretty chirpy with himself now because he's no longer a tenant, he's a landlord as he states himself twenty years later in *Moses Ascending:* 'After all these years paying rent, I had the ambition to own my own property in London, no matter how ruinous or dilapidated it was. If you are a tenant, you catch your arse forever, but if you are a landlord, it is a horse of a different colour.'

But Moses eventually ends up almost like a tenant in his own house. I mean he has these 'Pakis' who come to stay and the Black Power Party taking over the basement and then Bob and Jeannie take over his own flat, 'the penthouse', and he has to move out of it. So his house in the end seems to be taken over by the blacks, by the new generation of immigrants, not just West Indians but Pakistanis and everybody else.

Well, in the third novel of the trilogy, *Moses Migrating*, he finally makes up his mind that he's going to return to Trinidad and he gets back there where he stays in a hotel. He has to stay in a hotel room. And he is there in Trinidad, he looks around, he's casing the joint, he isn't quite sure whether he's going to stay in Trinidad or not, he still has the feeling that he belongs to Britain. In fact what he does is he sets himself up as a goodwill ambassador, who is going down to the islands to tell people that things are not really as bad in Britain as they have been reading about. All these stories about how the economy is falling right down and there are millions of jobless people and Britain is falling on the rocks. He is setting himself up as a kind of champion for Britain and he goes down there determined to try and tell people that Britain still rules the waves as it were.

So does Moses feel like a stranger in his own country, a West Indian Londoner in Trinidad? After all, he has been away from the island for nearly thirty years.

This is exactly how he feels, and these are some of the incidents that happen to him while he is down there in the island.

So he moves from a basement in *The Lonely Londoners* to a metaphorical attic in *Moses Ascending* and then back down to the basement when Bob and Jeannie take it over; then back to Trinidad in *Moses Migrating* to the 'upside-down' world of his hotel room in the Trinidad Hilton. What does he do at the end of *Moses Migrating*?

Well, he looks around at the scene in Trinidad. He thinks, 'Well I don't know, I'm not quite sure what I'm going to do here, you know, and I'm wondering what's going to happen to me now I've turned my back on Britain completely and what will happen if I try to get back in', and in fact he does take a plane and he lands up at Heathrow at the end of the book. He stands there and he faces the customs officer and the customs officer takes his papers and has a look at them and tells him 'Just wait a minute here' and that's how the novel ends.

So we're left there with Moses waiting, we don't really know where he's going.

That's exactly so. He gets back to the gates of Britain and he knocks on the door and I end the book right there.

Most of your London novels seem to be concerned either in fantasy or reality with this movement from Trinidad to London and now we have a Moses who is migrating back to Trinidad. What about you yourself? I mean you came to London in the 1950s and you stayed here until 1978 and you're now living in Canada. How did you find this experience yourself?

Well, I spent so many years in Britain taking in English culture and European traditions, that I felt I wanted to get back to the Western hemisphere really. It didn't matter so much whether I got back to the

Caribbean or the United States or Canada or Latin America for that matter. It's just that I wanted to get back to that part of the world. I had personally spent almost half my lifetime in Britain and I wanted to get back and see what was happening on the other side of the world. And this is really why I moved on. And in fact what happened during the years later on was that most of the writers who lived in Britain had already left. I guess I must have been one of the last ones to leave. All the other writers like Lamming and Salkey and others, they had already left Britain, I was about the last one to leave.

And how do you find your experience in Canada?

Well, I haven't regretted it. I am seeing Western culture really for the first time, which I had left as a much, much younger man. And now I think that my thoughts are working along different lines and that I am in touch there with things that are happening in the Caribbean. In a strange way I happen to be geographically living much further away from Trinidad than I did in London, but there is a great deal of Caribbean atmosphere in the United States and in Canada, which I find stimulating and which I want to get working into parts of a new book.

Why is there this Caribbean atmosphere in Canada? Were there a large number of people who emigrated to Canada at the same time as they came to Britain?

I think so, I think immigration has been happening to Canada for a number of years. People haven't been talking very much about it. But the fact is that the Caribbean is in that part of the world and many people have been going to the States and many more to places like Canada. So that there is a feeling there that is a new world feeling, whereas living in Britain was an old world feeling. So this is really what I went over there to try and get back into. And living in Canada, which is a developing country, I feel almost part of going along with the development, whereas in England I felt that there was already so much tradition established here, that I was imposing on it, whereas in Canada I feel I am actually helping to build it.

Sam Selvon died in 1994 on a trip 'home' to Trinidad.

Wole Soyinka
with
Mary David

Since his first emphatic emergence on the literary scene in Nigeria in 1960 – the year of the nation's independence – Wole Soyinka has successfully combined the roles of dramatist, actor, director, novelist, poet, memorialist, critic and agent provocateur. His policy of deliberate non-alignment during the Civil War of 1966–71 landed him in prison for several months in Kaduna and Lagos, an experience that he described in his memoir The Man Died *(1972), and he has since maintained an unremitting resistance to the corruption and oppression of a number of regimes. Other phases of his lively and alert existence have been covered in successive volumes of near-autobiography: in* Aké: The Years of Childhood *(1981), in the part-fictional* Isara: A Voyage Around Essay *(1990), and in* Ibadan: The Penkelemes Years *(1994). Early in his career Soyinka published two novels:* The Interpreters *(1965) was a fictional account of his generation, and* Season of Anomy *(1973) an allegory of civil conflict. But it is as a playwright that he is mostly known to the world at large. Rejected by an official committee,* A Dance of the Forests *(1960) was an alternative to the formal Nigerian independence celebrations, and he has since produced and published over fifteen plays, notably* The Road *(1965),* Kongi's Harvest *(1965),* Madmen and Specialists *(1971),* A Play of Giants *(1984) and* A Scourge of Hyacinths *(1992).*

Soyinka was awarded the Nobel Prize for Literature in 1986, the year following this interview, which was recorded when Dr Mary David was teaching at Ibadan and Soyinka was about to quit his job at the University of Ile-Ife to return to full-time writing.

Mary David Of the different forms of creative writing that you have done, are you more at ease in any one form than in others? Do you have a partiality for any one medium?

Wole Soyinka It is a fair question, one which I find difficult to answer with any precision. I think that different experiences and different objective responses as well as emotional responses call automatically for different mediums. There are experiences which literally go straight into the terrain of poetry. I never sit down and say, 'Which medium do I want to write, this or the other?' Some go straight into the theatre. The only time there is ever any kind of clash is in the case of plays. I'll give you an example. When I wrote *The Road* for instance, I saw *The Road*, I remember, as a film. But I wrote the play since I had no means of doing a film at that time. It is a film I'll do someday.

You once referred to *The Strong Breed* [1963] as your favourite one-act play?

You'll find that I never said a particular play is my favourite. I would say that it is one of my favourites.

Are you planning a sequel to *Aké*, which has given your readers a lot of insight into your childhood and the early influences on you?

No, I don't think so. That was a very special period, which as far as I am concerned terminated with that. There would be others but they would be more . . . for instance, since I've been reading a lot of material which has been coming out of the Civil War and that whole period, I've been provoked more and more into writing about my own experiences during that time. In other words a number of things which I deliberately left unsaid in *The Man Died* [1972] for obvious reasons.

And will it be as impassioned as *The Man Died*?

No, it will be quite objective.

At what period of your life did you make the decision to be a writer?

I don't think I consciously made up my mind to become a writer. I know that in school I wrote short stories, won prizes, wrote essays for school magazines, wrote sketches for our school social evenings. I contributed to the children's page of the *Daily Times*, wrote stories for the Nigerian Broadcasting Corporation and it just went on and my writing continued to reflect my progressive maturity.

What of the contribution of the universities of Ibadan and Leeds?

Oh, yes, of course. I continued to write for magazines. Then when I got to Leeds I wrote plays. I then thought I should send them to theatres to see if they were interested.

Wilson Knight was your tutor at Leeds. Could you say a little more about the influence of Wilson Knight and Boname Dobrée on your writings?

All teachers – if they are good teachers – must be influences on one in the sense that they open new perspectives of the mind and new approaches to literature which are slightly aside from one's own. In that sense Boname Dobrée, Wilson Knight and also Arnold Kettle first opened my literary perspective towards a Marxist – but a critical Marxist, not any doctrinaire Marxist – potential of literature, interpretation of literature. These were all specific directions which I did not possess before. Dobrée – I always refer to him as a pagan – sort of enriched my own, shall I say instinctive paganism as I had already rejected the Christian religion, all orthodox established religions. It was an insight into the literature of the world as being very often the expression of very basic paganistic instincts and relationships with Nature, with matter, with reality more than I ever suspected at that stage of my development. Wilson of course had . . . an ability to think off the beaten track. His spiritualism actually led him to quarry out vast riches in poetry, especially poetic drama.

The archetypes and symbols you have repeatedly used in your work are drawn from the myths of different cultures – Classical, Judaeo-Christian, Yoruba and even Indian. What does this mean?

I think it means very obviously that humanity has – civilizations have – a lot more in common than they profess, than they are willing to accept.

There is a trend in African literary criticism now that is obviously unaware of this – I mean the trend that frowns on 'universality' as a denial of Africanness. What do you think of this tendency?

To me it is a temporary situation with which one must be patient. It has to do with ignorance. Many of the people who are critics see only the text, they do not see the intertext with other texts; they do not see the relativity of the very process of literature. They know so little about the cultures of the outside world which exist right inside that culture. Those who are not academics in that respect do not find this difficult. If you look for instance at the writings and pictures on taxis and lorries you'll find a lot of Islamic iconography, Indian mythology which has come in a kind of bastardized form through Indian films and through pictures on the praying mats from the Orient, jewellery and so on. Now, the ordinary person who does not have this hang-up does not have any problem at all. Such people recognize this fraternity of responses, of images.

Your archetypes, your favourite images and your persistent themes are all centred on renewal. Could you explain how this theme came to be fixed in your mind from the beginning?

Well, it is very difficult to say this. Let us say, growing up in an atmosphere in which the seasons change. The harmattan when everything dries up, and then the rain turns the whole world green again. And recognition of periods of drought sometimes so severe that the whole town is praying for the rains to break and an end to the drought. Realizing that there are the fat periods and the lean, if you like. And also growing up in an atmosphere which embodied these experiences in rituals.

Your images of renewal are not only seasonal, but drawn from myths of various cultures: from alchemy, from metallurgy, from Christianity and symbols which have roots in mystery, religion and even from quest literatures. Clearly a lot of scholarship has gone into this, and certainly much is expected of the reader. Does it ever worry you that a lot of your meaning is sure to elude the grasp of the ordinary reader?

Ah, but my favourite answer to that is this [*pointing to a corner of the office*]. Look at that carving on the wall there, that sculpture. It is an African mask. On one level I appreciate it as an aesthetic object. The pastel shades, I think, are nicely balanced. I like the forms, I like the combination of the forms, even the elevation of the mask. I think it is sufficient aesthetic reward. Well, my appreciation of it is further enhanced by the fact that I actually can see it in motion, I know how it is worn. I happen to know the rest of the mask that the carrier wears. I know what shapes he makes as he dances. At such times I am able to go deeper and contemplate its meaning because it is also a ritual form – incidentally, of renewal – and it is part and parcel of the ceremonies. I know all of that. And therefore I obtain very many levels of correspondences with that mask. But is it futile to somebody who just comes in? Is it worthless as an object whose sum is zero to somebody who is not aware of the various levels of significances of that mask? The point I am trying to make is that everybody obtains from a work of art very many different things at many different levels, and one should never worry unduly that a certain section of one's viewers or readership is not appreciating it. The same thing applies to lots of Yoruba poetry, ritual poetry. There are many aspects of the poetry which are hidden from me. At the same time I can enjoy the use of words; I can enjoy the imagery, the allusions, but I know that at a certain level it is totally closed to me. I think the same is true of all works of art or literature.

Your archetypes of regeneration, Dionysus and Ogun, undergo dismemberment and reassembling. You have stated more than once that the contemporary paradigm for these mythical figures is Fidel Castro, who experienced total defeat and disintegration before he harnessed his energies for a successful effort. Do you think society can be reconstructed only through such exceptional individuals who undergo this ordeal–survival affirmation pattern so central to your works? What of the role of the masses, which you have been criticized for ignoring? You know you've been accused of championing 'bourgeois individualism'?

I've never at any time suggested that it is only individuals who redeem societies. Look at the entire history of mankind, look at the religions which, for me, have the strongest indices of the cravings of society and the fulfilment of those cravings. The religions are in themselves most obvious examples of this reality of the individual redeemer in society whether in antiquity or in 1985. I've never suggested at any time that it is individuals alone who can redeem, galvanize, reactivate stagnant societies. No. But I battle with those who suggest that the individual *qua* individual is not a significant factor in social change and even movement. And we know the effect on society when such individuals leave the scene. We've seen the results which show that those are rather special gifted individuals. Something that always amuses me, that strikes me as ignorant and dishonest is when this thing is coupled with bourgeois – 'bourgeois individualism'! – what is *bourgeois* about individualism? There are, if you like, peasant forms of individualism, individualism exists in all societies. The whole idea of community is to embrace and . . . to ensure, that these contributions of the individuals do not get smothered and submerged by the uniformity of the rest of society. This is what true collectivity is all about. Our folk tales – we cannot get anything less bourgeois than folk tales of the peasant world – usually have to do with heroes. All folk tales anywhere in the world have heroes. Now, do these tales emerge from bourgeois society? I am always amused at what they think is an unanswerable kind of criticism – bourgeois individualism. It is not in this society alone. You know, even when you go to real bourgeois societies, which, of course, have their strong core of die-hard Marxist-Socialists, you always find that when two or three Marxists are gathered together they have this sort of self-correcting, self-criticism session. Individualism can be a strong force for change. At the same time it can be a retrogressive force. It all depends on the circumstances. But nobody is going to persuade me that a Fidel Castro, a Julius Nyerere, an Indira Gandhi – or let's go back a little – a Mahatma Gandhi, or a Pandit Nehru – are not very special people. Where the thing becomes dangerous is when Gandhi wants to ensure that she develops a family dynasty. I object very strongly to that. She was an individual and that is that. But when it degenerates into 'My own qualities must be passed down naturally to my son', I find that disgusting and even reactionary. It means that the entire millions of Indians who may be gifted with superior qualities do not have the chance to emerge. Now that is wrong.

In your writings you have moved with ease from the martyrdom of altruistic saviour figures to the most hilarious comedies. How has this been possible?

For me it is a reflection of reality that everything has a tragic and a comic phase at one and the same time. It is recognized in a lot of Irish literature, Russian literature, remember?

Certain African critics have censured your bringing Christian symbolism into your writings while some others try to argue that since you renounced Christianity very early, you should not use Christian symbols at all. What do you think of such opinions?

I think it is illiterate to say that though I have renounced Christianity as a religion I should not get any aesthetic delight out of it. When I go to any new European city, my first pleasure is just walking around and admiring the architecture, and among the architecture I enjoy church architecture. If I am in a Muslim country, the architecture of the mosques. I literally wallow in them. I think they are glorious buildings whatever the motivation, the inspiration, was. And to suggest that I shouldn't appreciate the architecture of a church or appreciate a Christian tale or use a Christian symbol is absurd. And more especially, what these people do not realize is that Christian religion is a pagan religion. The dates, the rituals, the crucifixion, these are all symbols of renewal. Christianity itself was based on pagan religions.

That explains, doesn't it, your use of Christian rituals like baptism, the communion meal, etc., which have their origin in pre-Christian mystery religions?

Yes, or course. Rites of passage exist in all civilizations and they meet at so many points.

In the course of your reflections on your fiftieth birthday you referred to yourself as belonging to a 'wasted generation'. Were you speaking as a Nigerian or as a writer?

I was saying it definitely as a Nigerian. I don't feel that my creative life has been wasted. No. But now I am depressed and frustrated very often by the inability of many individuals like myself who have given quite a lot of their energy and capacity to energize one's environment. We find that we've been frustrated at every turn and we've had to do something like the labour of Sisyphus rolling the stone uphill all the time until it reaches the top, and instead of it being built upon, is given a push back down again. The political forces are such that they have thwarted our attempts to really build a viable society so that we do not feel like abnormalities within society or to use your expression to regenerate our environment in the same way as we regenerate ourselves. This has been thwarted by political forces.

I have to avoid Nigerian politics as an academic here, but I want to know how you respond to what is happening in South Africa, knowing your deep concern over that issue. What can the African writers do about South Africa?

Not much. You asked me just now what I was writing when you came in. In fact in the car the other day I was so provoked by the burning down of Winnie Mandela's house that I began to write a poem in the car. So one responds you see. That's all one can do. A few years ago in a lecture in England I said I was giving apartheid ten more years. A few years later in another lecture I said, 'A few years ago I gave apartheid ten more years. I am afraid something must have happened to me which made me so optimistic.' And I know what that was. It was the day Mozambique put itself in a state of war against South Africa. So, now that you see what is happening, maybe I'll go back to my former prediction. I don't know. Anyway writers should not busy themselves with predicting. I was so optimistic when Mozambique took that action, I thought it was going to be a sort of bush fire which would spread. I was so convinced that it would spread around. And then what happened? Nkomati took place, the ultimate betrayal. So I'll be publishing probably a couple of poems in the *Guardian* you know, triggered off by what is happening. Maybe one of these days if there is a sort of international brigade going into South Africa you may be sure that I'll be in it. By now it should have taken place. I've always looked forward to it. Well, anyway, all that is history.

Do you put a bit of yourself into your characters?

I know that it creeps in very often. I know that, because I take great trouble to expunge such instances wherever I find them. It is only when I see that to take something out will interfere with the structure, the integrity and the relationships of what I've already put on paper that I just leave them severely alone.

I have some difficulty in coming to terms with your women characters, who seem to combine the bitch and the madonna. I think your depiction of women is unrealistic.

Well, that is my attitude to women. But you see, women have become inseparable in my mind with nature. Their form, their being and the fact that they, unlike men, reproduce, cause them to become fused in my mind with nature in a way which men are not and never can be. I am aware of criticism, especially feminist criticism which has been rabid among one or two individuals. There is no compromise for me on this subject. A women's shape, a woman's reproductive capacity which is unique to the female sex just sets her apart from men. It does not mean that women are not equal to men intellectually, in capacities and so on and so forth. But the figure of a woman, the biology of a woman – for me nature is biology, obviously – just separate her; and I can never look at a woman in the same way as I look at a man and when I reflect her in my writings she occupies that position. But you'll admit that there are exceptions. The secretary – Dehinwa – in *The Interpreters* is obviously an exception because she was not treated as a symbol, but a member of the new generation.

Yes, but I wish your women characters were a little more well-realized.

But that's the role of women. It is women who must realize themselves in their writings. I can't enter the mind and body of a woman. No, let women write about themselves. Why should they ask me to do that?

My readers would be very much interested in your interest in India. There are a lot of references in your works to Siva, and Kali and the *Mahabharata* and the hermaphrodite gods of the Hindu pantheon, etc. Have you made a serious study of Hindu mythology?

When I was in England, as a result of my literary inclinations and the influences we talked about – Dobrée and Wilson Knight – I actually took time off to read extensively into many religions of the world. Apart from the religious precepts themselves, and the philosophies, I was interested in the poetry of the *Bhagavadgītā*, for instance, and the Buddhist literature. I went deeply into these for many years. I read more and more, simply because I was fascinated more and more by what I read. And in addition I've had some fascinating relationships with Indians. So you see, I am romantically attached to India as well as intellectually.

Yes, I can see that in Taila in *Season of Anomy*. Is she an individual or does she represent the oriental mysticism that left a deep impression on you, and charmed you without fully claiming you?

She was an individual, but a very special individual. She was very spiritual. She became in some sense a provocateur of these Indian deities on many levels.

In *Anomy* you have used the name 'Suberu' for the human version of Cerberus, which is akin to the Sanskrit 'Sabera', the name of the animal guarding Pathala or the underworld. Were you aware of this resemblance?

You know the Yoruba name is 'Suberu', and Cerberus was the name I was thinking about. I didn't know about the Indian name which as you've pointed out comes very close to 'Suberu'.

Have you visited India?

Yes, but not really visited. I've passed through a few times. Like China it is one of the two main places where I am trying to reserve a few months.

Do you think that the common colonial experience that India and Nigeria have could indicate some similarities between Indian literature in English and Nigerian literature in English?

I don't think so. I think colonialism affected India very differently from the way it did Nigeria. The literature I have read definitely suggests that. There are similarities of course. . . . But the British created a sort of lower middle class in India: the clerical, bureaucratic lower middle class which formed a class in itself, the like of which we did not have in Nigeria. This is something that I noticed.

English is a common legacy in both countries, isn't it? And that brings me to an aspect of your art which, one feels, is not being given the critical attention it deserves. I mean your brilliant use of the English language.

It wasn't always like that, you know. I am now talking not only of my writings but the forms of criticism which the works of Chinua Achebe, J. P. Clark and the late Chris Okigbo used to have. These things, I suppose, come in waves. Suddenly all this was overtaken by the neo-phytes to Marxism and they were incapable of using even Marxist criticism as a means of illuminating texts. They left the literature completely and would write pages and pages on what the literature is not doing rather than saying what it is doing and how well it is doing it. It is a kind of opting out, a kind of intellectual laziness, a form of opportunism in which they then become the centre, their propositions become the centre of debate, rather than the literature which provoked the propositions in the first place. Some examples are more notorious than others, I won't single out any. It is one of those things which happen but I believe you cannot defeat literature in the end.

3

Wilson Harris

with

Fred D'Aguiar

When Fred D'Aguiar interviewed Wilson Harris in 1986, Harris was already established as one of the most original writers of the anglophone Caribbean. Immigrating to England in 1949 after pioneering pre-war Caribbean writing in the Guyanese 'little magazine' Kyk-Over-Al from 1945, by 1986 he had published two collections of poetry, three books of criticism and seventeen novels, besides numerous interviews, reviews and essays. Prominent among these were his first four Guyana-based novels, republished as The Guyana Quartet (1985); Tumatumari (1968) and Black Marsden (1972). Carnival had appeared in 1985, just prior to this interview, and more novels were to follow.

The flux and mystery of his homeland's interior jungles, where he once worked as a surveyor, left an indelible print on Harris's imagination, and Guyana's history created a fascination with racial and cultural complexity. Yet he disliked being identified as purely a Caribbean or South American writer. His first literary influence was Homer, and his central concern is all mankind in time and space. While each of Harris's highly original novels is distinct, they contribute to one ongoing work in progress. His individual prose fractures the surfaces of conventional 'realism', challenging the reader to see the world in new and liberating perspectives. A polymath, equally interested in literatures, art, mythology, anthropology and the sciences, he invokes the creative imagination to offer insights that *might help lead modern civilization out of the impasse between the colonial past and a future locked in racial hatreds and blinding materialism. His concern with the responsibility of the artist, and the need to explore new forms and perspectives in the arts, has made his work a potent if largely invisible liberating influence on younger Caribbean writers, as this interview with Fred D'Aguiar – a British–Guyanese poet and novelist of a younger generation – illustrates. In addition, the insights of his many visionary critical essays – written as early as the 1960s – have anticipated by many years the questions of hybridity, cross-culturalism and transnationalism that concern critics today.*

Fred D'Aguiar I would like to start off by asking you about your use of the Guyanese rain forest in your fiction and about your years as a surveyor there. You were once described in the *New Left Review* as going into the rain forest and coming out with a changed point of view – that it had a profound effect on you as a kind of psychic experience. Could you say something about this in relation to *The Guyana Quartet*?

Wilson Harris I think this is an important matter. It may help if I were to touch on some aspects which arise from *The Whole Armour* [1962] and *Palace of the Peacock* [1960], and also in my new novel *Carnival*. When I first travelled in the rain forest it made an immense impact, the sort of impact which strikes at what I would describe as 'inner space'. It seems to me there are two consequences which flow from that impact; one has to do with the sense one has that one is travelling back into the very origins of creation. Now of course that is an impossible quest but the stimulation which springs from this is quite enormous in that one has a sense of the luminous fabric of the landscape within the density, within the play of contrasts, the play of life, and it is because of this luminous fabric that one is on the threshold of what I would call 'wholeness'; a wholeness which one could never hope to structure absolutely but which is there nevertheless and which enriches partial approaches to it – the partial images – as it stems from the stimulation of 'inner space'. The other is to do with the way one engages with the past. The past seems to have consequences that never die absolutely; they impinge upon one, they seem to involve one in a complex rehearsal of matters, events which have happened in the past. And of course that is true of the rain forest. As we know many cultures have appeared there and have vanished in South and Central America and our knowledge of the reasons for the demise of these cultures remains incomplete. So one is involved in this complicated incessant rehearsal in which one sees or senses these events which one approaches from different angles. I began to find myself involved in a fiction which in responding to the past made one aware of the biases of the past which one had to consume in some degree in order to move into another dimension.

The very first section of *Palace of the Peacock* implicates one in modes of dying which remain uncertain; Donne may have been shot, he may have been hanged, it is as if the bullet runs along a kind of rope. This is a crude paraphrase of that complex introduction to the novel. We know later on that he may have been one of the crew who were drowned, so there are three possibilities. Curiously enough my step-father disappeared in the rain forest when I was about seven or eight and we never discovered what actually happened. So apart from individual expeditions in which this kind of thing occurred there were cultures, and the reasons for the disappearance of those cultures remains very difficult to grasp in a complete historical way. Very early in the novel one is implicated in the gallows or the noose, which is a natural physical gallows or noose. We find that later on in the substance of the narrative – in which the crew appears to die again and again – that that image undergoes an alteration, a series of complex alterations, and in the end when Donne is hanging from the noose one discovers that the noose sustains him, supports him, and does not execute him as a noose would do in physical terms. What is happening is that various patterns in the novel are consistently broken and with each change the central image appears again but in a different light as if one sees it from another angle; it appears to pick up new content so we have a noose that is not a noose. A noose is a noose is not a noose, unlike the Stein dictum 'a rose is a rose is a rose'. A change occurs in the noose and the different content is expressive of the break in the pattern and therefore there is a sort of convertibility of images. This is something I have wrestled with a long time and tried to validate because one looks for validation. I tend to think that validation may lie in quantum physics with the quantum imagination, a particle is a wave in the way one looks at phenomena in quantum physics; one sees things consistently in different ways . . . the pattern changes and as the pattern changes the past makes a different impact on the imagination. The imagination picks that up, takes an image out of the past, that image requires new content; the image changes.

Let us take another example from *The Whole Armour*. The tiger appears, it is a symbol which comes from the ancient past in the South and Central Americas. It is a very important image of creation on the one hand and also of destructive powers and resources on the other. What I have done in the novel is give the tiger majesty but the tiger also exists within the territorial imperative. I think this is immensely important. Cultures and civilizations have been tormented by the territorial imperative. . . . To whom does this block of land belong? Men have died because of boundaries, the boundaries they inscribe into place – that is territorial imperative. But it is vital to transform territorial imperative into a web of processes, a web of life in which one senses that a community can sustain diversity and contrast. In *The Whole Armour* one has the lost child who is drawn into the tapestry of the tiger; the child is taken away and there is the regained child, the child who is found again. So there are two children, the one who is lost and the one who returns at the end. The child becomes a mysterious medium. We know that a great deal happens within the child in the first four years, there are mysterious faculties in the child. I have used the child as a very fragile resource and this brings me to the point of how one makes fragilities visible? We know that it is easy to make sensational episodes visible, but to make fragilities visible is an immense challenge; I am suggesting that the fragile child stands between the majestic tiger and the human frame which seems so vulnerable. . . . We know, in a sense, how far short we fall from our deepest aspirations and one of these is the transformation of the territorial imperative into a web of life which sustains private space – diversity. So that one has the fragile child occupying the middle place between majestic tiger and the vulnerable human frame and this translation is something that happens precisely because one is in a position to visualize these fragilities.

Can I ask you about the idea of translation? A lot of your narratives take place outside of history and rely for their content on a mythical history: your reliance on the Carib, or mythical notions of place. How fair do you think it is? Donne and the crew sail up the river and as they do you discover their journey is an exact replica of one that took place in colonial times, but their crew is made up of the racial consistency of present-day Guyana rather than colonials and employees going up river. You seem to be working outside history as far as we can glean, a history from an interior situation like Guyana where there are no historical facts and you are placing that past within a mythical framework, or one that is partly a negotiation between myth and imagination and what the imagination can actually deliver when history seems to have failed to do the job. We do not have any records of who actually lived in the Guyanese rain forest, what civilizations rose up and how they died. You are clearly letting your imagination move in a certain space and have come up with an integrated idea of what happened there and also an idea that can offer solutions for present communities which are deadlocked in problems of their own – race, class and others. How true is this? How much do you see the imagination 'delivering the goods' where perhaps the historical account has failed and how does this transformation translate into what is going on in society, because the books create a narrative that goes forward without giving a solution?

My judgement is that there exists a profound relationship between all

societies and that the imperial age, whatever ravages it may have
inflicted on cultures, did possess the seed of a covenant, simply a covenant between those who are governed and those who govern. This is a
notion which existed in these vanished cultures and it is a notion which
requires this translation, this balance between the territorial imperative
and the web of processes. What seems to me striking is that it is possible to sense the seeds of a civilization at the extremities of our world
and it has to do with the ways in which we gauge what this covenant
means. For example, in *The Far Journey of Oudin* [1961] there is a
continuous rehearsal; Oudin is a thief at first sight who is sent by the
money lender Ram to steal from a certain family. When he arrives there
they recognize him; he is the double of the murdered half-brother who
was the heir to the estate. Instantly he is burdened with this problem,
they project upon him their own fears and terror and guilt and remorse
and one discovers that as the novel mixes with the substance of the
narrative we are involved in a rehearsal. When Oudin eventually turns
against his master, the money lender, and decides to rescue the illiterate
girl Beti (which means 'daughter of the people') and to take her away
from the clutches of that family, we discover that the journey he makes
seems to recapitulate the circumstances of the death of the murdered
half-brother. We see various figures appear and these are frail figures.
Again it is this question of making what is frail visible. These frail
figures appear and when they do it is as if one is involved again in the
crime that was perpetrated but all the time one sees it from different
perspectives, though eventually we seem to sense that Oudin is not only
retracing this matter but is sustaining a covenant between forces, gov-
erners and governed, deity and humanity. There are all sorts of ways of
looking at it; he is sustaining it so we see there the burden of an entire
civilization which picks up the impact of the imperial age which, despite the ravages it brought, also brought that seed of value. But on the
other hand, the cultures that were devastated also possessed a seed of
value. In short, we cannot, I think, establish a genuine morality if we
live in a world which compartmentalizes cultures and people. There
must be this profound dialogue and to trace that dialogue in creative

terms requires us to see frail connections; there are no massive connections. . . . One also has to remember that when one speaks of the rain
forest it is a very fragile place. It could be devastated overnight.

There is a passage in *Carnival* which emphasizes this 'phantom
world'; it is not solid. I go against the notion that everything has to be
solid; it is the frailties that one looks for, the frail connections because
the things that appear solid may be much more frail than we think.
Therefore it is through these infinite rehearsals, where there is no final
play, that one takes up the uncertainties which lie in those regions, the
sensation that one is moving in the shoes of those who once lived there.
My judgement is that the present in which we live is completely mean-
ingless unless we can sense the impact of the past. Now one knows one
cannot physically go back, what happened yesterday has happened, but
in inner space one can return, and this is through the creative imagination. The values of inner space are values which allow us a certain kind
of fiction to ceaselessly digest its biases with each break in the pattern
and with each rehearsal. This is not easy, but the fiction which does
that, in my judgement, must be a complicated fiction in which no
pattern has an absolute command of the scene, all patterns are partial
and as they break, the image changes. It appears to be the same image;
in other words you have two forces which resemble each other but are
not the same. Thus one begins to open oneself up to new undreamt-of
dimensions and regenerative possibilities.

**You have often recoiled from spelling out your position as regards
writing, always going through the process of juxtaposing ... and
exploring. Is this because you are saying that fiction can only be
partial and therefore, if it tries to describe what 'wholeness' will be,
it is actually starting off from a false premise because it can never
grasp 'wholeness'? Is this why you have resisted giving us a blueprint of how society ought to be or a new world vision and have
written about the tensions that go into making that new world?**

The wholeness is there but it is something that cannot be absolutely structured, therefore the fabric of the world through which we move becomes luminous; the partialities which we discover in the world arouse us both in terms of a certain kind of ecstasy and in a certain kind of torment. Therefore the partialities which are biases, we pull back into, dig into and we discover something which seems partial and has connections with other parts elsewhere which we may not have realized.

I was thinking particularly of *The Angel at the Gate* [1982]. Mary says at one point, 'to behold one must endure the traffic of many souls'. She is receiving therapy at the time for a schizophrenic type disorder – a multiple personality – and one, according to psychiatry, that might be cured. But for her the experience is actually creating a 'wholeness'. How do you respond to the common psychiatric notion that a multiple personality indicates fragmentation when you are saying that the experience of several personalities is a premise for 'wholeness'?

In *The Angel at the Gate*, you may remember that the priest, Father Marsden, an old wise man, a man who appears to be filled with virtue and goodness, walks with a stick and this becomes something that, at first sight, you may discard. Later on you discover it has an importance which lies in how one assesses things which seem frail. You may remember that the woman who is sleeping, Mary, has a bottle of pills by her bed and the child takes the bottle and is about to consume all the pills. At that moment there is a thundering blow at the door and this wakes her in time to snatch the tablets from the child. When she looks out of the window to see who it was who had done this thing, she sees a grotesque figure who is exposing himself and you have the grotesquery and horror and yet she would not have saved her child if this horrible man had not arrived and hammered at the door at that very instant. Now the hammering at the door gives us a link with the wise virtuous man; what is at stake here is the reality of our moral vision. If one is to have a moral vision in which there is some degree of transcendental wholeness one cannot exclude anything that happens to all humanity. Now this is a painful fact, that there are things which are happening that appear horrible, grotesque and revolting, and yet one cannot exclude the fact that these horrible things are being committed by human beings who are as human as ourselves. To keep the balance, to have some sense of the depth of humanity, and not to lose the transcendental wholeness is a complex matter.

But the moral vision – the wisdom that springs out of that tension – is at the heart of creativity and therefore we have these real connections between figures that seem to belong to different worlds. The priest, Father Marsden, who is so wise, seems to belong to a totally different world and yet we can see that his moral vision is such that it cannot exclude any section of humanity. If he has to pass judgement on the criminal he does so not because of some technicality of the law. The law says if a man commits a crime he must be punished; Father Marsden passes judgement both in terms of the technicalities, because he has to obey the law, but also because he has a profound miraculous sensation of the misery or the potential misery which resides in the criminal. It is this sensation of understanding what the criminal is, because the criminal is related to him as a human person, that deepens his moral judgement and makes the law something more than a technicality and more than simply the administration of technical rules. The law then has its roots in creativity; in other words there is a complex interrelationship between the moral vision and the vision of the law and that is why you have these incongruities and yet these incongruities are the building blocks of our civilization. It depends on what frailties link them together . . . we can only sense [this] in terms of the way we connect things that at first sight seem to have no connection.

I wanted to ask you about how you see the idea of community and commitment in the artist. It seems that while you operate in a particular time and place there is this wider vision which moves outside of history and takes on board myth. How do you equate the

stance of the artist who is detached from his or her community (who seems to operate in a language where home isn't so much in a house in a street but is located in language almost) with what is actually happening with so and so in a particular area or society? How do you address this and bring your fiction down to historical events as they occur in order to see a direct analogy between fiction and 'reality'? Here you have been arguing for a wider vision for the artist.

You see my judgement is that in the civilization in which we live, we have for centuries seen the ascendancy of the European. One has to remember that Europe has drawn many of its resources from all over the world. It was necessary, for example, for a sculptor like Henry Moore to have entered into a dialogue with African and pre-colonial, Mexican masks. Such cross-culturalities have never been deeply underwritten. The reasons why we are locked in this kind of imbalance may spring from a difficulty to sense that there is a community of texts – what is lost to us in a purely historical sense may reside in texts of the imagination. For example my interest in say Dante is an interest that springs from Dante's texts. They are such that one can revisit the Inferno, the Paradiso, the Purgatorio, but not in the strict territorial ways in which Dante drew upon these. What one is saying when one looks at Dante is that the Purgatorio appears in the Inferno, the Inferno appears in the Paradiso, there is this overlap. In the Donne figure in *Palace of the Peacock* mentioned earlier, who hangs from the noose, there is the juncture of the Inferno and the Paradiso. That is when he perceived his deepest vision into the Inferno. . . . What is striking about Dante is that the guides that he worked with to me are real and true; they spring out of the collective unconscious. They are intuitive guides.

   To come to this matter of the community of texts, if you look at *Black Marsden*, the nameless section is a revisitation of *The Waste Land* [1922], the Chapel Perilous, which takes a completely different form from Eliot's poem, but the parallels are there. The Chapel Perilous appears in terms of the cluster of rocks in which you have this sense of the cathedrals of space. The assassin seems to loom. The man who is overlooking the chapel is conscious that at some level he has to turn and confront the assassin and if he can't do that he is lost. What is his connection with the assassin? Is he simply going to cut himself asunder and break the world so that they drift off into separate realms whether you call them Inferno or Paradiso? Is he finally going to find a connection?

What I am saying is that Eliot, who drew many of his resources from a variety of cultures, needs to be responded to from within those cultures. Now, I have come from a totally different culture, but Eliot drew some of his strengths from my culture just as Lévi-Strauss has done, just as Picasso has done, just as Henry Moore has done, and a response has to come from me and from others like me in which we return to this community of texts. *The Wasteland* is one such text; Dante's text is another such text. It is important to return to those and respond to those from an angle from which the establishment expects no such response. As far as the establishment is concerned, so-called 'Third World writers' must all the time present a mirror to the realistic world and point out how decadent their society is; this satisfies the establishment. It awards many prizes to such writers. But the response needs to come from a far different level.

Through language, you come up with all these possible solutions which you don't spell out but which are nevertheless there. Can I ask you about the notion, in *Carnival*, where the narrator claims that the characters there are almost writing for him, that they have taken control and are in the process of going through his own life. How much does this come from this community of texts and the idea of the Third World writer refusing to write the agenda, or delivering the realistic text, but instead being involved like any other writer in the exploration of the relationship between the writer and the community and in taking people's vision forward?

Of course one could easily be drawn into a response to your question but it takes us so far afield that I hesitate a little. The thing to recognize . . . is that this 'writer written' idea which runs through *Carnival* relates to a profound response to Dante. And in terms of this community of texts of which I spoke, one may be drawing upon resources which can lead one in certain ways. Therefore, one is writing as well as being written; one is being written by the past even as one writes the present. Therefore the whole question of tradition is a question of a community of texts; if our world was demolished we would have to scrape together what community of texts were available to us and we would also have to look at the gaps in those texts because one realizes that the intuitive imagination is of a profound significance. The thing leads into many areas. . . . There is a kind of text which can urge us on to find a response. The history of the world is incessantly incomplete.

4

Lorna Goodison

with

Denise deCaires Narain

Lorna Goodison, born in Kingston, Jamaica in 1947, is a poet, short-story writer and artist. She has exhibited nationally and her artwork has appeared on all the covers of her books. She has been writing since 1970. Her first published work, Tamarind Season *(1980), won her acclaim as a leading voice in Caribbean women's writing, combining Jamaican speech rhythms with the relaxed and sensual movements of her own poetry. She went on to write* I Am Becoming My Mother *(1986),* Heartease *(1988), her* Selected Poems *(1992) and a collection of short stories,* Baby Mother and the King of Swords *(1990). In her poems, Goodison creates a sisterhood united by the strength and continuity of the female body.*

Since this interview, which took place at the University of Kent, Lorna Goodison has become the most prolific of contemporary Caribbean women poets and her work has been translated into several languages. Although she now lives and teaches in Toronto, Jamaican culture, in all its nuanced manifestations, continues to shape the contours of her poetic craft. To Us, All Flowers are Roses *appeared in 1995, followed by* Turn Thanks *(1999),* Guinea Woman: New and Selected Poems *(2000) and* Travelling Mercies *(2001). Her new collection,* Controlling the Silver, *is due out in 2004. She describes the title poem as a praise song to the market women who are the abiding spirit of Jamaican life. 'I see myself ', she said recently, 'in a tradition of praise singers. I'm not sure that I said that to Wasafiri*

in 1989, but I'd like to say it now.' Goodison's work testifies to the possibilities
for a more subtle and varied delivery/performance of the poetic 'word'.

Denise deCaires Narain It struck me that in *Heartease* your identity has changed . . . it seems there's a new direction. I wondered if
you felt that was the case?

Lorna Goodison No, I don't think it was really new but merely submerged or hidden. It was always an underlying current. The process of
writing those three books was very different. *Tamarind Season* was like
a crying out. I always loved poetry; I always knew about the power of
poetry and (I keep telling this over again!) when I went to school I read
all of this great English poetry by the great English writers but none of
them were speaking to a young, black West Indian woman. A lot of the
women poets I later read were from a sort of suicide school of poetry
which I didn't want to have to deal with: I didn't want to kill myself; I
don't want to kill myself. So, while I recognized that this great stuff
existed, I never anywhere saw my own point of view. Although it wasn't
a conscious effort, I think in the end I needed to read those poems;
that's why I wrote them. So, *Tamarind Season* was just a need to cry out
about a lot of things . . . about myself, about other women, about
Jamaica, about the world in my own small way. In the end I don't even
know those poems very well . . . they came out of me in such an organic
kind of way. I'm not closely acquainted with a lot of those poems! *I Am
Becoming My Mother* is a totally different thing because I was much
more focused on the poems and a lot of them have to do with writing
down things which I knew had to be written about. But towards the
end of each book I began to see a certain kind of movement . . . you
know, those little poems towards the end of *Tamarind Season* about you
owe me a walk in the rain . . . it was a crying out to something much
bigger – it wasn't strictly this very ordinary plane any more. And then
in *I Am Becoming* I felt I had been given this job to correct some things,
to write down these things, to tell stories for people, their truth, their
version . . . like my great-grandmother, Winnie Mandela, and so on. I'd

been given this job but again towards the end, it always happens towards the end of a book where I just notice a particular kind of direction sweeping into the other book. Towards the end of *I Am Becoming*, you know the 'Letters to the Egyptian'? It looks like a letter to an Egyptian but they're much more than that; they're letters to the divine . . . it's a much bigger kind of thing. I've always felt my identity was African and especially Egyptian; Egypt has a lot to do with mine, as the cradle of civilization. So it's not that I just all of a sudden come up with this thing; the *Heartease* poems for me started in the poem I eventually placed at the beginning of *I Am Becoming*, that is 'My Last Poem Again'. I remember writing it and just being totally absorbed and taken away by it. I remember I was in a car one day with my brother and I said he had to drive because this poem was so insistent it was just coming in waves.

I felt in *Tamarind Season* and *I Am Becoming* that the poems were more contained. You used the word 'organic' earlier and that's how these poems seem to me, like they were born in one piece. Somehow the voice in *Heartease* seems more fragmented, as if you're experimenting with different voices. The use of biblical language is stronger. . . . I see what you mean about the currents already being there . . . but I was thinking in particular of the Gospel of St John with all the references to the power of the word and illumination and bearing witness and so on.

I don't have much to do with it, you know. They just come this way. I never thought they'd happen like that, but they presented themselves in a very strong way. What could I do? I had to write them down.

It almost sounds as if you're a victim of poetry!

No, seriously – it has to do with my own personal development, my internal freedom. When I'm supposed to go through all these things . . . I can't see myself when I read, but I've seen photographs of myself reading and I don't think I just stand there and read. Something happens sometimes when I read. I never used to read like that and I used to hate to read. I think that the way I read now is quite bound up with some kind of internal freedom that is taking place inside of me and it allows me to just stand there and read and it doesn't bother me. I get 'borrowed' as somebody once said.

A wonderful expression . . .

I think that's what real poetry is . . . there are all these levels . . . you can write about what you really feel. I remember reading these poems by Walter James Turner in the *Oxford Book of English Verse* edited by Yeats. There was such a power moving through those poems, it was astonishing, mighty. Yeats spoke highly of him in the introduction but I don't know why he's never been as popular as some of the other poets; perhaps he doesn't have a very big corpus but that kind of power I recognize. You get borrowed and it doesn't have very much to do with you. That's why I think real poetry or the inspiration to write real poetry is a divine thing; it is completely out of your hands. You just happen to be standing there and it passes through you.

That's interesting. You don't think that your working at it allows you to be that 'vessel'?

Yes, I think that part of it is luck and part of it is that I'm willing to do the work. You have to work at it because you don't get it so. None of these poems just happen . . . until maybe twenty drafts later. Every single one of them you have to work at forever to make sure you are taking down your 'dictation' properly and when one single word is wrong you have to change it. It's a lot of hard work; it's not as wonderful as it sounds.

This is a question I'm sure you've been asked lots of times but are there any poets who have influenced you greatly and, in particular, any women poets?

Because of our West Indian education, there are any number of male poets who influenced us because I was not taught about any women poets. The only woman poet I did know of when I was growing up was Louise Bennett and I didn't want to write like that. And then what I was presented with was the suicide school of poets and I didn't want that either. There were some women writing earlier in Jamaica like Una Marson but their writing did not have a great impression on me. I think it had something to do with the fact that I have six brothers and I didn't think you should approach what your vocation is in any faint-hearted way . . . or as Rasta would say 'with a weak heart'. So, I wanted to write strong poems as good as the men, but about women's business. There are all kinds of poets whose work influenced me, like W. J. Turner, but I particularly like a Russian poet, Anna Atmatova. I read her in translation because I don't read Russian, but she's elegant and she's great. I like a lot of Russian women's voices. My taste in poetry is very diverse. There's a Peruvian, Antonio Cisneros, whose work I like, and Lorca. I like a lot of people in translation for some reason . . . like Tagore. I like Derek Walcott and Emily Dickinson and many others.

I wondered about Plath?

But you know, like I said, I never succumbed to her because of this suicide business . . . Elizabeth Bishop . . . they're good. I understand that poetry when I read it but I always feel there are some things I should instinctively avoid and this sort of poetry was one of them.

I wondered about Plath because some of the poems reminded me of Plath in their intensity.

Yes, it's that very intensity that would warn me to stay away from her work.

Except you take that intensity in a completely different direction than Plath would. I was thinking of a poem like 'My Last Poem Again' [in *Heartease*] when you talk of poems 'bleeding' you 'shiny bottles of red feeling'. It reminded me of Plath, not in a derivative way, but in the sense in which writing is associated with pain.

Yes . . . I've written poems and felt I couldn't get up to face the next morning. There's a poem in *I Am Becoming* ['Invoke Mercy Extraordinary'] – it's about Marvin Gaye because I love his music and I think there was an extraordinary pull in him between the flesh and the spirit. These two things operated in him very strongly. He has a record called 'What's Going On' which is a most loving piece of work – the concern for humanity, the earth and ecology – it was such an incredibly beautiful piece; it was levitating; it was going to incredible heights. I think if he had continued in that direction he would have ended up in a monastery or on a hill by himself. But always that pull between the flesh and the spirit, that fight. I came to such an understanding of this in the process of writing that poem; it was like I had to go through the process to be able to write it. I was crying . . . it was very painful. Now I don't worry about it: if I have to cry, I have to cry; it doesn't bother me any more. I think *Heartease* did that for me – the process of writing it – if I have to cry and it hurts, then that's okay.

What happens after *Heartease*? You said earlier that you could feel the beginning of another volume starting at the end of *Tamarind Season* and *I Am Becoming*; do you feel that kind of movement after *Heartease*?

Not really. *Heartease* took me to a place where you can't stay . . . you must keep moving. I finished it in the year I was in Boston. That piece and that time was very special; it gave me the time. I had an office where I could go to every day – which I never had before – and I'd sit down and just write for a couple of hours every day and work steadily at it. It is very important to have the time to do it, to just carry on. I remember the last poem I wrote in that volume was 'Heartease New England' and it was kind of weird – it took me away; it was very special, that whole process of writing it. But I didn't write for a while after that. I couldn't.

'Heartease New England' is my favourite poem in that volume; it's beautiful.

Yes, I was very pleased with what happened in that. I really couldn't go into anything after that. Last year I finished a little collection of poems which are very different to the *Heartease* poems. They're about Jamaica and reminiscences of my childhood and even the language is very simple, not so lyrical. I think that's how it had to work itself out. What I'm working on now is more like *Heartease*, more like where it would have taken me if I'd had the strength to keep going right after I'd finished in Boston. I can't even describe what I'm working on now but it's more in keeping with the *Heartease* poems.

Did you find that you had a different perspective when you were writing the *Heartease* poems because you were outside Jamaica or do you move around so much now that it doesn't make a difference?

Yes! I move about quite a bit so I just try to bloom where I'm planted.

Do you do many readings in Jamaica?

No, I wouldn't say I do many, just every now and then.

Why?

There's not a lot of scope for all that many poetry readings in Jamaica.

Someone mentioned that you may be bringing out a selection of short stories.

Yes, I wrote these at the Bunting too. Some of them are from my childhood. Also some of them deal very much with relationships between men and women because I think that's one of my areas; I'm strong on feelings. Some of them are funny and they're not like the poems: I enjoyed myself writing them.

Did you find it very different writing in prose rather than poetry?

Yes, I prefer writing poetry.

Are there any women poets in the Caribbean that you are particularly fond of?

I just love what's happening now; it's like there's a big tapestry and everybody has a corner because everybody has a story to tell. I think that what Erna Brodber is doing is wonderful because she's coming from that extremely spiritual dimension which is so powerful. I think it's great. . . . Olive Senior, Velma Pollard, it's great.

Yes, it's really exciting . . .

Yes, but I hope you're not just limiting this question to the women. I was also very impressed with Caz Phillips's reading for an extremely different reason. I've felt for a long time that there's a big hole – no voices of men of his age from the Caribbean in a serious way. I have brothers his age and I've always wanted to know what they thought.

No, I'm not against the male perspective! It's just that they've had so much mileage in the past that it doesn't seem to me that we'd be doing them a great disservice if we concentrate on the women for a while.

Of course! I agree with you; we should have our turn; it's just I want to know some things. I was particularly interested in what he was saying because the older Caribbean male writers tend not to write from that kind of . . . you know . . .

From a more feeling perspective?

Yes.

There's a poem in *Heartease*, 'She Walks Into Rooms', which really intrigues me. I can't fully come to grips with it; it's mesmerizing but I don't really know why it's so powerful.

There are two things about that poem. . . . One of the things in Russian poetry that I really like is that the elements take on life in an important way. A lot of my poems are about water, so the whole concept of being saturated becomes a very rejuvenating kind of saturation because there is this thing about crying and rain being very depressing, but they are the very things that can make you 'as full of mysteries as the ocean'.

But in another poem, 'On Becoming A Mermaid', the water seems to be signalling death almost . . .

It's death to a certain stage of life – a metamorphosis to another kind of life. I like to think of it as a change in focus . . . to become more clear about a role.

Not sure that I follow you.

I think what I meant in that poem is the change from all distractions to something more simple. A mermaid is a very simple thing . . . a woman's head and a fish's body and that's it. You know what you have to do.

Yes, because you're sexless. I think in the poem you say you're a 'nixie' now.

Yes!

So, the real complications are gone.

It's not something that I want for myself but it's appealing. You're clear about what you are.

Yes, and what you do: you just thrash around in the water!

Yes . . .

Can I just ask you a few questions about your 'spirituality'. You dedicated your last book to Ali Darwish – it sounds like he was a kind of guru for you?

He's a friend of mine and he's important to me. He's an Egyptian writer; I've never met anybody like him before. What he was saying to me exactly fitted what I wanted inside me only I never knew it existed. I didn't know that was what I wanted until I heard him articulate certain things. He was good to me and for me in that sense of pointing me in particular directions. I don't think I need to tell you that I'm a very intense kind of person. I grew up in the Anglican church which is a very intellectual, distant kind of religion; an important religion for intellectual freedom but my whole personality is very affected by it: I feel things – sometimes I feel too much. I needed something that would speak to that aspect of me and that's what Ali did for me. I just love the way he dealt with his whole relationship with God, as a writer and as an integrated human being.

How did you come across him? Did you read his writings first?

No, I met him first. He has some things called 'prepositional writings' which are very short. He can build a whole story around one word. They're lovely stories and they have many layers of meaning, which is another thing that appeals to me; you can always go deeper and deeper into them, like Chinese puzzles.

Do you practise any particular faith?

Not really. I rejoice in my freedom. I think I'm being given an internal freedom; I see God in many things; I can go to a lot of churches. I think God is in everything and everything is in him. Let me be much clearer than that because I don't want to be misunderstood. No, I don't consider myself as belonging to any particular religion but I will happily go to whatever it is; if I'm drawn to a church I will go there.

Because of the kind of spirituality associated with it?

No, I think I'm being set free . . . someone like Gandhi had that kind of outlook on religion which I think is the best kind. You appreciate what is God and what is good in other people's religions.

So the God in the *Heartease* poems is whoever the reader wants that God to be?

I can't impose my God on anybody. I just write about my God and it's up to you to take what you want from it.

How do you feel about the American writers like Alice Walker and Maya Angelou and so on?

Yes, all respect is due to them. Toni Morrison in particular is important to me. Her powers are extraordinary.

I was thinking of Alice Walker's essays in *In Search of Our Mother's Gardens* **[1984].** *I Am Becoming My Mother* **reminded me of that.**

I think this is a time for particular themes to be dealt with and as much light needs to be thrown on them as possible. Everybody must bring their own portion of light. I think for black women, for all women, motherhood is an important issue. For example in Europe – I don't want to generalize, but when I was in Germany last year and speaking to students, many of them seemed to be going through an anti-mother phase. They saw the mother as the focus of everything that was wrong in their lives, and that was anathema to me. All I can say is that I cannot see my life without mothering a child. Even if I never have a child, I'd have to go and get one because it's just something I couldn't see myself not doing because to me having a child is the key to a whole lot of things in myself. I can't speak for anyone else but I know for me it's a key. I remember when I was having my son I used to have these dreams about a little boy saying you have to wake up now. And it's true: he did wake me up!

Yes, motherhood really transforms your life . . .

Like nothing else can. This little boy used to come and say, 'Mummy, you have to wake up now' and Miles has really done that for me now.

Someone recently said she felt slightly alienated by your references to 'him' in *Heartease* **(and I've said that too but for different reasons) because she felt that with the rise in the Caribbean of fundamentalist religions, particularly from the American mid-west, your poems might be playing into that?**

Well, if it's there . . . people will take whatever they want from it. The 'him' is very natural to me. In Jamaica we call everybody 'him', men and women; I don't know how good or bad that is. When we say 'him' we mean everybody – do you do that in Guyana? One of the things I'm looking at is the idea of God as mother, which is another view of the divine. I like to think of it as a continual search. If I'm at a stage when I call God 'him', then that's the stage I'm at and I can't pretend otherwise. I want to reach the stage when I can call God 'she' and be totally sincere about it. And when you read that I'm calling God 'she' you will know that I've arrived at an absolute and heartfelt conclusion that God is a woman. But I'm not there yet! I believe too in this 'Song of Solomon' thing of God as lover. A lot of Eastern poems are poems to the divine, so God becomes a lover or the object of the beloved. I would still think of my beloved as a man but I'm not forcing him on anybody else.

5

Chinua Achebe
with
Chris Searle

Chinua Achebe is Africa's best-known writer and is seen by many as the founding father of African fiction. His first novel, Things Fall Apart *(1958), not only told the story of the colonial encounter from an African point of view, but also gave life and validity to the Igbo village community which grappled with the meaning of that encounter. His subsequent novels,* No Longer at Ease *(1960),* Arrow of God *(1964) and* A Man of the People *(1966), continue the narrative of the consequences of British political and cultural imperialism in Nigeria before and after the achievement of independence in 1960.*

The massacre of many Igbos and a military coup in 1966 led to the declaration of Biafra as a separate and mainly Igbo nation state, for which Achebe wrote and toured the world as a spokesman until Biafra was forced to surrender in 1970. The physical and psychological disruption caused by the war in Nigeria, as well as the increasingly unrestrained economic and political corruption, made sustained writing difficult for Achebe. Never-theless he published a volume of poems, Beware Soul Brother *(1971), and a collection of short stories,* Girls at War and Other Stories *(1972). Achebe also established the literary journal,* Okike, *and continued to contribute forceful lectures and essays on African writing, its reception, and the fail-ure of leadership among politicians and intellectuals in Nigeria itself. In 1983 Achebe was elected deputy president of the People's Redemption*

Party, following the death of its founding leader, Mallam Aminu Kano. That same year he published The Trouble with Nigeria, *analysing and deploring the failure of leadership among politicians and intellectuals in Nigeria.*

This interview focuses on Chinua Achebe's fifth novel, Anthills of the Savannah *(1987) and its context. It is a part of Achebe's belief in the power of words and the integrity of the storyteller – the 'escort' whose language prompts those whom he or she accompanies to 'examine the condition of their lives' – that in his novel such word-makers are the people's protectors against lies, corruption and the abuse of power. Thus they are the last line of resistance against the President's drive towards outright dictatorship, and despite their own positions of influence, still seek contact with the peasants in regions far from the centre of power and the mass of the population. For Achebe's most trenchant criticism is of the form of government which separates and then insulates its rulers from the people in whose exploited name it rules. Colonial power is grotesquely substituted by a stratum of self-seekers and servers of foreign interests who have learned well from the words and deeds of their former masters.*

Chris Searle It is over twenty years since your previous novel, *A Man of the People*, was published. Why has there been such a long period of gestation for *Anthills of the Savannah*?

Chinua Achebe I think that one of the reasons could have been the civil war in Nigeria, the Biafran War. This was such a cataclysmic experience that for me it virtually changed the history of Africa and the history of Nigeria. Everything I had known before, all the optimism had to be rethought. I had found myself writing poetry and short stories, and writing for children in between, as it were writing, and trying to get acquainted with this new reality. The other factor was that I have never felt I *had* to write a book. I began this book fifteen years ago. I had the characters but I didn't have a story. So I put it away and five years later I took it up again and still wasn't ready. So I simply let it stay, until three years ago when I began again and this time it worked.

At that time the situation in Nigeria was deteriorating again very fast, particularly at the level of the leadership. The second civilian republic had failed and the army had returned. Things were seeming to get totally out of hand again, and worry was being created in all our minds.

How do you see *Anthills of the Savannah* in comparison to *A Man of the People*, which was also about the qualities and failings of leadership?

The writer is extending the story all the time. *Anthills* goes into more detail about the kind of people involved in leadership and I go from that to consider the kind of education for leadership such people need to acquire in order to be fit for its tasks. This education has to do with our leaders reconnecting themselves with the people and not living up there, unaware of their reality. Our leaders do not realize how quickly they become completely cut off. It doesn't take a year! You move in cars with sirens and everybody clears the route for you – they even pave the road for you before you make a visit. They paint everything before you see it. And if you are not careful you quickly lose touch. This is one of the key problems. So I'm making this point specifically. That this leadership has to connect itself with the source of its legitimacy: the peasantry, the workers, the women – the people. At the end of *Anthills of the Savannah* there is a kind of groping towards this reality.

How do you think that the major themes of your writing have changed since you wrote *Things Fall Apart*?

The changes are really in the direction that I've indicated. It has been a filling out of the story. It is the same story, the story of Africa in the modern world and our problem with Europe, our problems with modernization, the story of Africa in our time. What I'm doing is trying to see it from different angles like in the proverb about the masquerade. Africa is the masquerade and you don't stand in one place to see it, you move around the arena and take different perspectives.

I'm against those who see Africa as a one-issue case. It's a case of a multiplicity of issues, and you can take them one at a time, like the urgent issue of leadership. But that is not the only one.

Are you saying then that your whole life of writing is really one novel that includes all those perspectives?

It is, that's what I'm saying. It's like four synoptic gospels, I think that's what it is.

In *Anthills of the Savannah* you refer to the 'Bruised Heart' of Africa. Could you explain this a little?

What happened to Africa in its meeting with Europe was devastating. It was our people losing grip on their history, being swept out of the current of their history into somebody else's history, becoming a foot-note. So the history of Africa became the history of alien races in Africa, and the real history that had been going on since the millennia was virtually forgotten – especially because it was not written down. As a result of this, many of us lost our knowledge, our memory of Africa. I can't think of anything more grave happening to a people than this. Then you get into the details and humiliations of colonialism. Then independence came and we assumed that we would immediately take up the story as if nothing had happened and, of course, this has proved to be impossible. So the source of the bruise is a long one, and it has been compounded lately by the brutality of the kind of leadership we have had. So the people have lost their sense of person, their sense of worth. Yet the romantic would suggest that the people are okay, that all you need do is get the people and they would already know what to do. But this is not true and this is why I talk of this bruise. Our people need to be healed. They are the owners of the land, and we, the elite – and among them I count the writers too and we too are bruised in our own way – we must connect with them and we must also expect some disappointments.

A number of prominent African writers, like Ngugi and Sembene Ousmane, are using their novels to explain and contest the force of neo-colonialism in Africa, and its local leaders. *Anthills of the Savannah* seems to have a similar preoccupation. Would you see this concern with neo-colonialism as a highly important theme, perhaps the most important, for the African novelists?

This is a very, very important theme. But I hesitate to prescribe or to say 'This is it' or to be obsessed with either the one problem or the one answer. Some writers, for example, say that the only problem is imperialism. I don't think this is true. There are other issues in Africa beyond imperialism. Nkrumah used to say that if you seek the political kingdom, everything else will be added unto you. But we pursued the political kingdom and found that everything was not added to us. So we must learn to live and write on a broad front. Neo-colonialism is a portmanteau word for all kinds of illnesses – it's a real thing, it's colonialism regrouping and coming back using local jokers as leaders. This is very important, but there are other ways of looking at our problems and we must not get trapped in only looking at them through one vision. This leads to the using of more slogans and over-simplifying of the problem. This then leads to further disappointment because you have not faced the complexities of the issue. We are lazy-minded, we want to know the answers quickly. 'Cut out this long thing,' we say, 'tell me what to do to be saved.' But our problems have been there for hundreds of years and they vary from place to place, country to country. So we must be prepared to face this complexity, as untidy as it may seem, because this is the only way we shall make progress.

In *Anthills of the Savannah* you describe the writer as the people's 'escort'. What do you see as the role of the novelist in Africa and how has it changed since you first started writing?

A little correction, it is the *story* that is the escort. The *story* is more important than the writer, although they are related, naturally. If you look at the things that are happening in the society: the struggle itself, the inspiration to struggle, the story of the struggle; when you put all these things together and say what is the most important, then the choice falls upon the *story*. It is the story that conveys all our gains, all our failures, all we hold dear and all we condemn. To convey this to the next generation is the only way we can keep going and keep alive as a people. Therefore the story is like the genes that are transferred to create the new being. It is far more important than anything else. It has been the same right through my period of writing. I have been using different words, a new metaphor for expressing it. But I don't think that any change has happened to the truth that the *story* is crucial to the survival of a people. This is why those who say that the past is no longer useful to us are so mistaken. You cannot have a present if you do not have a past. The past is all we have. All we can call our own is what has happened, that is our history. If we consider the folk tales which our ancestors crafted, we must strive to do the same thing and communicate to the next generations what is important, what is of value, what must be preserved. If they decide to alter this and that, then that's fine, but they will be doing it in the full knowledge of what has gone before.

You clearly have a belief in the power of the African storyteller and the integrity of his words. In *Anthills of the Savannah* the most commendable characters are those concerned with the making of words. Your character, Beatrice, at the end of the novel also invokes the promise and hope of people and ideas. In what ways does your faith in the storyteller, ideas and the people point towards an Africa where the bruises are healed?

This is my belief and hope. But I say this knowing there are still dangers on the way, there is still a lot of work ahead of us before we arrive at this ideal state where the storyteller, the people and the force of ideas are working together in harmony. This is a great future, but it may never come fully, because our human condition is that we shall always struggle, struggle to achieve our utmost. I don't know whether what

I've done will bear any fruit, but whether it does or not I like to feel that when I go, then those who come behind will say that although I may have failed, I struggled. It is like the tortoise and the leopard and the way the tortoise put up a fake impression of struggle. You remember in the Igbo folk story that the leopard caught up with the tortoise. He had been trying to catch him for a long time. He wanted to kill him. So, when he finally caught him, he said, 'Aha, now prepare yourself to die.' So the tortoise began to scatter and push sand all around him on the road, to create the impression of a struggle. The leopard was mystified. He thought the tortoise would simply want to stand still and contemplate his death, rather than get involved in this frantic action. So he said, 'Why are you doing that?' And the tortoise told him, 'When I'm dead, I want people who pass by to say that here a man met his match.' In other words, that there was a struggle, that he did not go meekly. That is the metaphor of a writer.

Why is the writing in English that is emerging from Africa and the Caribbean so much more powerful and positive than that coming from the imperialist and old colonizing powers like Britain and the US?

It comes from that same source of struggle. The writer is involved far more in the world of struggle in our countries, real life-and-death struggle. We are not playing games. We are dealing with serious issues. I remember in Stockholm, at a conference, a European writer saying: 'You know, I envy you people. Here nothing I do will ever put me in prison!' We have the advantage that we can be locked up – that is what he was saying! But in a way he was acknowledging that what we are doing is more serious, more fundamental. In addition, we have the advantage of our largely unrecognized huge oral tradition. This is a vital source for us. We are now in a position to be able to use it and call upon it in our literature.

We have a massive diversity within our struggle in Africa. Wherever we are there is struggle and we must struggle ourselves to see the whole picture. We must not fall into the narrow view that we are a one-issue continent. One place where we must begin is in the area of leadership. Africa must link up, for we are all in this struggle, whether it is the elemental struggle against famine and hunger and Ethiopia having to appeal to the world for grain, or the struggle in South Africa against apartheid. In Nigeria we do not have apartheid but the fact that the South African people are locked in this struggle diminishes us and our potential for solving problems in Nigeria. For ultimately it is a struggle about the great wealth of South Africa and its economy and the way this wealth is *not used* for the benefit of Africa and its people. And, of course, the disruption it causes to other states, like Mozambique for example. So the whole continent is one war front, for anything that reduces an African in Ethiopia or South Africa reduces *all* Africans anywhere. So our writing *must be* political and must carry the vigour of these fundamental issues into it. There is no writing in Africa that can fail to be political. Whereas in the West, if a novel is said to be 'political' it means that it is not very good, it's used as a criticism. Or the critics say, 'Although it is political, it is a good novel', which is in itself a very political thing to say. For it means, 'The world is okay, we don't need to drag in any of these extraneous factors. Let's talk about Art, about style, about the use of language. Things are okay!' So there are two positions. One is conservative, the other is not – because it doesn't have anything to conserve, it wants a resharing of things.

You talked earlier about how the civil war in your country had shattered the optimism of your writers, particularly with regard to African political leadership. But don't Africa's great leaders like Machel, Cabral, Nkrumah or Nyerere give you cause for some optimism?

In 1983, in Nigeria, I wrote a little political book out of some desperation before the election called *The Trouble with Nigeria*. I was concerned with the question of leadership. I did point to a few great leaders by name. This was not exhaustive. But I did talk about the late Aminu

Kano in Nigeria itself, who at least had this record of going through all the offices of state and still coming out a very poor man. I also gave the example of Julius Nyerere, a legendary figure. Today there will be those who say he failed, that the Tanzanian economy crumbled in his hands, but that's not true. But even if he did, he was a man who was not helping himself to the treasury, which has been very common behaviour in our continent. So we have had our exemplary leaders, and we should talk about them, understand that it has never been one grim story of failure all the way. In fact, there is a need to get away from the pessimism and change our words and imagery and not harp on about failure. But it must not be simple minded, it must concentrate intelligently upon the examples and signs that have been positive and successful. For example, despite the immense difficulties that Mozambique faces, things would have been infinitely worse without a leader like Machel, or the same with Tanzania without a Nyerere. These are desperately poor countries, yet they have never made a fiasco with independence. They have free education, for example, which we don't have in Nigeria, even though they don't have oil. These characters in the story of Africa did not fail. Okonkwo in *Things Fall Apart* or Ezeulu in *Arrow of God* did not fail. We are still talking about them. It is the same with these great leaders. Machel is dead, but actually he is not yet dead, and the same with Lumumba, Neto, Cabral and the others. They stay in the memory of Africa; that is their greatest contribution. We remember them and their struggle. And now we also have the written word to keep their work in our minds.

In *Anthills* one of your characters condemns very forcefully the impact in Africa of US imperial culture. What kind of damage do you see it causing in Nigeria?

US culture is a strong force of debilitation, not just for Nigerian or African culture, but for almost all other cultures around the world. It is difficult to stand up, to be yourself as you ought to because the West, and America in particular, has so much power and influence. The music that my children listen to now is the same that American children listen to. The Nigerian High-Life is virtually dead because of this. In dancing too. We are the great dancers, but our own youth now shuffle like the Americans. This has been a very serious penetration of our life and culture. It is where everything is coming from and the world is imperilled by its influence. So, again, we need to insist upon the multiplicity of cultures to combat this and stand up also for the way in which our own ancestors did things, in order to give ourselves more confidence. In writing, too, we have a group of writers who create totally un-African settings and try to copy the fast-car, fast-murder kind of story that comes from America and the West. Again, it shows us that all of us, including our writers, must educate ourselves about our own culture in order to be strong enough to withstand this force.

How do you find that the particular qualities and strengths of your first language, Igbo, have become a part of the English that you write? Do you think they have given it a particular African quality?

I think it has done that, certainly. I don't know how and it would be difficult to explain in detail unless we are students of linguistics. But I'm not very interested in that. There is a way in which the vigour of one language, its imagery and metaphors, can be transferred across. And there is a certain irreducibility in human language anyway, which is what makes translation possible, even though we are not always satisfied with the result and we keep striving. If one has this respect for the integrity of language, you make this extra effort to get as close as possible to what you have in your mind. And that may not be what you actually manage to get down on paper. But you worry about it, work at it and try to get something better.

The other vital question is what happens to the African languages in the situation where we are writing our books in English, French or Portuguese? What happens to Swahili, or Gikuyu or Yoruba? As you know, there is a very strong lobby for abandoning the European languages. This is a very understandable passion, to move away from the metropolitan languages and to revive the African languages. We must respect this. But we can also get trapped in this one-issue mentality. 'If only we abandoned the European languages, our problems would be solved!' This is not true at all. Our problems would not be solved by this. We have got a very, very complicated situation in Africa, including the survival of the nation states. It is not for nothing that the most radical countries in Africa like Mozambique, Angola, Burkina Faso have chosen the metropolitan European languages as national languages and have more or less foreclosed the argument. They are the ones who are the most forthright in saying 'we cannot be without these languages'. The minister of culture of Burkina Faso was saying not so long ago, almost with a shudder, that if the sixty languages of his country were to be officially used, the one state would disintegrate into sixty states. So it doesn't do us any good to belittle this danger which the political leaders of all modern African states must be aware of, this peril of disintegration. Writers who are not responsible for keeping their country together must not talk or behave as if there is no real problem, as if you can simply go back to a pre-Treaty of Berlin situation. As an African and a nationalist looking at the situation now, there is a real value in keeping our countries together using a language that has been imposed upon us. It may not last for all time, but writers are not only there for all time, they're here for now as well.

6

Moyez Vassanji
with
Susheila Nasta

Moyez Vassanji was born in Nairobi, Kenya in 1950. He was educated at the Aga Khan Schools in Dar es Salaam, Tanzania, before attending the Massachusetts Institute of Technology and the University of Pennsylvania. On a visit to London in 1991, Vassanji discussed the background to The Gunny Sack *(1989) with the editor of* Wasafiri. The Gunny Sack *won the Best First Commonwealth Novel Prize for Africa in 1990; it is centrally concerned with the experience of the African-Asian diaspora in East Africa and explores the relationship between memory and the writing of histories amidst transient communities whose identities are mixed and shifting. Since the interview was conducted, Vassanji has gone on to publish a number of other award-winning fictions, including a collection of short stories,* Uhuru Street *(1991),* No New Land *(1991),* The Book of Secrets *(1994) and* Amriika *(1999).*

Vassanji has been highly acclaimed both as a 'Canadian' writer and as a figure who has excavated and narrated the stories of ordinary people's lives, stories which create a thread between past and present amongst the voices of East Africa's migrant Asian communities. In 1998 he edited a book of essays, Meeting of Streams: South Asian Canadian Literature, *and he won the Giller Prize for his latest novel,* The In-between World of Vikram Lal *(2003).*

Susheila Nasta You've just won the Commonwealth Writer's Prize for Africa with your novel *The Gunny Sack*. It is a book concerned particularly with the migrant Asian population in East Africa spanning four generations. I wonder if you could say something of how you came to write the novel?

Moyez Vassanji There are several ways of looking at that. One is that I live in Canada and at some point I felt a tremendous sense of loss at being away from the place I grew up in, and what I did was try to recreate the life that we lived. But I think a more important motive perhaps is that that life has never been lived . . . I mean never been written about. It's something that is slowly being wiped out, and as the people who've experienced that life die away, die off, then there's no more record of that life. I think all people should have a sense of themselves, a sense of where they come from, and it just happens that people in East Africa – I think Indians as well as Africans and especially in Tanzania – don't have that sense, a historical sense, of where they come from. There is a vague kind of oral history telling them where they come from but it's not something that you read about; it's something that's constantly changing, and if you just compare it with what goes on in the West, where everything is recorded, you can see that our lives have not been recorded and that's what I set out to do when I wrote the novel.

The gunny sack is the central image or symbol in the novel. I believe this kind of image has come up in different forms in other writings by Asians in different parts of the world. Had you seen this idea in relation to any sort of an Asian diaspora, the idea of history being carried with you . . . as a kind of trunk?

Well, I wasn't aware of that but once people told me I realized that yes, the trunk was very fundamental.

Particularly in South Asian writing.

Yes. But I wasn't aware of it. To me the gunny sack was just memory and when I began writing the novel I had a very romantic image of a person weighed down by memories, which is what I felt I was. And at some point I was looking for a way to deal with that past and that past to me was just a bunch of memories, very discrete memories that interlinked and combined in all sorts of ways. And then I had this idea of using a metaphor where actual objects, real objects stand for memories so they remind the narrator of memories, or they evoke his memories. But what happens eventually in the novel is that after a while the gunny sack again becomes a metaphor and objects are no longer that important; it is the memory, the imagination that's important.

And the stories which the memories evoke.

Yes.

It struck me that one of the main characteristics of *The Gunny Sack* was the number of different voices you tried to introduce into the text through the stories of Jibai and the stories the various women tell; the stories of all the different characters in the family are all interrelated and although you have the narrator there, there seem to be lots of different voices speaking. I wondered how you tackled that not only in terms of writing the novel but also in terms of writing the novel in English?

You mean how I did it technically?

Well not so much technically but how you approached the voices of these people who may not have been talking to each other in English, or telling their stories in English, how you transformed that into a novel in English?

In my writings the voice is very important and even the narrator's voice . . . I don't have a neutral voice, an objective voice that you find in traditional English novels. The voice or the accent of the person is there when I write so it was not that difficult for me to use different voices. If I imagine someone telling the story then there is a voice that was with the story – a tone – and I tried to recreate that tone in English.

So you don't find it difficult to recapture the content of how these people were living in English; you didn't find that using English actually in some senses changed the experience?

A little bit, but what made it easier I think was that even when we were young, as boys and girls when we talked English, the English always had an accent because we could switch between three languages. Our English was a kind of hybrid at least in terms of the accent of the voice because we could switch when we talked. All our three languages therefore merged into one voice and it was easier to reproduce them on paper.

The book has been compared to Salman Rushdie's novel *Midnight's Children* [1981] as a fictional history of India and independence. Did you have (apart from your own personal reasons for writing the novel because of your own experiences), did you have any sort of socio-political motive there, because obviously throughout the novel you have the development of the society after colonialism and the movement towards independence, and certainly towards the end of the novel the political side of it becomes increasingly significant and you seem, or the narrator also seems to be very wary of the politics at certain points. What were your objectives there?

The objective was just to record a life, and the lives on which that life – that is the life of my generation – was based. But I think because I lived away from my country it was easier for me to convey. I could name the country. I could name the political leaders. I could name actual events which many other African writers have not been able to do or have refused to do. In that sense the novel becomes very political because it obviously has a stand on real political events and real political figures. For example, it has a narrator's view of Nyerere and a view of Karume who was the vice-president and of the other political leaders, but that was not the only purpose; it just happened that way. I was dealing with the life of my generation. We cannot disassociate our lives from politics, from the politics of the continent. We are what we are right now because of certain political decisions made nationally and internationally.

Was there a sense amongst the Asian community of a future which was going to involve a continuous sense of movement or a continuation of the movement that was already part and parcel of their history?

I don't think there was a conscious feeling that there would always be movement. In fact consciously the Asians always thought – at least the Asians that I was in touch with in my community – that we were there to stay and these were very conscious decisions. British citizenships were renounced, we sent back our British passports and it was a wholehearted embrace of the new political situation. But subconsciously it's possible that the colonial legacy was very strong amongst the Asians because we had certain values which somehow seemed out of place in the emerging political reality. So in that sense it's possible that there was a potential movement and I think somehow it has to do with having been colonized.

Why do you think there has been so little African Asian literature or writing about the Asian community in Africa whereas with African writing in general there's been a lot published? In a sense your novel is one of the first novels to look at this question.

It's a very deep mystery that I cannot understand. One reason seems to be that Asians belong to very closed communities, and also very close communities, and to be able to write about them would require a tremendous sense of detachment which they did not have. I know of other writers, Asian writers, who could not detach themselves from their communities and therefore their writing does not deal with the life that was lived, but deals more with abstractions. But there were no Africans; we don't have that many writers in East Africa except perhaps Ngugi, who really touches deeply into the life of his people; I haven't seen many African writers having emerged from East Africa.

What do you think will be happening with the Asians that are still there? Most Asians left . . .

Well a lot of them left; but it depends where you are talking about, on the coast?

Yes. The areas that *The Gunny Sack* is dealing with.

Yes, there you have some very deeply entrenched communities, Asian communities, the communities that left were the more wealthy communities. They didn't start out as wealthy but because of the development in the 1950s and 1960s they became more Westernized and you can trace it to specific schools that were founded by these communities, and because of these schools, the community – my community – took the decision that it would get educated in English and once you took that route then you had to finish it and wind up somewhere in Britain or Canada or the United States. Whereas, other communities were more traditional, they believed more in the Islamic education, for example, and therefore Westernization did not appeal to them; they did not take the community decision to Westernize themselves and therefore they were quite happy. In East Africa if they ever left they would leave not for the West but they would go to Iran or some of the Arab countries, the Emirates or Oman, where a lot of Arabs came from, or they would go to India or Pakistan, but they would not go to the West.

When you started to write *The Gunny Sack*, how long had you been away?

I had been away ten years when I started *The Gunny Sack*, although I had been back and forth many times when my family was in East Africa.

Did you find the distance in a sense crystallized the experience in some ways?

It does, because there is the need to recreate and little details emerge which are quite important in your life. It's a reality that's impinging on you all the time, so you have one reality when you are outside looking at snow but in your mind you have some very precise images or events from the past.

The structure of the novel is not designed as a linear structure, it's more of a cycle. How did you come to terms with finding a form for this sort of oral history which doesn't follow a particular time scheme and doesn't follow what you might expect of a conventional plot? How did you find a way of structuring this story, because the novel is about there not being a structure?

It is. Yes. *The Gunny Sack* gave a structure to the basic memories that one has in one's mind so once I established the existence of the gunny sack, I was imposing a pattern and then I imposed another structure on that which divided into three parts, although the three parts are interlinked, and go back and forth. Every part is a focus of a certain period in history and that made things easy. Also, the narrator is a unifying force and his interaction with his memories is also a unifying force.

And he's linked to all these generations before him, through the family. There are sixteen or seventeen characters who are all interlinked with each other. That must have been quite difficult when you

were writing it. I remember when I was reading it, it was hard trying to keep track of all these people.

I did not really find it difficult, because in our lives there are so many people whom we interact with that somehow it didn't seem that difficult, and also some of the characters were based on real people so again that helped.

Another thing I'm curious about is the ending of the novel, or the way you close it, not necessarily the ending. When you talk about the figure of Amina, I suppose. Could you say something about her?

Which Amina?

Well both of them. That's really what I mean.

Well there is the Amina who doesn't work for him, and there is the Amina who is the possibility. The novel ends with the rejection of the Amina that doesn't work, who in fact has rejected Salim. The new Amina could stand for hope and faith. For any country, especially a Third World country, the only possibility that I could see when I was finishing the novel was that there was nothing you can do except have faith in the country and hope, and by faith I mean you have to have a stake in that country for good or bad and only then can it work. If everybody abandons something that doesn't seem to work then obviously there's no hope.

You end on the idea of redeeming the wounded souls and you also set up a kind of opposition between writing, creatively, i.e. writing this oral history that the narrator's been writing in the novel, and a different kind of writing – academic writing – represented by Salim's brother. They are trying to pull the same things out of the cupboard maybe but they don't have the same results. There are other instances of this in the novel. Do you find that critical writing

on your work is useful or do you find it essentially a not particularly creative process?

One needs readers and I think the reality that exists for my kind of writing, African writing, Third World writing, is that unfortunately one has to depend very heavily on academic readings, because there isn't that big readership that writers in the West normally have, so I wouldn't want to put down those people who are taking the trouble to actually make the work more relevant to a wider audience. Of course what that means is that the work is very much dependent on a very small number of readers and that disturbs me: that the channel between my work and the rest of the world is so small. That is frightening.

I wonder in a sense whether the tension at the end is also about a different kind of sack of memories which maybe an academic can pick out, or a different way of writing history, whether this is also linked to language and the way the story is told, because there are alternative ways of writing about history, as you said earlier, giving voice to the people that haven't had a voice.

Yes, to create a mythology or a new nation which I find more exciting than academic history, but I introduced this tension because at one point I was very interested in the academic digging up of history and the two brothers represent two sides of my own interests. I am also very interested in looking at manuscripts and editing them or just being aware that manuscripts need editing, and philology and stuff like that. I was very interested in this and almost took it on seriously but gave it up in favour of doing something more creative. But the research that I did for a few years is very much part of this book; so even though the novel talks about the imagination and creative history, it also has depended on written reference.

Where would you place a novel like this? I mean does it irritate you that you're set up as the writer who's won the African section of the Commonwealth Writer's Prize? How do you feel about those sorts of labels?

Well in one way the label is an honour because it means that it is an acknowledgement by my peers who are African writers; it's an acknowledgement of me as an African writer which is more important than an overall prize. I wasn't quite sure how I would be taken or accepted by the other Africans, but it seems that has not been a problem. On the other hand one doesn't want to be labelled as only an African writer or only an Asian writer.

Or, Canadian writer?

Or, Canadian writer.

Could you say something about what you're involved in writing now?

In the midst of writing *The Gunny Sack* I wrote a collection of short stories [*Uhuru Street*] which deal with a view to recreate Dar es Salaam where I grew up, during a specific period. And what I thought of doing was just to basically turn off and turn on lights, in a manner of speaking, one by one so each short story would be a flicker of light and then you would have a whole street emerging or a whole city if you like. A few short stories don't do that but essentially that's what I was trying to do as that street and that life will in a few years almost be non-existent. But after I wrote *The Gunny Sack* I wrote, purely for fun, a novel that is set in Toronto [*No New Land*] and deals with some of the Asians who left Dar es Salaam for Toronto and how they coped with the life there, how they redefined themselves in Toronto.

And how do they redefine themselves?

There are several ways of doing that. There are three men – and they do it in different ways. There is an older person, a middle-aged man who is the main character, and going to Toronto is essentially a liberation. At least after a while he sees it is giving him lots of possibilities but the question that the novel asks is whether he is capable of taking them on. The answer is it's not possible because he is essentially where he came from and that puts certain restraints or constraints on him and he cannot do everything that he would have liked to do; he cannot break free from the past. And there are two other younger characters who more or less have escaped the past because they're younger and they have been educated in the West or in the Western style.

Do you have any regrets about living in Toronto now in terms of writing?

Well I realize that living in Toronto made it possible to write what I'm writing right now, and especially to examine the life that was lived, but at a more basic level I would of course have preferred that I was still in East Africa in the community there and that we could be doing something constructive in a country which seems to me at least to have degenerated in many ways. I think if the Asians had remained there and been allowed to maintain the structures that they had set up – the educational system, the health system, businesses – then the country would have been in a much better shape than it is now.

7

Jamaica Kincaid
with
Gerhard Dilger

Born in 1949 in St John's, Antigua, as Elaine Potter Richardson, Jamaica Kincaid is one of the Caribbean's most distinguished women writers. She left Antigua at seventeen, before independence reached the island, and travelled to New York where she worked as an au-pair and a receptionist, and wrote for a magazine. She changed her name in 1973 and became a staff writer for the New Yorker *in 1976. Her first stories appeared in* Rolling Stone *magazine,* Paris Review *and the* New Yorker. *She received her first literary award in 1983, for her collection of short stories,* At the Bottom of the River *(1983); this was followed soon after by the publication of* Annie John *(1985). That year she visited Antigua and was shocked by fourteen years of government neglect following independence. The visit led to the writing of her controversial non-fiction work* A Small Place *(1988). In* Lucy *(1990) Kincaid returns to the relationship with her mother and mother-island first explored in* At the Bottom of the River *and* Annie John, *a suggestive metaphor in all of Kincaid's fiction for her ambivalent relationship to her colonial and postcolonial past. Since this interview was conducted she has published* Autobiography of My Mother *(1996),* My Brother *(1997),* Talk Stories *(2000),* My Garden Book *(2001) and* Mr Potter *(2002).*

Gerhard Dilger *Lucy*, like all of your other books, is very much based on your own personal history. Why did you leave Antigua and go to the United States?

Jamaica Kincaid I left at the time, in 1965, because I wanted to. People left, they went to England – I happened to go to America – they left for economic reasons. I left for the same reasons people tend to leave the places they live in, because they feel they will find happiness of some kind somewhere else, they feel that they'll feel better about themselves. They hope to be prosperous. I did not hope to be prosperous. I was only sixteen years old. It wasn't a particularly important thing for me then. I was a very depressed person, I wanted to leave, I wanted to go to America and I would make sense of myself to myself. If you saw me at the moment I was leaving, you would say, 'This is someone who is leaving and will work and help her parents', and if you had asked me I wouldn't have said you were wrong. I really didn't have a choice in the matter; it was something that happened and I was glad it happened.

Were there any regrets?

No, I never regretted leaving at all. Not at all. It's one of those things with no regrets. There were moments when I was homesick, but no matter how homesick I got, I never wanted to give up. I was looking for control of my own life although I didn't know it. I was looking to close my door when I want to, open it when I want, come when I want. I was looking to have some idea of myself.

How did you start writing?

I don't really know. People ask me that all the time, and I wish that when it had been happening, I would have made note of it. I started to write when I was in college. I wrote poems – I think everyone who begins to write begins to write poems because it seems to be a way to express your feelings. I was studying to be a photographer, and I ended up leaving school and going to New York. I think it must have had more conviction than I'm remembering because you don't really start to do something in the haphazard way I describe it, but I can't remember.... Now that I know how difficult writing is and what it really takes to do any kind of writing, good or bad, I'm astonished that I was so bold. I think it was one of those things of fools rushing in where angels fear to go. If I knew what I know I would have been more cautious, but I'm the kind of person who is deliberately ignorant about whatever I'm going to do so that I can do it.

You have said you were not conscious of any kind of literary tradition when you started writing. Looking back, do you see yourself in the Afro-Caribbean tradition of storytelling?

I did not have any African type of storytelling traditions. I had gossip, essentially. I had my mother telling me about her life, and about my life before I knew myself, and about her mother, her father, her sisters, about their marriages, their loves in a very sanitized way, it was rather mythic and fairy-tale-like. I heard what the other people were doing, who was trying to kill whom through secret means or was getting brutal.... My storytelling from my family was gossip and things over-heard, things that I should not have heard, things that I made myself listen to. So this is my storytelling tradition. The great griots did not exist in my life. All the great traditions of village life in Africa just absolutely escaped me. I'm very much against those new attempts to bind people of colour to traditional things. One of the reasons why I left home was that I was a victim of tradition. I was on the verge of being a dead person because of tradition, and I think women especially have to be very careful of these traditions. They are the first to go when you start talking about traditions, because there is no tradition of freedom, they have to make it up. So I don't have any tradition.

What literature were you exposed to in school?

The thing that I knew was English literature. It was not told to me because the English cared for me and wanted to educate me and thought it was a good thing if I had a mind. It was taught to me to reinforce their superiority. It's one of the few cases where it didn't work. It just hasn't worked for all of us to write, I suspect with the exception of V. S. Naipaul. It worked on him, he's in awe of it. But if I have influences, it would be English literature, of the greatest kind. Mind you, they really did show us their best in a tantalizing way.

This reminds me of the passage in *Lucy* where the protagonist remembers how she had to recite Wordsworth's 'Daffodils' – for me, this is a very impressive example of how Classical English literature can turn into a nightmare for people in the Caribbean.

Yes. Has anyone else told you of their experiences with it?

Well, I think people like George Lamming or Austin Clarke wrote about it. When I was in Jamaica, I was surprised to find how much teachers and pupils still take English culture and language for granted as the thing to teach, as compared to the classroom use of the Creole language. I had the impression that in many places little has changed from the way you describe the colonial type of education in *Annie John* and *Lucy*.

Well, it's hard to know what to do with all of this because the other alternative is to change your name and call yourself Kenyatta, which means that you have to ignore the fact that Kenyatta was not a good man, you just ask the average thinking Kenyan how marvellous Kenyatta was, and you'll quickly abandon this idea, so it's hard to know just what to do. Then you'd have to learn a new language; it doesn't really take in your past, the new language, it takes in what you're learning now.

But Creole really is the language spoken by most of the people in the West Indies, and in your books you also mention French patois . . .

. . . spoken in Dominica, and in Antigua: ten people would read it.

I mean the spoken language.

Yes, but then a writer like me should have two languages. I'm telling you how confusing the whole thing is. The minute you start this discussion of the 'people's language', 'the imperial language', you have to arrange your own little Stalin for yourself in which you enforce all these rules for yourself or you send yourself to your own little Gulag and you die. It seems that a very very hard thing for someone like me or people in the conquered position is to understand that we live with all sorts of contradictions and it can make you crazy and it can make you sad and it can even cripple you but it's a reality . . . These teachers, what can they teach, there are no books written in these languages. Even if there were, what would the students do with it later? They'd still have to learn a language of the world.

I'm not suggesting that students shouldn't learn English. Don't you think that the fact that Standard English – in its spoken and its written form – is not dealt with as a foreign language contributes to the high drop-out rate in Caribbean schools?

No.

Certainly the major cause is the little amount of money put into the education system, with underpaid teachers and sixty pupils in one class . . .

. . . you would drop out, too! They're having that drop-out problem in the United States, with the African American students. They have

Afro-centred schools and they say the drop-out rate is much lower, but what I suspect is happening is that the kids just get better attention, so you would learn anything. You know, I have my own quarrel with all of this, when I hear people saying it, and I have the quarrel again with myself because I don't even know how to speak English patois any more.

Who are the readers of your books? People in the USA and Europe, or is there also a readership in the Caribbean?

I would have no audience in the Caribbean if I had not had an audience in the United States and elsewhere first. It's a very bitter thing, but true all the same that all these people in the Caribbean, in the island I come from, would not be interested, and would have thought I was foolish. One reason I changed my name is because when I started to write I didn't want anyone I knew to know I was writing, because I knew – and I was not wrong – that they would laugh at me, they would say that I was a daughter of a vain woman attempting doing this terrible thing. So if I sound very bitter about the place that I come from, I am and they deserve it. . . . Well, they behave just like the people everywhere, I suppose. Everyone coming from a small place will feel the provincialism of their compatriots particularly. I started to write about people who wouldn't read me for people whom I wasn't sure would be interested, and that was just a risk I took.

When you write nowadays, do you think about the white readership at all?

No, no, it wouldn't be helpful. It's very hard for me to think of white people, because I don't know these terms particularly well, and I use them for shorthand, but I don't believe in them.

In your books, the protagonists are strong, hard-headed women. In particular, there is this very intense love–hate relationship between daughter and mother.

. . . I don't really know what to say about the mother–daughter relationship . . .

Reviewers tend to enhance that aspect.

I don't know why. It's not the only theme in my work, but actually, it has wider implications than just the immediate mother and daughter. I'm suspecting that I'm really writing about mother country and subjective daughter country. It certainly led me to see that I was obsessed with the powerful and the powerless, and the strong and the weak, and it led me – in examining this relationship between a child and a parent and in particular between the mother and the daughter which has its own female configuration – it led me to see politics, and it led me to see other relationships in the world, mainly as I say, the relationship between the colony and the 'mother country'. So if you had asked me this question a few years ago, I would have been able to give you the answer you perhaps might like to hear, but I've outgrown the domestic implications of the mother and the daughter, and it now has wider implications for me. So that's where I am with it, I have exhausted the domestic colouring.

Critics have praised the poetic and 'dream-like' quality of your earlier writing. I see a certain correspondence to the thematic shift you described in your way of writing. It has become more straightforward, more 'realistic'.

I obviously have grown in awareness, I think, since I started to write. Either that or I'm able to express some things more than when I started and that makes sense.

Does the distance help as well?

Oh, I could never write these things in the place I'm writing about. I mean, I need to be away from it and to hold it closely in my mind. The reality of it is overwhelming. I've always found my reality in this place crippling, but it's the only thing I really want to write about. I can't write about America, I mean I can, but I'm not an American and America has so many writers it doesn't need one more person peering at it. I come from this small place where no one looks so perhaps I look and get damned for it. It's clear I'm not really the same person starting to write the stories in *At the Bottom of the River*. In those stories I was deeply interested in words. Each word in that book is carefully weighed. I no longer do that because I'm in a big hurry to get to say something, and I don't have time for nice weighings, I just sort of want to crash through. So I just now use this slash-and-burn policy of writing, I just say what I have to say and get it out. That sort of long contemplation of each word, that sort of hymn to each word and each comma and each full stop, I no longer have time for that.

In *Lucy*, you manage to bring the two worlds – the Caribbean and North American – together. You characterize very accurately certain upper-middle-class white Americans, like Mariah, Lewis and their trendy friends. What were the reactions to that?

Well, the strange thing is that this book got the most unsympathetic review from an American black woman. The most sympathetic reviews of it were from people who were not black. In America, black people are obsessed with skin colour, to the point that they write those long articles about who is really black, and who isn't, and who is part white, and this sort of nonsense, just absolute nonsense. They've just never really gotten beyond the question of the colour of your skin to see humanity, and it's a great problem because there was a moment when that was being done, I think with Martin Luther King, when we were just going to rescue human beings from this dustbin we were all in, and that failed. . . . Now the people, it would seem, most interested in racial classification are black people, or non-white people in the United States. And so they got very annoyed at me because I wouldn't say Lucy is black and that kind of thing. When a white person writes, he or she doesn't say 'I'm white', and Lucy simply assumes her place in humanity. Well, that was very annoying to people, they wanted to hear about her oppression and her racial discrimination, but she is someone who is going to be disappointing for a small-minded reader. If you are in the world, and if you are beyond certain limitations, I think she's a very satisfying companion. These words, 'white' and 'black', are really representations of power and powerlessness. When you say 'white', you know the winner, if you say 'black', you know the loser. If you just said, 'the people who lost', everyone knows who they are, 'the people who won', we all know who they are, and that's what you say when you say 'white' and 'black', and I'm really beyond that, because in my mind, everybody loses and everybody wins at this point.

At some point, Lucy herself talks about the victors and the vanquished.

She does, but that's how she talks about them, because I think that I now can see that sometimes you win and sometimes you lose and you cannot predict – as you know all too well looking at your own history – when you'll win, and you cannot predict when you'll lose and we cannot know how it will look in the next hundred years.

This year, we remember Columbus's arrival in America. Looking back at five hundred years, there seems to be a clear continuity of European white exploiters on the one hand and the exploitation of African, Asian and Native American people on the other.

That voyage is one of the biggest wins in history. Do you know why Columbus and the Europeans, went that way? The Muslims had conquered Constantinople, which then was the gateway to the riches; it was through that way that you could get to Asia. It had fallen into the hands of the 'horrid infidels' and closed off Europe. Europe then was looking into this abyss. It looked as if the capture of Constantinople was the biggest win when it happened. Five hundred years later, nobody remembers it. Nobody knows what happened. You could ask the first ninety people you met, 'Why did Columbus go that way?' They'll say, 'Oh, he wanted to see if the world was really flat' or something, but the reason these people went that way is because the old route wasn't available any more. When that old route became unavailable, the people who won Constantinople looked like the biggest winners, and we know where they are today. They are begging to come into the Common Market, they are nothing really, they are waiting on tables in Germany, they are cleaning toilets, that's where they are. So you just do not know how these things work, you don't know what the thing is. It's true that the way European power looks in the world today, they look unassailable . . .

. . . especially in the Caribbean. *A Small Place* **is, after all, a very pessimistic book.**

Yes, I'm a pessimist when I think about the Third World. I just went to Kenya, and that was pretty discouraging on many levels. Obviously you just look at Africa, and it's a disaster . . . but it was discouraging in another way. I met these Kenyan intellectuals, very intelligent people. They would say things like 'Have you been to Africa?' and I'd say 'No', and they'd say 'Welcome home'. Well, Africa is not my home. In telling me 'welcome home', they implied that my presence outside of Africa was not permanent. This word diaspora is a very odd thing. In the first place, the people it used to apply to . . . I don't see how anyone in their right mind would imitate the experience of Israel or would hope to imitate it. However necessary it may have been for the Jews to have Israel, it's not been pretty. In that part of the world, Israel's existence has not led to great happiness for most of the people living in that part of the world, for whatever reason. So this idea that I'm living in a diaspora which means that at some point I'm going to go home . . . but won't I get in the way of the people there, I mean, if all the black people in the West went to Africa, wouldn't that cause incredible tension? Wouldn't that have its own horror? So you just wonder why people say this nonsense. If I am in a diaspora, my 'diaspora-ness' has huge problems if I return home.

That is one thing; the other thing about this welcome-home business is that it became clear to me that they would be very inter-ested, if I did 'go back home', in making a distinction between Africans in this way: there were Africans who had remained in Africa and there were Africans who were descended from slaves. I was descended from slaves, and if they could find an advantage in that, and they could, because being a descendant from a slave is not pretty – it's not exactly the ancestral family you hope for, you know, the founding member of your family is a captured person – they were looking forward to this distinction in which they could be better. So I gave up. This was very sobering. I came back and I thought, well, I'm just nobody. In this world I live in, I'm nobody, and it's quite fine with me. I choose that. I'm not African, I'm not anything. In fact, I have the blood of quite a few different people running around inside me, but I don't claim them. This is dead. I'm now.

In *A Small Place*, you very strongly attack a certain type of wealthy tourist coming from the US or Europe, and you mention the fact that the US administration wouldn't tolerate another charismatic leader like Maurice Bishop from Grenada.

. . . They would get rid of him.

. . . What were the reactions to that book in the United States?

Again, that book got the most vicious attack from a black man, a black American man, and the most sympathetic views from people that are not black, so you see, you just can't tell who'll be nice, who'll understand better about these things. *A Small Place* was meant to be an article for the *New Yorker*, and I really wrote it for the *New Yorker* reader. The *New Yorker* changed hands, and the new editor didn't like it. He didn't say that, but it was obvious that they thought it would offend the advertisers. But then it became a book, my wonderful American editors printed it, and the people in Antigua who read it would say to my mother, 'It's true, but did she have to say it?', and that I think is a very revealing statement and a very typical statement of people where I'm from. They think you shouldn't mention the unpleasant truth, and then maybe it will go away.

You come to the conclusion that Antigua is worse off today than when it was a British colony.

Apparently, if you look at the surface, Antigua is very prosperous. But it has the highest incidence of malnutrition in the eastern Caribbean, 35 per cent. Antigua used to grow enough food to support itself. Do you know the French painter Millet? There is a great tradition of painting agricultural workers, people enjoying the cutting of the weed, the way the golden sunlight falls on them they're in touch with God. In the West Indies, this cannot happen, because agricultural work is associated with enforced labour, with slavery. You cannot see any heroic cane-cutting, or any heroic cotton-picking. It's associated with conquest, it's associated with hell.

Your main target in *A Small Place* is the corrupt ruling elite of Antigua.

Powerful countries try to do these things all the time, but what's particularly mean about these rulers is that they take everything, so OK, Mr Kohl is a corrupt man, and he probably has done horrible things, but he doesn't rob the German people of essential things. When German students get upset, he doesn't close down the university, because that ultimately harms the wealth of his country, and the power of his country is very important. Being a ruler of a powerful country, a lot of his efforts are devoted to keeping his country. . . . But it's a kind of patriotism black rulers don't seem to have, the idea that these people get in their eyes, Greater France, Great Germany or something. We don't have people like that. They have Swiss bank accounts. The schools are bad, the hospitals are bad. I was reading a report about a hospital in Zaire, where people came in, they'd been hurt, and the doctors were just waiting for them to die. They were beyond treating. You go to the hospital to see the doctor, he looks at you, he gives you a prescription to go elsewhere and get the medicine, there is no medicine there. The president of Zaire is one of the richest men in the world; François Mitterrand is not among the richest men in the world. That's what I mean.

8

Joan Riley

with

Aamer Hussein

Joan Riley was born in Hopewell, Jamaica in 1958 and raised by her father after her mother died during childbirth. She moved to Britain in 1976 and studied at the universities of Sussex and London before beginning an active career in social work. Many of her novels engage with the realities of 'care' or the lack of it in the community, particularly as far as women's issues are concerned. Riley's first published novel, The Unbelonging *(1985), was seen as the first novel by a woman about the black experience in Britain. This is a theme she continues in her subsequent fictions,* Waiting in the Twilight *(1987) and* Romance *(1988). Her fourth novel,* A Kindness to Children *(1992), signalled for many a new stage in Riley's career. Structured around the intertwined lives of three women of Caribbean origin – born and brought up in Britain – it explores the psychological implications of return.*

Since this interview was published in 1992, Riley has edited a collection of short stories with Briar Wood: Leave to Stay: Stories of Exile and Belonging, *which came out in 1996. In 1992 Riley was awarded the* Voice *award for her fiction and in 1993 the* MIND *prize for* A Kindness to Children. *The discussion published here with short-story writer Aamer Hussein took place at London's Institute of Contemporary Arts.*

Aamer Hussein Joan, let's talk a little bit about Jean. Her illness is a sort of postcolonial dis-ease, and her mental condition disintegrates as the novel goes on. She presents a very powerful depiction of a woman in pain and, at the same time, of dislocation. She left the Caribbean as a young woman to study in England, she's had a fairly successful life, a handsome and successful novelist lover, two children, a sort of . . .

Joan Riley Well I suppose Jean didn't leave the Caribbean in such a planned way as it seems. Jean ran away from the Caribbean, to escape from a lot of the luggage of her growing up, a lot of what basically formed the seeds of her mental illness. She went to England and I suppose there's the whole theme about the mother country, themes which obviously aren't the subject of this novel but it's really an underlying thing. But going back to the Caribbean question. I suppose that circular journey is a circle of disintegration because you can't really run away from the past; you carry your past within you and Jean does that. The problem is for Jean to go back unsupported to the Caribbean and to survive. The thing is that you can never go back. You can visit a place, but once you've left you have left, particularly a place with small horizons. The Caribbean, Jamaica, is a small place with very small horizons. You've still got the luggage of that past but you can't fit back into that small space, so Jean is dislocated in Jamaica; she has no answers and she disintegrates as a result.

Why do you think her experiences with religion, which form the subtext of the novel, affect her?

Well I suppose it's about betrayal. Religion is very essential to Jean's rural Caribbean past. Religion for me too has always been male; it's either a white Jesus or a black Jesus but whichever way Jesus is a man. For Jean it was a white Jesus; it was about some place or something that is supposed to be safe. In lots of ways men are what Jean sees as safe, and yet men always fail to live up to her expectation: her father failed to live up to her expectation because he always undervalued her. Because she was a girl she couldn't carry on his name and he disintegrated because of what happened to his favourite child. The pastor who is the figure of real security betrays her, and Jimmy, for all that he's seen as a good man, he betrays her too. So in lots of ways betrayal and security are wrapped up in the same gender.

Let's now look at Sylvia, apparently a very confident woman with a different attitude to, and relationship with, the Caribbean, which she doesn't know very well. She idealizes it to a large extent, doesn't she?

Sylvia is of the Caribbean and yet not from the Caribbean. Sylvia has English mores, English norms, she has always looked out from eyes that saw a dimmer sun, a different sun, an urban sun which is also an industrial one. She is Caribbean in the sense that she's born into a Caribbean household and some of that actually has coloured her life, but a big part of your life is how you associate with society. So she goes to the Caribbean and yet the actual nitty gritty of associating with that society shows basically how un-Caribbean Sylvia is. I mean Sylvia is not the central character but she's the main character, and in lots of ways I suppose I see Sylvia very much as the potential the Caribbean throws away, because she is incredibly articulate, very educated, a highly skilled woman, but a woman who is out of sympathy with the local norms.

You said the potential the Caribbean throws away, which makes me ask you another question, which is that taken together the three women – Jean with her two worlds, and Pearl and Sylvia each with their one in a sense – are a gallery of portraits of the Caribbean and in some way serve as metaphors for national states and attitudes. Could you say something about that?

I thought about what really makes up the Caribbean. The migration which happened in the 1950s has changed the Caribbean, in the sense that people come back, people interact, they have an impact, people from elsewhere who are of Caribbean origin have an impact on the Caribbean. And then you have the people like myself who left later or whatever, we also have an impact. And the people who remain; all these three facets mix together in lots of ways. I see all three women as one metaphor and that is the metaphor for the Caribbean, each of them represents an aspect. Sylvia, as I said, is the Caribbean export of surplus labour, it's always this kind of exterior look-in situation; she is the potential the Caribbean threw away. Jean, I think, represents for me the schizophrenic nature of Caribbean society, of Jamaican society in particular. She is sick and I think Caribbean society is sick, for historical reasons, for reasons of where it is socially in terms of the larger world, and for reasons of its policy to the humanity which lives within it, particularly the 90 to 95 per cent who do not have a name given to them by economic wealth. So Jean represents that kind of very painful reality and that is the person who has to balance between two worlds, because it's very hard. Being emotionally attached to the Caribbean, I cannot leave the Caribbean, I cannot go back and I cannot leave; it's too much a part of my reality. I carry with me that space and yet I've made connections in another space and so I feel torn all the time. It is a form of psychosis, sometimes. And then there's Pearl, she's Everywoman. I suppose you could throw in [her husband] George and say he's Everyman. Pearl is every woman you pass on the street every day in any country who is doing the shopping, screaming at the kids, holding stuff together, networking; she's the factory worker, she works in the fleapits, she's the woman who doesn't work but who is having to make do. But she has a lot of strength and she has a lot of ability, a lot of creativity. Pearl is the potential the Caribbean overlooks, that's how I see her.

One of the things I've often heard some of your Caribbean contemporaries say of your work is how immediate and how alive your sense of the Caribbean, Jamaica in this particular case, is. But you yourself have not lived there for several years, you have come

and gone. How do you maintain this connection, how do you keep the images alive, the lifestyle, the voices?

You carry it within you. Okay, I don't live in Jamaica, I live here, but I think it's funny you should say that because I remember a story of yours I was reading and you had this image of a lake and a man grieving by this lake and I said to you it was very real, I could almost feel the breeze coming off the lake. I suppose in lots of ways you do because landscape doesn't really change and that is something about a rural society as well; there are changes which happen but it doesn't really change. You carry what has made you within yourself, so the images and the people and the flavours of my homeland are within me. I suppose in lots of ways it is all about my inability to divorce myself from the Caribbean as much as anything else.

Yes, but there's also a tremendous guard against nostalgia in your work and I think that has to do with the fact that you've maintained connections in another way, by tackling public problems within the individual characters you create.

I suppose it has, but it also has to do with the fact that I still have a commitment to the people from whom I originated. Of course I have nostalgia; there are times when it's very hot in England and I feel this absolute total haunting sense of homesickness, this need to smell the air, to smell all the Caribbean things. But you know people make a landscape. For me people are what plot a landscape and when I think of the landscape I think of the people. And 60 per cent of that is suffering.

Is that why voice, language and the registers of speech are so important in your work?

Well, yes, I think the other thing about people is that when you see somebody, the first thing you see is what they look like, but that's very superficial; what defines the person is what comes out of their mouth, because as you know the person, they're redefining themselves for you because what comes out of their mouth is the nearest approximation to what's inside them that you're going to get and what they look like becomes a secondary thing in terms of how you experience them. I suppose for me that's why voices are very important. It's also because if you come from a culture where there's a lot of orality, what society passes on to you, how you experience society is verbal and that becomes a part of what is part and parcel of the people of the landscape.

But as a novelist you constantly work with a double perspective because you often have people who have been divorced from that reality, going back and discovering it, so those vocal registers are quite different; there are the people who belong and those who are outsiders. How do you find that your sense of form differs from your Caribbean contemporaries?

I'm always wary of making comments about other people. I suppose that if I'm going to make a statement, I think that most of my contemporaries come out of an English-language tradition where the form is quite often set; and even though they live within it they do not come from an oral culture, they come from a very highly structured and highly literate sort of subculture within a wider culture. The thing for me is that because I'm so used to hearing voices, to listening to voices, to defining where I am by voices, defining how people are feeling by the nuances within voices, I tend to define people wherever I go by voices. If I'm writing about an English person my formal English becomes very formal; I learnt formal English and so I always think of English people in terms of formal English. It depends on who I'm talking about. I think it's all about how I see the person, because I can't divorce landscape, I can't divorce context from content if you like, I tend to write context around the content, i.e. the person. I've no literary background so I don't know what I'm supposed to be doing, you see.

Speaking of context, not very long ago I heard a writer complaining very bitterly that those of us who come from the Third World, whichever country it may be, are constantly read and asked to speak in terms of statistics, sociology, psychology and medicine and that's quite a burden. You've had your share of the labels: a Caribbean, a Jamaican woman writer . . .

. . . black . . .

. . . etc., etc. Third World.

I just refuse to engage. I think it's quite important to refuse to engage because in lots of ways you validate something which is somebody else's perception of what you should be. You know you get asked to do these things, but basically, as a writer of fiction you're a sort of anarchist because you're just making it up as you go along; you're not bothering about what facts or statistics say is a reality because quite often people don't experience that kind of reality. It's interesting that you forgot to mention history, or you deliberately didn't mention history.

I deliberately left it out . . .

. . . because it is the one thing which I think is very important. I mean the historical content is something (and I don't mean history as something which the dominant ideology decides is history – I'm talking about history in terms of how it's actually been experienced generationally) that is important because it's about context. History in a wider sense is important as well because one of the things I like about London is that I can make connections with other histories which have differences and similarities. I can actually connect with other realities which feel a part of it. This gives me a sense of having a wider context in lots of ways.

Speaking of other histories, do you think that the fact that people from so many different cultures or geographical locations are writing now in England is something that creates a community wider than one which you would have had elsewhere?

Ah, well, definitely! In rural Jamaica, anybody who came from anywhere else got labelled and named according to the place they came from. It really is a very isolated society, not so much now, but even now it's monocultural in lots of ways, and I am excited by differences. I think making connections – writing across that space, but writing in a way which means that dialogues can happen – is very exciting. The variety which I find in London in particular is something which I think must of necessity colour my perception and I think it actually gives me a lot more depth in terms of my own writing.

Do you feel that that is happening in general, or is there too much fragmentation that one has to overcome?

There is a lot of fragmentation. I think the tendency amongst the white population is to look for examples and because of that there is the tendency to actually even fragment within a particular cultural group, and it becomes very difficult because then there's so much in-fighting about a small space that it doesn't happen. I like to think that the literary world is irrelevant to my writing. Therefore I tend to seek instead what I need to sustain my writing and I think cross-cultural dialogue is one thing I do need to sustain.

And having said that, who do you write for? Who do you see as a perfect reader; where is your constituency?

I write for myself, it's something I get lots of stick about, but I do write for myself. I mean my writing's almost like a dialogue with myself, my internal life is about this dialogue that I'm having within myself, but having said that I want to be read, I'm sufficiently vain to not hear what people say . . .

You want to talk to yourself and be overheard.

Yes, I want to be overheard. I think that's a good way to put it. And I want to take my dialogue and put it in a ring and get other people's dialogue within the same circle. I also like to make dialogues with the reader. Having said that, well, who is the reader? I suppose for me I have a sneaking wish to be read by my own kind, those similar to my kind, and of course anybody else who wants to read me, but for me I think what is important is that I don't feel that the people who I come from and with whom I can make connections can't have that dialogue with me.

9

V. S. Naipaul

with

Alastair Niven

On 15 March 1993 V. S. Naipaul was awarded the first David Cohen British Literature Prize. This prize, administered by the Arts Council of Great Britain (now the Arts Council of England), sought to be the supreme accolade for a living British writer and was awarded for a lifetime's work. Its monetary value was the highest of any literary award in the country at the time, totalling £40,000. Subsequent winners have been Harold Pinter, Muriel Spark, William Trevor, Doris Lessing, Beryl Bainbridge and Thom Gunn. In an interview specially recorded for the presentation, Sir Vidia spoke to Alastair Niven about his writing career, which spans several decades since his arrival in Britain in the 1950s.

Since the publication of his early novels set in Trinidad, a phase which culminated with the publication of A House for Mr Biswas *(1961), Naipaul has published nine other fictional works, including* The Enigma of Arrival *(1987),* A Way in the World *(1994) and* Half a Life *(2001). He has also written several major works of non-fiction based on his travels and journeys across the globe. These works, such as the books on India* An Area of Darkness *(1964),* India: A Wounded Civilisation *(1977) and* India: A Million Mutinies Now *(1990) or his numerous autobiographical essays such as* Finding the Centre *(1984) or* Reading and Writing *(2000), parallel closely the concerns of his fiction, reflecting a lifelong dedication to the writing of a life.*

Born in Trinidad of East Indian extraction in 1932, Naipaul left the island to go to Oxford as a student in the 1950s; he continued writing in London after this and has remained based in Britain ever since. Few writers have committed themselves so wholeheartedly to the vagaries of a writing life and few have commanded such worldwide attention. Perhaps the most incisive insight into Naipaul's oeuvre is through the creation of his fictional selves. The words he gives to Salim, narrator of A Bend in the River *(1979), are indicative of some of the major preoccupations of his work. As we are told towards the end of that novel: 'The world is what it is; men who are nothing, who allow themselves to become nothing, have no place in it.'*

The interview reproduced here was originally conducted on film for the David Cohen award. Since that time V. S. Naipaul has gained further worldwide recognition and was awarded the Nobel Prize for Literature in 2001.

Alastair Niven Sir Vidia, your cultural background is partly one of great storytelling in India and the Caribbean. Your father's writing is also very important in your work. What drew you particularly to narrative as the way you wanted to express yourself in life?

V. S. Naipaul This question about narrative: we should first of all leave out traditional backgrounds because they played no part. One just went to school and led that kind of life rather than being part of a more traditional culture. The novel ambition was given to me by my father. He had derived it from his reading and to me that was where the nobility in writing lay. When I developed problems with moving on, having exhausted the early impulses, I discovered that there was a whole world to write about in other ways. The novel assisted people in the nineteenth century to get at certain aspects of truth that earlier forms like narrative poems and essays couldn't get at, and the novel began to do things that hadn't been done before. That is part of the excitement and the validity of the great nineteenth-century work. I also began to feel that those of us who had come after were simply borrowing the form and pouring our own experiences into it. This meant that we were really writing other people's books and falsifying experience, because experience has to find its own form. So a lot of my creative life after the early impulses has been to find the correct form for expressing what I feel and what my experience has been of the many mixed worlds in which I have lived.

In *The Enigma of Arrival* you seem to be merging fiction with a kind of documentation. Is that how you saw it, that it was a hybrid form you were creating?

No, actually it was very simple the way one thought about that. When I began to write *The Enigma of Arrival* and found myself writing about the English countryside, I felt that there had been so much said about it in the English language that this kind of writing immediately set up associations which I had to undo. I had to identify my narrator, my seeing eye, my feeling person. I didn't want to invent a character and give him a bogus adventure to set him there. I thought I should make the writer be myself – let that be true and within that set the fictional composite picture, because you can't use real people to hang philosophical ideas about flux and change. That's where creation comes in. So there were the two aspects. To me I didn't do it out of any sense of being experimental. It just seemed natural.

But you have in fact created a new form. Sir Vidia, you have moved in and out of fiction over the years. Graham Greene tended to describe one set of works, his travel writings, as entertainments, differentiated from his fiction, which he regarded as his serious work. In your case I don't think you make any distinction between the fictional writing and the travel and documentary writing; they are of equal status.

Yes, both the fiction writing and the travel writing, or books of enquiry conducted in other countries, are aspects of one's looking at the world one has lived in. They are both equally important. The other thing to remember about the fictional form is that it would have been impossible for me to be a writer and to stick to the same form for forty years. Consider how Dickens developed between 1836 and 1870, and Balzac, beginning one kind of romantic drama and ending with his realistic description of France. Twenty or thirty years is a very long time and one has to express the movement of one's soul and of the world.

You seem to have a great sense of movement in your writing. It's not writing that ever stands still to contemplate, but you look at a world that is constantly in a state of mobility and flux. Is that correct?

The world has changed and I am aware more and more that I have lived in this last half of the century when one has been adult and active through a period of the most prodigious change. I am very glad I had the courage to follow difficult instincts about the truth and was therefore able to capture something of the changes in the world, the changes in empire, the changes in the colonized, the changes in countries like India, which from being colonized have developed some new sense of the idea of renewal. These things seem to me immensely important.

And yet at the end of *In a Free State* [1971] you seem to suggest that we are all engaged in a cycle where things come back to the point at which they had begun, and they go on repeating themselves.

At the end of *In a Free State* I remember the writer saying that that was perhaps the purest time when everybody lived in their own little isolated world. I think that what was contained in that observation was the knowledge that such a world probably never existed. The world has always been in a state of movement and flux. I can think of no culture that is entirely of itself, self-generated. Africa has had movements all the time from Roman times. India – people crossed and recrossed: there is no one thing which is India. Europe: who can carry in his head all the movements of people in Europe? So the world *has* been in movement.

You began your career by writing satirical and very humorous novels. Your work seems to have become more truly serious over the years, but some people would argue that a sense of comedy and the ebullience of life has disappeared from it.

I know that people talk about early comedy and later seriousness. I think that there is a good deal of comedy right through the work, a good deal of humour. It is contained in the actual tone of the writing, which probably comes over best during one's reading of it. I write for the voice. I read aloud at the end of the day what I have written to someone who judges and helps me in that way. The other point is that the early comedy was really hysteria, the hysteria of someone who was worried about his place as a writer and his place in the world. When one is really stressed one makes a lot of jokes. You can make jokes all the time. That's not healthy. The profounder comedy comes from greater security.

And you feel you have achieved that, presumably?

Yes, I feel I have become more serene because of the work and because of the way I have solved problems in my own mind. It was quite late – I was in my mid-forties – when I felt secure in my writing ability. By that stage I knew I could do certain things. Until then I could really be desperately worried about going on.

It's that question of 'going on' which has fascinated me about your work over the past twenty years. I wondered what on earth you could do next because each work seemed to be a kind of summing up. *The Enigma of Arrival* especially left me with a sense that it was such a completely achieved work I really could not see where you went next. The novel seemed to be a form from which you were moving

away and yet you presumably would not want just to return to more travel observation. I am trying to imagine the form you might be moving towards now.

One must write every book as though it is the final work, the summing up. I can't do things again once I've done them as well as I can do them. For example, having done the last Indian travel book I don't feel that I can go and do it for somewhere else. I've done it. I have taken myself through various stages to writing that kind of book. So it's time to do something else. There are always more things to do. I have a restless mind. It is my age, my health and my vitality that are now getting in the way and making me slow up a little. The world is full of excitement for me. Reality is always changing. It changes constantly and the writer has to find new ways of capturing the reality.

This is the British Literature Prize and it is in recognition of a British writer. Are you surprised to win it and do you feel that the British- ness of your work is something you have been developing over the years?

I haven't thought of being British in that way. I have always been very grateful to the country for allowing me to develop my talent here with absolute freedom. I have never done a single thing which I have not wanted to do. I could not have conducted this career in other countries in Europe for the language reasons and for political reasons. I couldn't have done this in China, Japan or India. I could really have done it only here. I could not even have done it in the United States because the American interest in my subjects and my attitudes occurred very very late. You would not believe this now. No one is more anxious to embrace the oppressed of the world. You would not believe that this has developed in the past ten or fifteen years. It wasn't there before. The changes have been immense. If you consider small places like the islands of the Caribbean, if you consider their history in the past two hundred years, what they've moved from and where they are, you see they have begun again to undo themselves. That's an immense cyclical thing almost. In *The Mimic Men* [1967], a very early book, one's already seeing the seeds of decay in that situation. When one began to write one simply recorded. One didn't question. Then because I was writing from a certain physical distance and time I began to question and see in a different way from the way I had seen in my earlier books.

The questions and answers ended at this point, but Sir Vidia then recorded short readings from some of his work. The text of his acceptance speech on winning the prize follows:

I know very well that there has been an element of luck in all this. The prize that has been given to me could have been given to many others. I thought myself of two names when I was told about the prize and its large purpose. I thought of Anthony Powell and Harold Pinter. One man finding a way of dealing with accumulations of experience through the changes of the century; the other apparently narrower, but also more lyrical, finding the exposed nerve ends we all continue to have. Opposed talents, it might appear, but really also aspects of the sensibility of our time. At a certain stage there is no real competition between writers, since every serious writer has his own concerns, makes his own explorations, and (with luck) finds his own audience. To twist the famous quotation, every writer is at once an island and part of the main. Every writer is entirely of himself and part of the general flow.

But my luck pleases me. I like the name of the prize, first of all. It is the British Literature Prize, and I like that because this writing career of mine has been conducted here. Writing is more than a matter of spirit. A book is a physical, commercial object. It requires a well-organized society. If you are going to make a living as a writer you need pub-lishers, magazines, reviewers, bookshops, libraries, a public looking for new work: a book trade. You need quite an apparatus. When I was starting, in the mid-1950s, there was no other place where I could have set up as an English-language writer, and found encouragement. It is, of course, different now.

So as a writer I was separated, and sometimes doubly separated from my background – if you take Trinidad as my direct background and India as my ancestral background. This separation helped with the early books. They dealt with the past: a complete, limited experience; distance helped with that. The way ahead was less clear. Adult experience seemed formless. It is so for others as well, but for me there was also an internal pressure to stay with the past, the smaller world. And even when I saw that my English experience has become as much my material as the other, and that there was also India to look at and write about, and Africa, and other places, I wasn't sure how I could add these new layers, while always making a whole of my experience. The English language came with a literature, came with certain forms. The forms helped when I was writing about the smaller, complete world. But they didn't help at all when I was trying to get at the nature of my wider experience. I always felt the need for example to establish the identity of the writer, the narrator, the gatherer of impressions: to make the point that, whatever associations came with the language, this English-language traveller in the world was not English but colonial, and carried different pictures in his head.

If I were starting today I would have no sense of anomaly, because there are now so many colonial English-language writers. But I am talking of thirty years ago. This is a very rough, elided account of what was a constant creative anxiety for many years. I give it here to say how glad I am that the prize seeks to acknowledge all of a writer's work rather than a single book, and that it doesn't lift one literary form above another. In my mind I have made a long journey; bits of the record are scattered through the books I have written; no one book or one kind of book is true to the effort.

In the modern period the rendering of reality has always been an issue. Judgements and forms have constantly varied. Hazlitt (who died in 1930) thought that Byron's personality display obscured the world. Scott was the truer writer, because Scott didn't stand between the reader and the world. To render the truth of his own life Hazlitt had only the essay. And so did Lamb. It wasn't enough. The novelists who

came after used the novel form to get at truths the essay couldn't get at
– truth about society and mental status, for instance.

The great novels of the nineteenth century still have this quality of
truth; and part of their excitement is that the writers can be felt to be
writing about certain things for the first time. They were not versions
of what had gone before, and novels like them cannot be done again.
Form and content go together. You cannot simply pour new experience
or new material into an old form; that is not only to write somebody
else's book all over again; it is also to falsify the material. The traditional novel never really existed; good work was always new. Reality
always has to be captured. Methods will change as the world changes.
Everyone will find his own way.

So there is no tradition of form that comes with language. The
tradition that does come, from the nineteenth century, is a moral one.
It is the striving after truth, the hard look at the world, and its effect is
subversive. That may be too strong a word, but many of the great
original writers of the nineteenth century and this have helped to
underline and remake their civilization. The ideal of truth and revolution – truth as revolution – is well described by Leonard Woolf in his
account of his time at Cambridge in the 1890s. This idea inevitably
spread out of Great Britain. It did so in at least one extraordinary way.
Gandhi wasn't a great reader – though I once read somewhere that in
1942, at the time of the Quit India campaign, somebody saw him one
day reading Richard Llewellyn's *How Green Was My Valley*. Anyway.
This is a story from 1904. Gandhi is thirty-five. He is in South Africa,
has been there for ten years, working among the Indian community on
what I suppose can be called civil rights. Stubbornness at this stage is
his principal virtue. He has no political dogma; he has read too little for
that. Every situation is new and at every step he has to think very hard
about what he should do. He has developed an idea of being good, but
he doesn't know as yet how he might express this in his way of life. He
is going this evening from Johannesburg to Durban, and Polak, a lawyer
and a friend (first met in a Johannesburg vegetarian restaurant), comes
to the railway station and gives him a book for the journey. It is

Ruskin's *Unto this Last* (1860). Gandhi, after he gets into the book, simply cannot put it down. The journey to Durban lasts twenty-four hours. Gandhi at the end is a transformed man. The latent goodness in his heart has been brought out by Ruskin: only a poet, he says, could have done that.

He says he learnt three things from the book. First: the good of the individual is contained in the good of the all. He says he knew that already, but really it was something he had learnt only from the general anti-Indian South African prejudice. The second is that the barber's work is as valuable as the lawyer's: he had begun, he says, in a vague way, to know that. The third Ruskinian truth was something he had never known at all. It was that the life of labour, physical labour involving the use of the hands, whether by craftsmen or by tiller, was the life worth living.

He knows now what to do. He founds a commune, he translates Ruskin into Gujarati, he elaborates his idea of a movement called 'The Welfare of All'. When he finally leaves South Africa and goes to India in 1915, these inward ideas – of perfectibility, bread labour, which contains the idea of internal caste reform – go with him. They balance and give a universality to the political fight. He finds an emblem of labour: the village spinning wheel. It is really the mahatma's tribute to the Victorian sage.

Let us stay just a while longer with Ruskin's followers in England. The Arts and Crafts movement, Ashbee, William Morris and the Kelmscott Press. The Press, when it fell on hard times, passed to an Anglo-Ceylonese, Ananda Coomaraswamy, who had inherited a fortune from his father. Coomaraswamy, who was born in 1877, applied Ruskinian ideas of the craftsman and medieval art to his study of the arts and crafts of India and Ceylon. He collected Indian paintings, mainly on paper. He established categories, he interpreted. There had been no one before him. This kind of Indian painting was not a public art; it was hidden away in the libraries of princes. He was a prodigious man; his work still has to be taken into account. In 1917 Coomaraswamy offered his great collection to the new university of Banaras. In return he wanted to be made Professor of Indian Art. They roughed him up and sent him away. He took his collection to the museum in Boston.

Coomaraswamy to Boston, Gandhi at almost the same time back to India – two men following different paths, it might seem. But seventy-five years on we can see them both as aspects of Indian renewal; and in the most unlikely way both careers contain a tribute to Ruskin. The irony is that Ruskin, after the Indian Mutiny, had no time for Indians.

This is just one chain of ideas and influence in our mingled civilization. There must be hundreds, thousands, more. They will multiply as the English language spreads, and the various literatures of English grow. The connections will become more subtle; sometimes they will be hidden.

It is with a consciousness of some of these connections that I welcome the luck of the prize.

10

Caryl Phillips

with

Maya Jaggi

This interview, which took place in London, was conducted soon after the publication of Crossing the River *(1993), which spans 250 years of the African diaspora and of relations between black and white people. The novel won the James Tait Black Memorial Prize and was shortlisted for the Booker Prize in 1993. Among Caryl Phillips's other novels are* The Final Passage *(1985),* A State of Independence *(1986),* Higher Ground *(1989) and* Cambridge *(1991). His latest work,* A Distant Shore, *was published in 2003. He has also written plays for stage, radio and screen and several collections of non-fictional essays such as* The European Tribe *(1987) and* A New World Order: Selected Essays *(2001). Much of his work focuses on the question of diaspora and the black Atlantic recovering the unwritten histories of black people in Britain before the large-scale migrations following the arrival of SS* Windrush *in 1948 or the civil rights movement in the United States.*

Born in St Kitts, Caryl Phillips came to Britain as a child and grew up in Leeds. He is currently Professor of English and Henry R. Luce Professor of Migration and Social Order at Barnard College, Columbia University.

Maya Jaggi What's the relationship between your radio play, *Crossing the River*, and the novel?

Caryl Phillips The radio play lasts eleven minutes. I wrote it in 1984 or 1985 for Radio 3, and it explored the guilt of a father who has sold his children into slavery. It was just voices, a strange, haunting piece which I'm not sure many people understood. When I started to think about the novel, the structure of the play, which was fragmented yet held together by the father's guilt, appealed to me. I thought, let me clarify this.

The novel draws inspiration from different periods in history. What kind of sources did you use?

In terms of pure research, before I did any writing, it took about sixteen months of inter-library loans, travelling to Washington to look at documents on the American segregated army in Britain, travelling to Sheffield City Library to find out about English villages, communicating with historians in Britain and America who specialized in Liberia and the history of the slave letters, checking out the catalogue of an exhibition in the Smithsonian in the mid-1980s called 'Blacks in the West'.

How much did you find on blacks who pioneered west, like Martha?

Not a lot. There's quite a lot on black cowboys and the early black settlers in San Francisco, Los Angeles, Denver – the first black millionaire in San Francisco. But there's not much about the migratory aspect, pioneers who rode the wagon trains and headed west. And, being a masochist, I chose to go with the aspect in which there was the least research because then there was more latitude for the imagination. Also, to approach it from the point of view of a woman, because there was quite a bit about black male cowboys but nothing about black women and their role in the West.

Where there are letters and documents, how do the characters' voices emerge from them? Do you immerse yourself until you're thinking in that language?

I have to hear the people, and I can only hear them after I've immersed myself in the research and the background. Once the characters begin to speak back to me, when I recognize their voices with all of the syntax, the vocabulary of the period, then I realize I'm on to something. I have ideas about various pockets and avenues of history in the hope that one of these ideas becomes an obsession. Only then can I commit myself to a year or two or three of writing. Ideas alone are too flimsy to sustain a book.

This novel repositions black people in histories from which they're usually excluded. What's your purpose in this?

It's to look at that history from a different angle – through the prism of people who have nominally been written out of it, or have been viewed as the losers or victims in a particular historical storm. You take something which people presume they know about – like the West from John Wayne – and you make them look again from the point of view of people who have been written out. You take something like the Second World War, and you make them see that it was not like *Brief Encounter* or *Mrs Minever*. It contained a lot more pain and poignancy, more anguish. And perhaps some of the seeds of the current British racism were sown in the Second World War. So you subvert people's view of history by engaging them with characters. I don't think you subvert it by arguing schematically about ideas.

You said some of the seeds of racism were sown in the Second World War. Could you explain?

The American army was segregated, and it was the first time many Britons outside of London, Liverpool, Bristol and the slaving ports had come into contact with black people in any numbers. Most black Americans remember their time in Britain fondly because they were more popular than the white Americans – they weren't arrogant. Most of them came from the South, from Alabama and Mississippi – they had no idea that white people could even vaguely treat them as equal. The British 'appreciated' their lack of arrogance, but they did so because they knew these 'blackies' were going to go home eventually. Less than a decade later, when the new black people, the West Indians, arrived, they had a totally different attitude because they were British. They didn't feel like outsiders that they had to be apologetic or polite – they had 'attitude'. They arrived because they were asked to come here, because they held British passports, and they had the temerity not to show any visible sign of going home at the end of three or four years. This is one of the contributing factors – not a major factor – to British hostility, because their only previous encounters had been with these rather playful American chaps who had a return ticket.

What would you say to someone who asked why a writer in the 1990s was still writing about slavery?

If you don't know where you've come from, you don't know where you're going to. The root of our problem – of all those people, white and non-white, who live in Europe or the Americas – is to do with the forces that were engendered by the 'peculiar institution'. You can't expect something to characterize the relationship of Britain and the outside world for two-and-a-half centuries and for it not to have deep reverberations still today. If we don't understand, and I don't think we do, the 'multiple ironies', then we have no possibility of understanding where we are or where we might be going. Look at the work that's been produced out of the Second World War, which lasted six years – the novels, films, non-fiction. Slavery as an institution lasted from 1572 until 1834. We're talking a huge period of history, and I'll bet you could fill more shelves with books about the Second World War than over the whole two-and-a-half-centuries span of slavery. British people forget they know very little about history. Why? Because most of their history took place in India and Africa and the Caribbean, where they could pretend it didn't happen. Having said that, I don't consider slavery to be my theme, or my 'thing'. But it's the biggest of those shadows where the history of Europe meets the history of the Americas. Under that cloud, you have a myriad of stories – of the slave fort, the guy sailing across the water, the auction block.

You've chosen to tell two of the children's stories from the point of view predominantly – and in one case almost exclusively – of a white person who loved or 'loved' them: Edward [Nash's former master and lover] and Joyce [Travis's girlfriend]. What made you do that?

Seriously, I don't know except it's a matter of voice. I tried to find a voice for Travis. I travelled down south during the research, drove round Georgia and Alabama for days in search of Travis. I couldn't find him anywhere, but I wasn't prepared to invent a voice. It just wasn't working, and if it's not working, I don't care about balance for the sake of balance. You approach it through the route that seems to you to cut through to the truth. One thing I know is that Joyce was speaking to me forcefully, powerfully, in the dialect I grew up speaking, which is Yorkshire. I understood that intuitively. I understood every twist and turn of that dialect. It was a bit like *Cambridge*. I had no understanding of why I narrated the last part of the novel through Emily's eyes till about a year afterwards. There were two reasons. First, she grew up in the north of England at the beginning of the nineteenth century feeling marginalized. The position of women is not analogous to the position of black people, but I grew up in the north of England feeling totally marginalized. Second, Emily made a self-defining journey to the Caribbean, and so did I. She made it but the journeys changed her life dramatically, and mine. And the supreme irony in *Cambridge* is that the black man becomes the character you're supposed to like the least, because she grows, he shrinks. The ley lines and undercurrents that feed your communication with a character, which on the surface may appear completely invisible and a mystery, do eventually make themselves clear. As yet, where the hell Joyce came from, I don't know. But it's very painful wherever it is. It's probably the most painful thing I ever wrote.

**Both Joyce and Edward are in a sense outside their own societies –
Edward is homosexual, and Joyce is more open, curious. What
makes her different?**

The clue to her is the same thing that binds the other three characters
together: she doesn't have a father. What holds the novel together is
that the father has lost these children. That's why at the end of the book
the father says 'My Joyce' too, that's almost the last change I made to
the book. What makes her different in that society, in this rather brutal
and painful relationship with her mother, is that she grew up without a
dad. She has bitter arguments with her mother which revolve around
her father. And it seemed to me emotionally correct that she should
belong with the other three kids.

**Was the fact that Joyce grew up without a father one of your routes
into her character?**

I don't know, probably. I hadn't thought of that. Normally, when you're
writing, you don't think about those links because you're just too
obsessed with the characters. You've just got to go with what's presented itself. As Eudora Welty said, dare to do with your bag of fears. If
you stop, all you're doing is drawing back from those painful junctions
which appear every two minutes for any of us in the day; there are
certain things we'd rather not think about, confront. But if you're going
to write, your job is to approach those junctions and just keep going . . .
It's no secret I came from a divorced family. I grew up in the north of
England, like many kids from the Caribbean, with a father who had,
shall we say, a very on-and-off relationship with the household. I suppose that domestic instability, coupled with the other feelings that any
black kid growing up in this country in the 1960s and early 1970s has,
of wondering when they say, 'Go back to where you came from', just
where they're talking about, provided me with some sort of insight.

Joyce has a vision which is non-racist in an unusual way – almost an antidote to Emily's pervasive racism. You don't know till quite far into her narrative that the soldier she's fallen for is black. Was that natural?

Absolutely. I think there are people like that, and they scare the shit out of me. She possesses an admirably non-racist view of the world, we love her for it, but at the same time we fear for her because she's so fucking naive. That's what makes her vulnerable. We want to shake her by the shoulders and say, 'Wake up and smell the coffee, girl, do you realize what you're getting yourself into?' Yet at the same time we want to hug her because she's not aware. It's both a strength and a weakness. Maybe there aren't so many people like her now, but fifty years ago, I'm sure there were. People didn't have the context of the Notting Hill riots in the 1950s or Carnival riots in the 1970s. If Joyce had been born now, she'd have been going to Sheffield United games, or Sheffield Wednesday games, and would have seen black players have bananas thrown at them. She'd have had *The Black and White Minstrel Show*, and all the racist comics on the northern club circuit. But back then, there was an admirable period of naivety. She frightened me because I kept thinking, get real, man.

There are differences of sympathy towards the characters, inevitably. But you always seem to have more sympathy, or a different kind of sympathy, with women characters. Do you think that's true?

Probably. Again, I don't know why. It may be as simple as the fact that I was brought up by my mother. It may be because I have an interest in voices that are not heard, and historically, women's voices have not been heard. It may be a combination of personal and professional interest.

What do you make of Edward? How do you feel about him?

I don't have that much sympathy with him. I see him every day, man, I see him if I go in the Arts Council, if I was ever to go near Parliament, in every university: the professional patron. But there's no such thing as a free lunch, is there? I'd love to sympathize with his plight, because he feels deeply, so you stop and listen, but only for so long. I have a lot of time for Madison, who shows him the place and leaves him, just says, 'Fuck off, it's your problem, mate.' It's hard to talk about because you don't judge your characters in the process of creation. In retrospect, you can talk about them, but it takes a long time to get the distance. That's one of the problems about adapting novels for films. I'd love to see a work of mine filmed, but I never have enough distance until a long time afterwards, and usually, by then, people's interest has waned. My intuitive feelings right now are: Edward, I don't like you very much. But I had to have sympathy with him when I was writing. I had to understand the guy, or try to understand him.

As with Emily, as you've said, though you wouldn't necessarily like her, there are many points of sympathy. With Edward, the way in could be his outsider status, his sexuality?

One thing I've consistently tried to deal with is sexuality. How it intersects with power and race seems crucial to understanding what's going on today, and in any of those periods I've looked at over the five novels: the taboo of sex, and using sexuality as power. That maybe half answers the question of why I'm particularly interested in women: women – both black women and white, but particularly non-white women – have always been the victims of that form of abuse. That sex and race aspect still completely messes people's heads up today. Anybody who tries to argue that who you sleep with is irrelevant to questions of power, class or race is crazy. Until two minutes ago in South Africa, you were talking about being thrown in jail. It was illegal in the majority of states in the USA at the time of the Second World War for a person like Travis to marry Joyce. In 'The Pagan Coast', a black man is the victim of sexual exploitation, and I look at Edward and Nash's relationship as one form of colonial exploitation – the way white men exploited black men for sexual gratification. It screwed up Nash's head good and proper.

You said in *The European Tribe* [1987], 'I felt like a transplanted tree that had failed to take root in foreign soil', and the metaphor recurs in *Crossing the River*, in the father-Africa's voice: 'sinking hopeful roots in difficult soil'. Yet there's an optimism in the last few pages of the novel, as the children 'arrive on the far bank of the river, loved'. Despite the anguish of the children's stories, what unites them is an almost jubilant sense that they're survivors. They're buoyed by a father's redemptive, healing love.

That's definitely right. I perceive a healing force that comes out of fracture. I wouldn't say I've always wanted to be an explorer of the fissures and crevices of migration. I have seen some connectedness and celebrated the qualities of survival that people in all sorts of predicaments are able to keep hold of with clenched fists. I didn't want to leave this novel as an analysis of fracture, because I felt such an overwhelming, passionate attachment to all the voices, and I kept thinking it seemed almost choral. These people were talking in harmonies I could hear. That doesn't just come from survival, but from something more than just getting to the next day. There's an underlying passion which informs the ability to survive, and it's that word that most people shy away from – the word that Salman [Rushdie] finished his review of [V. S. Naipaul's] *The Enigma of Arrival* [1987] by pointing out was completely absent from that book – which is a love, an affirmative quality present everywhere I looked in those children of the African diaspora, from Marvin Gaye to Jimmy Baldwin to Miles Davis. I've always been interested in what makes people survive the most vicious upheavals: the two qualities of faith and love, rooted in a family love. In the voice of the father is a love for all those who have crossed the river – a scattered diaspora and family.

And there are also the bonds of sexual love between Joyce and Travis, who cross different rivers.

Yes, there are all sorts of references: on one bank of the Missouri you were a slave and on the other you were free, and you had to cross that river. Martha crossed that river in search of her daughter; Edward crossed the Atlantic in search of this man, Nash; the captain of the slave ship crosses the river writing passionate letters back to his love in England, but without understanding that what he's doing in these cold, mechanical diary entries is actually smashing families.

Your work has focused on the spectral triangle of Europe, the Americas and Africa, particularly the England–Caribbean axis – whether linked by migration or slavery. This novel, though there were precursors, marks a shift to the United States, where you teach. Are you pulling out of Britain?

I'm almost better known in America now than in Britain, which I admit disappoints me. The easy, and rather foolish, thing would be for me to attempt to replace what I grew up with, with what I've discovered in America. But what I find in America – like the rich, strange, fertile relationship between those of African origin and mainstream society – is interesting, but it's not me. My primary axis of frustration is what happens between the Caribbean and Britain – particularly Britain. I remember what Nathan Zuckerman said in a Roth novel: 'England made a Jew out of me in eight weeks.' There's no other society on earth that can do that to anybody – or make a nigger out of you in eight hours, before you've even left Terminal 3. That society is the society I grew up in, and it'll always be the touchstone of what I write.

In *The European Tribe*, you described starting to write as a need to 'express the conundrum of my existence'. Is writing for you still that kind of personal quest, a sifting through of identity?

Yes, totally. Except there's one additional thing. The break for me came after *Higher Ground*, with the realization of responsibility. Graham Greene said childhood was the bank balance of the writer. It's true, and it's out of that bank balance that you begin to construct your work. But what Graham Greene didn't have, I, and many other writers who are non-white, have: the need to work against an undertow of historical ignorance. Our history is also our bank balance. And we have a responsibility to the people who produced us. I wasn't dropped here on to this planet, beamed here from Mars or Pluto. The forces that produced me are characterized by a lot of suffering and sacrifice and pain, and their stories and voices are important to me. I don't sit there worrying about what people are going to think, but it's a different kind of responsibility.

When I finished *Higher Ground*, in the summer of 1988, I remember thinking, I've written about Africa, about the USA, and about a Jewish girl – slavery, civil rights, the Holocaust in one book – and I thought, your canvas is a lot broader than perhaps you realized, but a terrific amount of responsibility comes with it. I come from a place which is characterized by survivor guilt. I don't have to be a Jew who survived the Holocaust to have survivor guilt – although my grandfather was a Jew. A few years ago I felt quite strongly that I didn't want to deal with Britain, I wanted to go and live in the Caribbean. But it's not that I want to grapple with Britain to become an exotic addition to the British literary scene. I want to grapple with it because too many people over the years have cut too much sugar cane, and sweated too many buckets for me to turn round and say I'm just going to write about the Caribbean or the US. Both my parents, all of my grandparents, were born in St Kitts as British people. The pain of their lives, the fact that they never went to university, the fact that I was the first person from my family on both sides to go to university, is a comment on the lack of opportunity that Britain afforded them. It afforded me that opportunity, and it would be crazy for me to turn round now, having been given a language and a religion and a history, to curl up in my shell and say I don't want to know. The forces that produced Emily produced me. What produced Joyce, Edward and Captain Hamilton produced me. I'm positive that in my parents' generation, my grandparents' and great-grandparents' generation, there were people who were able to make the same connections I can make, who had the same kind of insights I have, but who were denied access to publishing houses in London and New York, who didn't know how to set their thoughts down, who couldn't afford paper, pens, who thought these things but were illiterate. I don't see myself as speaking for them, or as some kind of wonderful byproduct the vortex of history has thrown up. I'm just lucky to have been born at this time.

11

Salman Rushdie

with

Alastair Niven

Salman Rushdie is the author of seven novels: Grimus *(1975),* Midnight's Children *(1981),* Shame *(1983),* The Satanic Verses *(1988),* The Moor's Last Sigh *(1995),* The Ground Beneath her Feet *(1999) and* Fury *(2001). He has published two collections of short stories,* Haroun and the Sea of Stories *(1990) and* East, West *(1994), as well as two volumes of critical essays,* Imaginary Homelands *(1991) and* Step Across this Line *(2002). Rushdie has been the recipient of a number of major literary awards for his work, including the Booker Prize for* Midnight's Children *and the Whitbread Best Book award for* The Satanic Verses. Midnight's Children *was produced by the RSC as a stage play in 2003 and Rushdie is currently working on a film version of one of his short stories. In 1993,* Midnight's Children *was nominated as the Booker of Bookers.*

In the autumn of 1994, just before the publication of East, West *and whilst still under the fatwa, Salman Rushdie was present at a conference on the literatures of the South Asian diaspora in Britain. He talked to Dr Alastair Niven about his recent work and his own position as a writer of Asian background resident in Britain. This conference was the first to take place on the subject of Asian writing in Britain since Salman Rushdie delivered his now frequently cited lecture in 1982 on the situation of the Indian writer in Britain, a lecture which later provided the title for his non-fictional collection of essays,* Imaginary Homelands. *The following is a transcript of the discussion that took place twelve years after that original conference.*

Alastair Niven Now, Salman Rushdie, you're clearly the Hamlet in the scenario we're playing out at this conference; to have not had you here would have been a notable absence. But, do you like being labelled a writer of the Asian diaspora?

Salman Rushdie I don't mind it. I mean I think I'm one of the people who tried to construct the label I guess, so I can't blame anyone for sticking it on me. I think there's been nothing more important in my life – as a writer – than that fact; both the fact of originating in India and then coming from there – both those things. I think I would not be this writer if I had never left, and I could not be this writer if I hadn't come from there.

I sometimes feel that the more distinguished and excellent a writer is, the less they wish to be labelled.

Well . . . I suppose there have been attempts to label me in slightly less complimentary ways recently, so . . . you just want to be read as a writer, but at the same time you know that that's not what's going to happen. People do have a desire to put people into categories and I guess writers have a desire to break down the categories all the time. I don't mind it because it's true; that's what I'm saying. There are certain labels that I have protested about. I'm slightly resistant to the term 'Commonwealth literature', which is something I've written about before, just because it seemed to me that if there's an alleged form, all 100 per cent of whose practitioners claim not to practise it, then that's at least a factor in the argument. But in this case, so far, the fact of my coming from India has been so important in my writing that I can't deny it. On the other hand, of course, what it does mean is that there's a kind of assumption that that's what you're always going to write about. There's a kind of ghettoization which I think needs to be avoided.

You have indeed written about Commonwealth literature. This conference is not described as a Commonwealth literature event, but many people in this room will have attended occasions which were. In your essay 'Commonwealth Literature Does Not Exist', in *Imaginary Homelands*, you talk about a kind of 'muddled' defining of the term:

> It occurred to me as I surveyed this muddle, that the category is a chimera, and in very precise terms. The word has of course come to mean an unreal, monstrous creature of the imagination; but you will recall that the Classical chimera was a monster of a rather special type. It had the head of a lion, the body of a goat and a serpent's tail. This is to say, it could exist only in dreams, being composed of elements which could not possibly be joined together in the real world.

And, indeed, you do have a story in your new collection where you actually use an image rather like that of a creature that is composed of the trotters of a pig. I wondered if you can elaborate that a bit, about your objection to Commonwealth literature?

Well, one of my friends is Nadine Gordimer, another is the Australian writer Peter Carey. Now, if you just take Nadine Gordimer, Peter Carey and me, I can't think of what definition would include the three of us in any useful way. You could say that we have some common experience of coming from parts of the world which were former colonies. That is, if you like, a kind of political description. But in terms of anything other than that political description, what's different about Nadine Gordimer's writing, Peter Carey's writing and mine is much more important and interesting than what's similar. Apart from the political description of the world as having been composed of the pink bits; the idea that the pink bits now constitute some kind of literary meaning seems to me to be more or less ridiculous, especially if you look at the way in which Commonwealth literature actually is constituted.

Academically, it excludes English literature. Now, when last examined England was in the Commonwealth. For large periods of time Pakistan and South Africa were not in the Commonwealth but they were in Commonwealth literature, so it became this very peculiar object, which seemed to me to be defined purely in order to create a certain way of studying things at universities, a way of creating a separate budget for a separate kind of academic hierarchy, which could study these other literatures and leave English literature nicely alone with its big budgets and its large rooms, etc. and you wouldn't, as it were, rain on their parade. It seems to me that at the very least if you're going to study something called Commonwealth literature it should include English literature. Otherwise, we may as well not have a Commonwealth.

I'm not going to try to defend the term, or indeed to dispute most of what you've said, except to suggest that maybe there are common points of contact between the development of parallel Englishes; that there is a possibility that as English has developed its own persona in the subcontinent, so it has been doing in Australia or in South Africa.

Sure . . . I think that's true and certainly that linguistic project has been something that I've been very interested in, but if you want to look at where that started, you could at least say it starts with Joyce. You know, it seems to me quite clear that a part of the reason for Joycean English was precisely anti-imperialist; Joyce was trying to construct an English that didn't belong to the English by deliberate use of a lot of European words, a lot of European borrowings. So, it seems to me to be more interesting to study G. V. Desani, for instance, in *All About H. Hatterr* [1948], in the light of the Joycean project rather than under the category of Commonwealth literature. What I mean is that if you reunite the literature of the English language you find more interesting things than by hiving the split off. I think if you look at Anita Desai in the light of Indian literature you leave out her very close affinities with, say, Jane

Austen. You leave out her affinities with writers that have nothing to do with India or the Commonwealth.

Yes, it obviously leaves out a great deal, not least American litera-ture, whose history of language and so on might in some ways be parallel again.

And also, you could define American literature as being a postcolonial object, you know, par excellence.

Now, on 6 October [1994] you've got a new book coming out. I also know you're at work on a major novel at the moment, but this book is a collection of short stories. It's called *East, West* and I've just read an advanced copy of it. I'd like to ask you a little bit about this: you haven't written many short stories although some of these have appeared in earlier versions in the *New Yorker*, *Granta*, *London Review of Books*, and so on. You are quintessentially a teller of tales. All your books to date are fictions which have had storytelling woven into the central part of them, so the short story would seem an absolutely obvious genre for you to be working in. Why is it that we really only have a few?

Well, it's really because they keep getting used up in the novels, I mean that's broadly speaking why. It seems to me that really there's only two kinds of books. There's what I would call 'everything books' and there's what I would call 'something books'. You could either try and write these books which try and be about everything, or you could try and write books that are about some particular thing. Both of them work, if they're done right, and I'm not trying to say one's better than the other, but there are those two kinds of writing, and broadly speaking, my novels have been attempts to be everything books. Now, when you do that, you use up what would otherwise be ancillary material. For instance, when I wrote *Midnight's Children*, one of the ideas I had about it was that . . . the first thing to think about India is its multitude, its crowd, and I thought: 'How do you tell a crowd of stories?' 'What is the literary equivalent of that multitude?' One strategy that was adopted in that book was deliberately to tell, as it were, too many stories, so that there was a jostle of stories in the novel. Your main narration, your main storyline, had to kind of force its way through the crowd, as if you were outside Churchgate Station trying to catch a train; and you had to really do some work. When you do that, you have to deliberately waste material, you have to have ideas that you know as a writer you could turn into a twenty-page story or into a novella or something, and you have to throw it away in a paragraph. You have to have this profligacy, there's just so much lying around. It was not an attempt to show off, but to try and represent the reality that the novel was describing, as being this place where you bump into novels in the street, where you step over them sleeping in doorways. There are simply so many stories going on that it would be absurd, I thought, to tell just one. A similar kind of project occurs in *The Satanic Verses* as well, and so there's nothing left over for short stories, except these.

Aren't you slightly belittling these stories, because it implies that they're kind of the woodshavings in the carpenter's workroom?

Well, they're not really. . . . It's a funny thing, the stories that revolve around a novel . . . you often think when you're writing a novel, 'Oh well, I can't really make that work but maybe I can use it in a story afterwards.' Actually, when the novel's finished, in a funny way those stories become ghosts and disappear, they become uninteresting to work up. These stories were always conceived as stories, they were thought of as stories and they never had any other function. But what I'm saying is that one of the reasons why, unlike many writers who write many more short stories than I do, one of the reasons why story-shaped ideas haven't often come to me is because of this other storytelling project in the novels. One of the things that really surprised me this year – because the later bunch of the stories in this collection were written at the beginning of this year – was the realization that I'd been, without knowing it, doing a rather strange thing. The book has three sections. The first section is called 'East', the second section is called 'West' and the third section is called 'East West' – because that's what they're about. But oddly I found that the first three stories, the 'East' which has India and Pakistan stories, were all written before the three stories in the 'West' section, which basically takes icons of Western culture like Hamlet or Christopher Columbus or the Wizard of Oz. Those three stories were all written before the three stories in the last section, which are about cultural crossover. Now, that was completely unplanned and not even conscious of the discovery that I was somehow making this step-by-step journey, I suddenly found that I had done this and that's why it's a book. That's why I decided to put them together into a book. There are other stories that I've written, two or three which aren't in here, because really they don't fit with that shape.

They do make a nice shape, perhaps in the way that *In a Free State* [1971] by V. S. Naipaul does. They read as individual stories but there is a kind of construction in the grouping of them.

And rather surprising to me, internal echoes which I never knew about. They are not put there on purpose.

I was also interested in your remark about your big novels being about crowds and working your way through the crowd, because in fact one of the things that struck me reading these stories was that you are also able to handle a sense of crowd in the few pages of a short story. You know, a story set in London, for example, does have a sense of the vitality and movement of London.

Well, thanks. There's a kind of literary gripe at the moment that you see in a lot of book pages, which is that there aren't any writers who are able to write about contemporary England or contemporary London. That seems to me to ignore an awful lot of writers who are doing exactly that, Martin Amis, for example. One of the things that has really irritated me about everything that's happened around *The Satanic Verses* is that nobody points out that it's a novel about London and that by far the longest chunk of *The Satanic Verses* is an attempt to describe this thing that it calls a city visible but unseen, which is right here, which is not so far from here anyway. So, yes, I've always been interested about writing about London, if only because I've lived here for a very long time.

These are obviously short stories, and the short story is a genre that people say, or have been saying until very recently, is a neglected form. Is it really true that the short story is the neglected genre people always say it is?

Certainly not in America any more, thanks I think largely to the effect of Ray Carver. I think ever since Carver's writing there's been a fantastic resurgence in the short story in America – not always as original as one would wish because I think Carver has a lot of not-quite-as-good-as-Carver imitators. But certainly the fact that he was able to create a major American body of work, exclusively in the form of the short story, did energize that form again in America. In England, generally, I think you're right. I think Antonia Byatt is as least as good a short-story writer as a novelist and often really wonderful in a novella length.

There's a sense of discipline that she's imposing on herself which isn't perhaps always so obvious in the longer books.

And she also gets more unbuttoned in her stories, she lets her hair down more.

If someone were to put a label on the kind of writing for which you are most famous – *Midnight's Children*, *Shame*, *The Satanic Verses* **– I think capaciousness is a word that might come to mind, a sense of breadth and panoramic scale and so on. I recall just a few years ago, I was asked by the British Council if I would write the text for an exhibition that was going to go around the world on the post-war British novel. I was thinking of a way of shaping it, and long before**

other events happened to you that made your name celebrated in non-literary ways, you seemed to me the natural writer to make the kind of culmination of this exhibition, which began with Graham Greene and Angus Wilson. It seemed that you were bringing back to the novel a sense of that rumbustiousness, humour and range which the English novel had in the eighteenth century in Fielding and perhaps obviously had in Dickens but which it had lost, certainly since Lawrence. I don't know whether you identify with anything that I'm saying.

I think the eighteenth century is the great century for English literature, and it's no secret that I've been very affected by *Tristram Shandy* or *Tom Jones*. They are those things that Henry James called 'loose baggy monsters' – I actually don't think they're that loose or baggy; I think it's easy for people who write Anita Brookner novels to think of them as loose baggy monsters (sorry Anita).

Well, they come out of a century of immense discipline, rigour and classicism.

I spend much more time on the architecture of my books than on their writing. It takes me a very, very long time to understand the book, to understand how it goes together, and what connects with what and what its machine is. That's why it takes me five or six years to write one of those big books, and I should think probably three or four of those years are architecture, are skeleton constructing. And that obviously means writing lots and lots of versions and passages and ways into it and seeing how it works out in practice, but they're certainly not loose in the sense of just falling onto the page. Kundera has this essay, doesn't he, about how the novel has two parents, one of which is Richardson and *Clarissa*, and the other of which is Sterne and *Tristram Shandy*. He says, and I think he's right, that broadly speaking the children of Clarissa Harlow have populated the earth, and there are not that many children of Tristram Shandy, not surprisingly.

They would have to be illegitimate children.

Exactly. He's not good in the procreation department for a start. I think Kundera's point, which is a very good point, is that the first strand, the realistic descriptive social novel, derived from *Clarissa*, doesn't have that much left to explore, whereas the other thing, the stunted, weird, misshapen, three-legged children of *Tristram Shandy*, leaves the whole universe to be explored in that way. And so I was always more drawn in that direction. But that sounds too theoretical really. In the end you write the way it comes out, and then you find echoes in what other people have done, and then you draw them close to yourself and see what you can learn from them. I never thought to myself, 'Oh, I'll write like this.' It came out that way. I'm glad you mentioned that they're supposed to be funny books, because I do think it's something people don't mention often enough. *The Satanic Verses*, for example, is supposed to be a comic novel, which is why I said, and then got in more trouble for saying, that it seemed to me that the real dispute in *The Satanic Verses* was between people who had a sense of humour and people who didn't.

I can promise you that *East, West* is full of good laughs. I'm going to ask you one more question and it relates to your present circumstances. It is a kind of double-headed question: has the fact that you have been living under the monstrous shadow of the *fatwa* for several years either intimidated the subject matter of what you want to write about, and made you feel, no, there are areas that I had perhaps ought this time not to explore, or alternatively has it given you subject matter? I was very struck that here there is a story called 'The Prophet's Hair' which I thought was a fairly risky story to be writing in your present situation.

Well, I think 'The Prophet's Hair' is the answer to the intimidation question. If I was being scared off writing about Islam it wouldn't be in the collection, would it? 'The Prophet's Hair' is based on a genuine incident, by the way. There actually is a mosque by the lake in Kashmir which claims to contain a relic of a single hair of the head of the Prophet Mohammed and it got stolen in the early 1960s, and there was a terrible scandal and then all kinds of political ramifications. . . . Actually, it's mentioned in *Midnight's Children*. There's a little passage about it in there as well. The government almost fell, all kinds of things happened, there was almost war with Pakistan about it. And then they announced that they found it and everybody believed them. Then they had a meeting where all the peers, and the holy men of Kashmir were all brought to the mosque and were asked to authenticate it. It was passed along and they said, 'Yes, that's unquestionably it.' Then it was put back in the shrine and there it is again. So that incident, which as I say happened in the early 1960s, I'd remembered as being rich in comedy, and I'd often wanted to write about it, but actually had never succeeded in writing about it as it happened. And the way in which I was able to find a story to write was to imagine a second theft, was to imagine that the thieves who had stolen it panicked when there was this huge hullabaloo and threw it away, and that somebody else found it. The moment I had invented that second, that secondary purloining, then I had a story to write, because who found it? What happened to them? etc. How did it get back? There's a game that one used to play when I was studying history, that you would try to invent a century in between two actual centuries, and you would try to invent it in such a way that it would cancel itself out by the end. So, what would be the century between the nineteenth and twentieth centuries which could allow the twentieth century to happen at the end as if this intermediary century hadn't happened? This story is like that, it's like the story between two historical moments which allows history to pick up again as if the story hadn't been there.

It reads almost like a spoof Jacobean tragedy. All the main characters get slaughtered on one page.

Well, actually, in one paragraph.

12

Nayantara Sahgal

with

Minoli Salgado

Nayantara Sahgal was born in 1927 into one of India's foremost political families. The niece of Jawaharlal Nehru, daughter of Vijayalakshmi Pandit and first cousin of Indira Gandhi, Sahgal's writing has been informed by her unique upbringing and by her espousal of the secularist political ideals of the freedom movement. A stoic defender of the Nehruvian idea of India, in both her fiction and her political writing she affirms the values of cultural pluralism, religious tolerance and non-violence, and presents them as having a historical home in the Indian nation. It is a stance that has led her to openly criticize key political and cultural developments, including Indira Gandhi's Emergency Rule, Hindu fundamentalist practices, and, more recently, the war against Iraq.

The author of nine works of fiction and eight works of non-fiction, Sahgal's novels include Rich Like Us *(1985), which won the Sinclair Prize, and* Plans for Departure *(1985), which won the Commonwealth Writer's Prize. She has also written a political biography of Indira Gandhi,* Indira Gandhi: Her Road to Power *(1982), and published a collection of essays,* Point of View: A Personal Response to Life, Literature and Politics *(1997). She has served as vice-president of the People's Union of Civil Liberties and as a delegate to the UN General Assembly. Her most recent publications include a novel,* Lesser Breeds *(2003), which explores caste communal prejudices and the enduring relevance of non-violence, and a collection of letters,* Before Freedom: Nehru's Letters to His Sister (1909–1947) *(2000).*

This interview took place in Brighton when Nayantara Sahgal was on a UK tour giving readings of her work. The opening comments refer to an extract from Rich Like Us *in which the narrator's grandfather witnesses the death by* sati *of his mother.*

Minoli Salgado I'd like to begin by asking you about that passage in *Rich Like Us*. Is it because there was a particular theme in it that is central to your work?

Nayantara Sahgal Well, yes. One thing that comes across in the reading quite strongly is the way I portray women. This is represented by the boy's idea of his mother. She has made as he puts it 'journeys of the spirit' regardless of the fact that she has almost never left home. She is like one of those migratory birds which flies thousands of miles. Nobody knows of their tremendous journey which has spanned seas and skies but only sees their arrival. She is a symbol of those Indian women who despite not having education, opportunity, travel and all the things which their husbands have, yet achieve a tremendous breadth of vision – a kind of arrival in modern times without anyone realizing how they got there. Yet their 'private shrines remain lit' as I have said in that piece. They don't desert their traditions or their past – there's no break away – but they flow into whatever is expected of them in an almost noiseless kind of way.

Is that meant to make her death, through the practice of widow-burning, seem all the more violent? The disposal of widows is a central idea in *Rich Like Us*. It is there in Rose's death.

Rose is a modern-day *sati* and this is a *sati* earlier on, in another century. It is that women are sacrificed in this way – the boy's mother for the greed and ambitions of men, then in the case of Rose for the greed and ambitions of her stepson.

You're suggesting that times haven't changed very much.

That's right, and nor have women. That immense quiet strength is there, and in my earlier novels it's there in contemporary women who do not struggle in the radical sort of way recognized as struggle in the West. Yet they experience an even greater struggle to my mind, because they are coming out of much deeper roots and they endure to the utmost. When at last they can't take any more they make no bones about leaving, about doing what has to be done. They do not stay to remain slaves at that point. They go.

This reminds me of Simrit in *The Day in Shadow* [1971]. Here you also use *sati*, this time as a metaphor for what Simrit is going through and the way in which women are treated. It seems to me there is a real development in your fiction from using *sati* as a metaphor in *The Day in Shadow* and using it as a metaphor and a reality in *Rich Like Us*. Was it a conscious move or was it something that simply evolved?

You might well ask whether *sati* was in my consciousness or my sub-conscious because I had a great-grandmother who was a *sati*. She's supposed to have been the last *sati* in her village on the west coast, in the village of Bambuli. I remember the story being told to me as a child with some pride as of a sense of history. Of course as time passed and I came to question this more and more I was increasingly filled with horror at the very prospect of such a thing having happened. I suppose all things grew out of the consciousness that there was such a woman in my own background. I am personally descended from a woman who did this deed.

Does this put you in a paradoxical position of someone who can understand tradition and see the value in some approaches that women take, but at the same time are against what is being done to them in the name of tradition?

The difficulty here is the way people use the word 'tradition'. To my mind it is not something static, it is something we make as we go along. We are constantly carving our tradition, blocking out parts of it deliberately as being useless to us, hacking it away like old wood and otherwise refashioning it in ways that strengthen and mean more to us. So tradition is something that moves. It's not something that obscurantist leaders and fundamentalists understand. They will insist that tradition is something back there and we have to hark back and tie ourselves to it, insisting that women can't move forward because that's tradition. That is not tradition. Tradition is our living selves and what we are making out of our lives and building for the future. Tradition is something which changes just as we ourselves do.

It's interesting you say that because I think what is central to your work is this ongoing attempt to assess the changes that India is going through over a period of time by articulating specific political views through your characters. Would that be a fair way of looking at your work?

Yes. I would say that my continuing character is India. It is this that I am considering and translating into people's experiences, men's and women's, through the political and social scene and the implications of politics and Hinduism on character. I am particularly interested in Hinduism and the kind of characteristics and qualities it produces in people – the very fact that for hundreds of years it has taken a back seat even though it has been the surviving culture and kept hidden for purposes of survival. Now of course the next stage will be one of coming out of hiding, it will be on the rampage, almost, in a fundamentalist incarnation. The next thing I write about will probably be about that because that is what is happening.

One thing I find very interesting is that there are some analogies between your last novel, *Mistaken Identity* [1988], and your very first work, *A Time to Be Happy* [1958], in so far as both set up a

debate between the Muslim and Hindu which is resolved through romantic love. You moved to a position of being rather critical and ironic in your last novel. Bhushan Singh is presented ironically as a poet and idealist. Is this a reflection of a shift in your approach to a secular India? Is such an India a possibility?

Well. First of all Bhushan Singh is a failed poet and a loafer and a delinquent – I think that's central to the story. Here's a man with no ambition whatsoever, who knew his real talent was for ballroom dancing and making love to women. Here's a man whose one ambition is to find his beloved and be reunited with her. He's obsessed, like mystics are with god, with wanting to find Razia. He can't see any possibility other than a Hindu–Muslim India, an India which is neither Hindu nor Muslim but which is Hindu–Muslim of which every Hindu and Muslim partakes. There I had in mind the legend of Kabir, the poet of the sixteenth century. He's a great figure even today. All secularists will point to him as a great example. He was an abandoned baby of a Hindu family found by a Muslim weaver, brought up in the household as a Muslim boy and grew into a great poet. His works have been incorporated into the Sikh, Islamic and Hindu traditions. He was great in his time because he wouldn't tolerate the high priests of either religion and said that god is not only one but that god is in you, you don't have to look for him in a mosque or in a temple. When he died and his followers were quarrelling over whether to bury his body or cremate it, they lifted up his shroud: there were only flowers there, no corpse. This has become a kind of metaphor for the fact that Kabir wouldn't confine himself to any one imprisoning label. So that's one thing I had in mind in *Mistaken Identity*, that there's no difference between Hindu and Muslim. We are one, from the gut. It's not that we partake of each other, we are each other. This is what India means. Secularism not only has a chance, secularism has been bred into our bones – through the national movement in modern times, and centuries ago through being good neighbours, living side by side, sharing each other's festivals.

On the whole are you optimistic?

I wouldn't say that I am optimistic. I would say that as long as you live you have to work for certain things. I have kept my Indian nationality by choice because to me the meaning of India is the values that it represents, which are worth fighting for. It's no good my doing it from six thousand miles away. If you live in a society where you want to see change then that's where you have to be.

With respect to these values, what does the figure of Gandhi represent to you now?

What he always did I suppose: a man who stated bare fundamental truths which will always be true. Some of them are very basic to India. For example he propounded that large industry alone won't solve problems, that the machine is not necessarily the answer.

What about the critical comments made by the comrades in *Mistaken Identity*? One figure refers to his 'treacherous politics'.

That's how the communists talked of him. They thought he was a useless, archaic specimen who had no place in modern society. But the communists constantly missed the bus in India.

We've been discussing the way in which religion and politics are entwined in India.

It hasn't been in India no, not until recently. India was unique in that respect because it was certainly not a theocratic society and called itself a secular republic. Now religion is being injected into the body politic by the BJP [Bharatiya Janata Party] who are using Hinduism as a platform to get power. It's the first time this is happening.

The reason I suggested that was because I've noticed that you often use religious terminology to express political views in your work.

I am terribly interested in religion and particularly Hinduism because it's the sky we as Indians live under. By that I don't mean just religion but the kind of psychology and behaviour that it sets up. For instance passivity may be the result of a people who've had to lie low. And it may be a very active characteristic for it's the only way to keep yourself whole and alive at certain periods of crisis. Hinduism was up against Islam for seven or eight hundred years and so passivity and sycophancy may have developed in the process of staying alive. These characteristics which became inbred in Indians, and maybe the society as a whole, are the characteristics to observe.

I find it intriguing that you select Hinduism as being of specific importance to you because you often use Christian symbolism in your work – I'm thinking here of the point at which the crowd forms the shape of a cross in *A Situation in New Delhi* **[1977], and you refer elsewhere to a moral crusade and the Holy Grail. Why?**

They're deliberate. One belief I hold is that there's no end to the debt we owe strangers. The Hindu fundamentalists will tell you that there is no other civilization in India but a Hindu civilization, that all others are impostors, they came later and don't count. This is a lie as far as India is concerned because everything counts. When we say that the past is important, well the past is yesterday as much as five thousand years ago. The kind of history that India has gone through, waves of invasion, conquest and occupation, and through that the criss-crossing of races, the cross-fertilization of ideas, religions, languages – there is no such thing as a pure strain there. Bhushan Singh in *Mistaken Identity* falls for Razia because of her face, which is the future of communal harmony. She has Hindu eyes and Muslim cheekbones. Similarly here the question of Christianity, Islam, all these things are part of the very fabric of India, and certainly part of every Indian like myself who's been educated in Christian schools and Indians unlike myself who live in a country where foreigners have come and gone leaving their marks on us in various ways. In *Rich Like Us* too there's Marcella, the aristocratic English woman who crosses Rose's path and changes her life by having an affair with her husband and then crosses Sonali's path at the end and changes her life because she, just by the words she says, opens up to Sonali the possibility that there's an end to the Emergency. So the stranger who crosses your path changes your life; and as it happens in life so it happens in countries, so that we can draw on Christianity, we can draw on Islam, it's part of us.

Your mention of Sonali made me think of one point in _Rich Like Us_ that has puzzled me: when Sonali has just read the manuscript and drops off to sleep. Is it meant to be an ironic commentary on her incapacity for action and the way some people felt unable to challenge the system during the Emergency?

She doesn't just drop off to sleep. There's a line I put in there for that purpose:

> I put the manuscript down. My eyes ached. I felt shaken. Illumination seems to come to me in the dark. When I switched off my bedside lamp I saw a world revealed, but strangely enough it was not the evil in it I saw. On a narrow parapet enclosing a funeral pyre I saw a boy of nineteen balancing dangerously, unconscious of the danger to himself, as he fought savagely to kill his mother's murderers. Not all of us are passive before cruelty and depravity. He had not been. Nor the boy in Connaught Place who had struggled desperately all the way to the police van. Nor even Rose's beggar, undaunted by his armlessness. . . . And I fell asleep to dream of heroisms whose company I was scarcely fit to keep.

Suddenly she's awake to all the heroisms that there are, that people do not accept evil lying down. They never have. She drops off to sleep dreaming of heroisms which form a kind of beacon light in front of her.

It's interesting that you've emphasized dreaming, because in your next novel, *Plans for Departure*, there's an emphasis on the imagination. This novel is quite different from anything else you've written, partly because it's not a political novel. It's very much a romance mystery. What led you to write it?

When I finished writing *Rich Like Us* I seemed to be so full of surplus energy I just went into another novel. As always I never have a very clear idea what it's going to be about and the only time when I feel I'm on the right track is when I don't know where I'm going. . . . A fragment of conversation came to me right at the start about a cutlet. I just carried on from there. Then it struck me that the period prior to the national movement must have been very fascinating – a period before Gandhi was even known, when Tilak was the giant on the political scene. I thought it might be fun to hark back and see what I can make of that time before non-violence.

In your earlier novels you are concerned with political reality and the transition to a focus on the imagination hinted at in *Rich Like Us* where you were questioning the nature of reality. Since then you have been focusing on the past more. I wonder if you could say why you're doing that?

In retrospect the novels I wrote before *Rich Like Us* seem to chart a chronological progression of India, reflecting the contemporary hopes and fears. Then it seemed that things were getting increasingly worse in India. Idealism had degenerated to the point where there was almost nothing left of the old dreams that nationalists had for India. Then came the Emergency and dictatorship. After that there was no further to go in that chronological progression. We'd hit bottom. I went into the past because I didn't see a way ahead. The past is always open. So I went back to 1914 and then 1929.

Why did you choose a non-Indian as a central character for *Plans for Departure*?

It's part of the freedom I acquired when I left the chronological progression. It seemed to me that I could write about anyone. Foreign writers have written about Indians – why shouldn't we be just as free?

Which particular writers do you admire?

One whom I admire greatly is Iris Murdoch. I used to read her a lot and I think she's very political in much of her writing.

Given your interest in contemporary Indian politics and your own political involvement, what do you feel the role of fiction is? Do you see your work as a form of political intervention?

No. Absolutely not. Being a political journalist I have another field for that. In that sense fiction was a love and journalism a duty. It was a matter of conscience for me that I said what had to be said through journalism. Fiction remains a field in itself.

That's very interesting because your early works can be read as interventionist . . . your characters seem to embody political perspectives and argue amongst each other in such a way that it seems they are making a call for action.

I never had such an intention in mind. I think I suffer from the disease of reticence, and always have. I've never felt that it was my job to change the world except by example.

If you hadn't gone into political writing what would you have done?

I don't know. Belonging to a political family there was always the possibility of entering politics. But nobody wants a person like me in politics. It would be extremely embarrassing [*laughs*]. I fall between two stools. I belong to the Nehru family and as you know I fought Mrs Gandhi during the Emergency. I stood out against many of her policies, wrote a whole book about that in fact. There was no place for me in any set-up which she headed. And I was not one to ever compromise my beliefs. When she fell from power there were those in the new government who were not keen on me because I belonged to the Nehru family – except in the various ways in which they used me when it suited them to campaign in the elections because they knew I had a voice and eloquence. I did all that because I believed certain people should get in.

What might you have done?

I think what is needed today is a person with courage and integrity who will not compromise on the basic issue which is the meaning of India. India is a unique proposition based on the most civilized human instincts – all religions and cultures have lived there for centuries and must always do so. Religion must never be confused with politics. There's no one out there saying any of this.

You mentioned the role of women and women's issues earlier on. One thing that has puzzled me is that there is a real dearth of fictional writing covering women's involvement in the national movement. I wondered if you might ever think of writing something – along the lines of *Mistaken Identity* perhaps, where you focus on a man's experience in prison during the nationalist struggle – which would portray women's part in the struggle? It's brought into your novels but has, as yet, never been central to your work.

That's very interesting and you're quite right, it isn't. I think that it may be that I am not gender conscious in quite the way that Western women are. There's a reason for that. I come from a family where the men were the feminists and they brought the women out into the limelight and helped them to achieve their potential. My mother for example would have held back and probably not even have gone in for a political career if her husband and her brother had not encouraged her. And then, after her husband's death, Gandhiji pushed her into diplomatic life. So the nationalist period was an age in which women were called upon to take part in political activities by men. Gandhi brought women into the national movement partly because it was non-violent, it was particularly suited to women. It was a happy situation because at Independence suffrage for women was not even debated – the only country in the world which gave women the vote without a debate or a fight. So I've never been gender conscious in that sense because women were being helped and a climate was being created for them in which they could involve themselves politically. Of course there are some dreadful situations in which women are still struggling for their basic rights. I do realize that.

13

Vikram Seth
with
Sudeep Sen

Throughout his career, which began with the publication of Mappings *(1980), his first volume of poetry, Vikram Seth has written fiction for both adults and children, poetry, travel narratives, translations and even a libretto,* Arion and the Dolphin *(1994), which was performed by the English National Opera. The book which followed was a travel narrative, an autobiographical tale of his journey from Nepal to India entitled* From Heaven Lake *(1983) which emphasized that his influences and interests extended beyond the Indian border. He returned to poetry, publishing* The Humble Administrator's Garden *(1985), which was structured around the plants of China, India and California, and for which he won the Commonwealth Prize for Poetry, and* All You Who Sleep Tonight *(1990), which combined Seth's sharp humour with the dark side of history, especially Hiroshima and the Holocaust. This was followed by* Beastly Tales from Here and There *(1991) and* Three Chinese Poets *(1992).*

Seth's first novel, The Golden Gate *(1986), prompted Gore Vidal to comment that he had written 'the great California' novel, and perhaps also set a precedent for the novel that was to follow,* A Suitable Boy *(1993). This classic realist, heavyweight tome, which took Seth almost a decade to write, was described by one critic as 'three and a half pounds of perfection', placing the author alongside the likes of Leo Tolstoy, Charles Dickens and George Eliot. Some felt it was a welcome break from the magical realist style that Rushdie used in his novels. Commenting on this, Seth said that 'the kind of books I like reading are books where the authorial voice doesn't intrude . . . [or] . . . pull you up with the brilliance of their sentences'. Set in Brahmpur, it explores the relationship between a Muslim boy and a Hindu girl and the interaction of four families: the Kapoors, Mehras and Chatterjis (Hindus) and the Khans (Muslim). Since then Seth has published* An Equal Music *(1999), a romantic novel set in England and featuring Michael, a musician, and an old flame whom he met in Vienna as a student.*

Sudeep Sen Much has been written about your novel *A Suitable Boy*, but what I would like to know is, what got you interested in that specific time period of post-independent Indian history, a period when you were, perhaps, just a year old?

Vikram Seth Well, actually I'm born just after the book is finished. Though I do mention a date when Mrs Rupa Mehra goes to meet a friend in Calcutta on the last page of the book. That's actually my birthday. I began with that period because it was quite a pleasant and safe period. I thought I'd begin the book on a low key, and then heighten it as I went along as the times themselves were heightened. But I never got to those heightened times – the times of Indian conflict with China and Pakistan, the Emergency, the assassination of Prime Minister Indira Gandhi, and so on – I just got stuck in this early period which I initially thought was a dull one. So that's what happened, I got involved in it and stayed with it for eight years. As I talked to people about what happened at that time, I realized how interesting it all was. The first general elections were taking place. People who had stood side by side fighting the British were now fighting each other. Land reforms were taking place: the large land estates were collapsing, and the patronage for the musicians and courtesans was disappearing as well. Some farmers were benefiting but not the landless labourers. Then the wounds of Partition – Muslim and Hindu antagonism – were still fresh, and a most unfortunate clicking together of the Muslim and the Hindu calendar took place, where Muharram [the Muslim month of mourn-ing] and Dusserah [the Hindu month of rejoicing] coincided. So the Hindu–Muslim tensions were heightened. All these things worked together. . . . It was a much richer period then I'd imagined it would be.

Was this something you found out as you went along?

Exactly, I stumbled into it. I thought it was a dull period, but . . .

I read in your piece 'To Cut a Long Story Short' in the magazine section of *The Times* [20 March 1993] that you were planning to write a major quintet of novels – *The Bridge of the World*.

Yes I was. . . . Shortly after finishing *The Golden Gate*, my novel in verse set in California, I had the idea of writing five short novels, in prose this time, set in India. The five novels would form an arc, beginning in the 1950s and ending whenever I put my pen down. The whole world would be a kind of post-Raj quintet. . . . The first one would have taken me up to the 1960s, the second one somewhere in the 1970s, and 1980s, and so on.

Were you consciously thinking of portraying Indian history in a fictional mode, or was it more that you wanted to tell a story which you were personally interested in?

The latter. I think books are most effective when they are story-led and character-led.

A Suitable Boy **is massive – whichever way one looks at it – its sheer monumental size, it is almost 1,400 pages, over 600,000 words long, and has taken you eight years to write. In fact the novel in an uncut form would have been about 2,000 printed pages. Can you tell me something about how the narrative evolved – this great love story, the quest for a suitable boy for Lata, and the life and times of the** four protagonist families? Did you have a larger blue-pencil sketch before you began, or did it unravel fairly naturally as you went along?

No, I had a few inklings about the first part of the book, and when I realized that it was going to spread into many different areas – the countryside, Calcutta, law, the leather industry, courtesans, Zamindari, elections – then I realized that my sketch would have to be thrown out of the window, that I would have to reformulate things with more research, and then work again in the remaining eighteen parts of the book.

When you say that it took you eight years to write the book, do you mean eight continuous years?

By write I mean everything from conceive to revise.

Two elements – the use of dialogue and the use of poetic forms – interest me most about the book. First, the successful use of dialogue, an aspect many novelists find hard to contend with satisfactorily, comes across with a sense of great ease. It must have involved a lot of research, especially when it comes to speech patterns outside the world you have grown up in or been familiar with.

A lot of research . . . Well, although research was an important part in the writing of the book, it's the least important part of the book itself. Because you don't want a book to smell of the midnight oil. But living in villages, by-lanes and gullies where my Buaji lives, not far from Jama Masjid in Old Delhi . . . staying with courtesan families, interviewing people who were freedom fighters, visiting families who worked in the leather trade in Agra . . . things like that . . . Reading newspapers from 1951 to get a sense of whether certain laws were still used then.

And of the eight years, how much of the time was taken up with this sort of research?

God knows, some time . . . I'd find it impossible to say exactly, I would
have to look at my diary to see how to attribute a particular day. See,
part of it is researching, but while you're doing that, you are also thinking of characters, ideas, and making notes. It is such a mixed process.

**The second element is your use of poetry. The 'word of thanks' is a
sonnet; the contents page is set as a long-line poem in alternating
rhymed couplets; then the poems Amit Chatterji writes himself;
and others throughout the book. What I am curious to know is
whether, at the very heart of hearts, it is pure poetry that you are
drawn to, over the prose genre.**

Well, you know the heart contains two auricles and two ventricles, and
so I suppose I can divide them between my love for poetry and my love
for prose. I really do feel that poetry is one of my deepest passions,
although over the course of writing this book I've realized how difficult
it is to write good, clear prose. It's not an easy matter compared to
poetry.

How much of Amit Chatterjee is really your persona?

I'm likely to be forced into a circumstance where I'll sue myself if I say
he's too much like me. . . . There are bits and pieces . . . it's a typical
novelist's evasive answer. You know, bits of me, bits of people I know,
and quite a lot of imagination. He's not really me. Obviously, he is set
up as a kind of alter ego. But he is only a part of me, and there are other
aspects of him that I wouldn't really subscribe to.

**If one looks at your other books, there are also characters which
could be identified as alter egos.**

Well yes, Janet in *The Golden Gate*.

Was the poem 'The Fever Bird' written specifically for the episode, or was it something you had written earlier and which happened to fit this section well?

I can't remember now, let me think. . . . When I was writing 'The Fever Bird', it kept me awake many a night. . . . It must have been a little of each, because during the time I was writing the novel, many of the poems flavoured the novel, and the novel flavoured the poems that I wrote . . . it was very much an integrated process. I can't quite understand where it comes from. On the other hand, 'The Fever Bird' keeps appearing in the book in other respects. For example, those two Englishmen talk about it, and then Maan hears it again when he's out in the countryside in Bihar.

Another admirable quality about the book is the use of the Indian idiom and words without italicization, such as kutti, gajak, etc. What are your views about glossaries, and over-explanation within the text (for foreign readers)?

Well, I think as an Indian reader I'd be very irritated if I kept finding italicization or explanations in the text or glossary. For example, if every time I used 'kutti', I described what one does with one thumb in one's teeth . . . or if I described 'gajak' as a jaggery sweet with sesame seeds.

But when it transcends the Indian parameters?

Well I think that's the point. I hope I'm not confusing the Western reader. I hope I'm not exoticizing India. I hope the story and characters would carry it through from country to country. At least in England it appears to have done so. It's not a Raj book. It doesn't have any important foreign characters. As you say, 'kutti' and 'gajak', no glossary, no italicization. So something has appealed, but it's clearly not a complete comprehension into that world that's appealed. There are things that they won't understand. If I were to explain what 'paan' is, would they still understand what it meant to us? You see, that's the thing. You get used to it after a while, you begin to realize what a 'lakh' is, what a 'crore' is, even if you are a foreign reader.

Let me now go back in time. Could you tell me about your childhood days? What sort of family atmosphere did you grow up in?

I've never known any of my grandparents, my proper grandparents, let's say, except for my mother's mother, my Nani, and the book is dedicated to her memory, as well as to my parents who are both of course alive. My father is in the shoe and leather trade and he's now semi-retired. My mother was a lawyer for twenty-five years, then a judge, and later the chief justice of·the Himachel Pradesh High Court, though she too has just retired on her sixty-second birthday. My father, my mother and the three kids . . . I'm the eldest, my brother is five years younger to me, and my sister five years younger to him. We are a very close family, although we've lived abroad . . . my brother and I have lived abroad for many years. My sister is now married to an Austrian diplomat and they live in Washington. But we are a very very close family when we are together. Now when we were brought up, we were brought up with two working parents, and say an 'ayah' or servant or someone or the other. Yet we spent a lot of time together as a family. I went away to boarding school, and that was time taken away from home, and yet the family is still the centre of my life in many ways.

Did you enjoy school, first in India, then in Britain, and then after that in America?

Well, did I enjoy school? I suppose my brother enjoyed school. I don't think I enjoyed it quite as much as I might have had I been different, or less uptight, or something. This year I was back at Doon School as chief guest and I gave the Founders' Day speech, and said clearly that though I owed a lot to this school, I also had not been happy there. I told the authorities to think about that before they invited me, [they said that would be fine] . . . but the boys appreciated the speech. I think people do have a tough time at school sometimes. They think that there is something wrong with them rather than the fact they are at a certain age. . . . England, then the States, and then China for two years . . .

When did you first start writing poetry? Was poetry something that always attracted you?

I started writing poetry, I suppose when I was at university in England. I must have been nineteen or twenty. I'd written stuff earlier. But that's when I really started writing, which is an expression of passionate feelings, let's say.

Who were your favourite poets at that stage?

At that stage, I can't remember now. But later when I started writing in America, I must say, my two favourite poets, one American and the other an Englishman, were Timothy Steele and Philip Larkin.

How important was [the experience of living in] Britain, America and China in shaping your sensibilities? Did it also give you a more mature feeling about your own relationship with India?

Yes. I think when you live in a country and you have friends there, you take on at least a little bit of the colour of that place and look upon the world differently. You look at your own country differently; it may lead to a greater affection, but it may also lead to a greater objectivity.

What are your views on the teaching of creative writing? Does it actually help a writer at all? In India, especially among the academics and older modern poets, there seems to exist an archaic view – that poetry is almost always feeling or content-based, with the structure or formal elements of poetry being hardly important.

Modernism [in India] has had a very long innings, of about eighty or ninety years. You can hardly call it modern, it's rather entrenched. And we have a tremendous habit, sadly, in India of taking the fashion of the West which has already been discarded in the West and hanging on to it. Instead of that, we should just think for ourselves. And that is not to say that there is no good verse written that is free verse, there is, but to close your eyes to a poem just because it is written in a particular rhyme and metre is silly. Having said that, I do agree that the most important thing in poetry is feeling and the content, but I'm just saying that's the most important thing. It is critical that the thing should be shaped well verbally so that it can be remembered, and rhyme and metre help in that regard. Also they are very suggestive in their own right.

How did the idea of *The Golden Gate* come about? How long did it take?

The Golden Gate was like a gift from above. I stumbled into a book store and started reading *Eugene Onegin* [1833], and couldn't put it down. I was obsessed by it for a month. It was around the time for me, when *From Heaven Lake* had just been published, and I needed to start something to distract me from reviews and all that. I began writing *The Golden Gate* and the whole thing was written in nine months and revised in four months, that's about a year. . . . Amazing, nothing like that has ever happened to me before.

Do you really think it's so much a gift from above?

I don't know. I'm very dubious about words like inspiration and the muse, but in the case of *The Golden Gate*, I came very close to saying that's what happened.

An important aspect about this book is that it is set entirely in America, and that you make no bones about it being Indian or the

need to be Indian in any way. It is thankfully free of all that. In a sense, it ties in with your earlier comment, about the fact that some Indians tend to have a peculiar tendency of criticizing: [*mimics* Indian accent] 'What is this, why are Indian writers not writing about our own culture?'

[*joins in mimicking the accent*] 'You are there, we would expect you to write about your own country, and now you are writing foreign things'. If Janet had turned out to be an Indian American as opposed to a Japanese American, no doubt I would have been spared some flak.

Your latest work, the libretto *Arion and the Dolphin*, is a story of Arion, a young musician at the court of Periander in Corinth. Thrown overboard on his return from a musical contest in Sicily, Arion is saved and befriended by a dolphin.

That was performed by the English National Opera last year. I took a commission for the first time. The Royal Shakespeare Company wants to commission me to write a play, but again I'm not entirely sure whether I should take a commission or whether I should write the play and see if it is any good. As I said, the previous play I wrote I think was not much good.

Did they propose the subject in the case of this libretto?

They proposed dolphins and said I could propose something else. And so I thought of something else: 'Wait, there is that myth, Arion and the dolphin, which has a human element as well as a dolphin.' So I decided to do that.

In present times, there are so many different movements. In the variety and latitude of writing appearing globally – Caribbean, Australian, Scots or Indian – there seems to be a remarkable diversification of the English language and excellence in writing. A recent article in *Time* magazine, 'The Empire Writes Back' [1993], took stock of some of that. Where do you see British and American writing vis-à-vis writings from these regions now and in the near future? There are many who say that British fiction is down in the dumps.

All you have to do is come up with one good British or one good American writer for people to say, 'Oh, it is out of the dumps and on to the pyramid again.'

You think it is more of a trendy sort of thing?

I don't think it is purely a trend. I think there are some very good Indian, Caribbean and African writers, as well as Australian and so on. But all it takes is one or two good writers, and then they'll say, 'Oh, look at her or look at him. Single handed, he or she has revived British writing.' Whereas all it means is that there is another good writer. The media looks for trends, where there are none.

You mentioned earlier some of the poets you like. Who are some of the contemporary novelists you like? Who are some of the contemporary Indian novelists and poets you like?

I don't read very many novelists. While I was writing *A Suitable Boy* I tried to avoid reading Indian novelists ... but who could resist Narayan? There is an American woman called Janet Lewis, a very good novelist. She has written *The Wife of Martin Guerre* [1967] and *The Trial of Soren Qvist* [1947].

What about younger Indian writers?

That is difficult to say. I haven't read very much. I have not read Rohinton Mistry's novel, but I have read some of his short stories, and they are very good. One of the great pleasures of having finished *A Suitable Boy* is that maybe I'll have more time to read.

14

Kazuo Ishiguro
with
Maya Jaggi

Kazuo Ishiguro was born in Nagasaki, Japan in 1954 and came to Britain in 1960. He was awarded the Booker Prize in 1989 for his third novel The Remains of the Day, *following* A Pale View of Hills *(1982) and the Whitbread Prize-winning* An Artist of the Floating World *(1986). The* Remains of the Day – *produced on film by Merchant-Ivory – tells the tale of an English butler, Stevens, who, after squandering opportunities for life and love through an excess of characteristic reserve, looks back on his service at Darlington Hall in the 1930s. In contrast, Ishiguro's novel* The Unconsoled *(1995) is in part a study of creative drive. Its narrator, Ryder, a fêted English Classical pianist, arrives in central Europe to give a concert but stumbles across acquaintances from his Worcestershire youth, or characters who mirror stages of his own life from boyhood to dotage.*

In this interview, conducted in London, Maya Jaggi talked to Ishiguro about the creative processes which informed the composition of The Unconsoled, *a work which signals a break with realism in Ishiguro's oeuvre and draws on slippages in time and place as well as the voices of memory. Since this interview took place, Ishiguro has written* When We Were Orphans *(2000) and is currently working on* Never Let Me Go.

Maya Jaggi The landscape of *The Unconsoled* is surreal or imaginary. Much of the novel takes place inside Ryder's mind, with his

acquaintances from England moving in and out. What made you set
the book in central Europe?

Kazuo Ishiguro It doesn't have to be central Europe, but it has to be
somewhere. I've been dogged by the problem of setting, partly because
of my Japanese ancestry. People have scrutinized the settings of my
books, assuming they're key to the work. In some senses that's true, but
it emerged as a major problem. When I set my books in Japan, their
relevance seemed to be diminished in the eyes of some readers. People
seemed to say, 'That's a very interesting thing we've learned about
Japanese society', rather than, 'Oh, isn't that indeed how people think
and behave – how we behave'. There seemed to be a block about apply-
ing my books universally because the setting was so overwhelmingly
alien. I thought that by dropping Japan, people would focus on the
more abstract themes, the emotional story. And by and large, *The
Remains of the Day* was read more for the inner story, though there
were still people saying this is an interesting piece of social history, a
recreation of life for servants between the wars. Then you get into a
debate as to how accurately the texture of life was reproduced – the set-
design question. I could see it was fair enough, I was working in this
realist mode, trying to make the setting as convincing as possible. But
there was a problem that people thought it was about the 1930s, or was
some parable of the fall of the British empire. There was a tendency to
locate it physically, as an extension of journalism or history, except with
dialogue and characters. I thought I should try to set a novel in a world
that is so odd, so obviously constructed according to another set of
priorities, that it must be obvious we're not in the game of trying to
faithfully recapture what some real place is like. One of the last things I
decided was where *The Unconsoled* was. I didn't name any place, but I
always thought it was the western part of central Europe, like Austria
or Switzerland. I just needed to have an English guy who was not in
England. He had to be away, travelling, for the techniques to work. But
I'm hoping people won't get too hung up on where it's set, or read it as
some strange allegory on the fall of the Berlin Wall.

You once said you first write scenes and dialogue, and then look for a 'beautiful landscape', a location, to set them in. Is that how you wrote *The Unconsoled*?

No, I did write *The Unconsoled* differently. I used to map out my novels very carefully before I started to write. This is a key question for anyone writing: how much have you worked out before you start writing the prose? That decision goes to the heart of a writer's approach. At one extreme you have writers who like to put in a blank sheet of paper and see what falls out, then they shape it. Whereas I find that process rather terrifying – perhaps it's something to do with having a cautious nature. I was always at the other end of the spectrum. I'd spend two years working things out – the themes in particular, and the characters – before I started writing. But with *The Remains of the Day*, I was both pleased and disappointed by the extent to which the targets and aims I'd written down at the planning stage were fulfilled. The book I ended up with was almost exactly the book I'd planned. That's fine, but it's something to do with the point in my life, and in my writing, that I didn't want to do that again. With *The Unconsoled*, there was much more a sense of exploration, and improvisation. I deliberately wanted to try shifting the starting point. I started to become aware after *The Remains of the Day* that by adjusting the stage at which I started, it would take me into areas I perhaps wouldn't get into with a more controlled approach. There was also a strange dovetailing. *The Remains of the Day* is about someone obsessed with controlling every aspect of his life, to the point where the emotional life gets stifled. Somehow he misses the most important things. Because it was a first-person narrative, there comes a point when you ask, am I writing about a person like this, in a voice like this, because I am afraid of losing control in the writing process? Some of the things I'd gone through in writing the book, looking at the benefits and costs of being so controlled in all aspects of your life, as the butler is, led me to think I should write about more messy areas of myself and start at an earlier point, when things aren't completely mapped out.

You've remarked that the same words recurred in reviews of your first three novels – 'understated', 'restrained'. Was that partly what pushed you to write a different kind of novel – in particular, the broad comedy towards the end of *The Unconsoled*?

These adjectives that kept turning up, like 'spare', 'subtle', 'controlled', surprised me because I wasn't trying to create an understated, calm voice in the first two novels. Because they're first-person narratives, people weren't sure if this was me or the narrator's characterization. I concluded it was to some extent me, although I didn't let on; I said, 'Yes of course, that character is very formal, isn't he?' *The Remains of the Day* was the first book I wrote when I was conscious these things were being said about my style. It was like an exaggerated version of this buttoned-up stuff. It was an easy step to take something attributed to me and make a stylized version, almost a caricature of it. At the same time, there was an uncomfortable realization. Some of the themes I was dealing with with Stevens did lead me to ask questions about myself: to what extent do you open yourself when you write, take risks, allow in certain things you might not be able to admit into your consciousness – and all the attendant technical problems that come with that? You can't have the same technical control, but you have an instinct that this is where the interesting stuff lies, and that you shouldn't keep going over old ground but should be digging around where it's uncomfortable. This perception of me as a writer did lead me to take a more risky approach – certainly more emotionally risky. The humour is perhaps a defence mechanism. We often use humour in that way when things are getting dodgy, dangerous. A safety net. I wouldn't want a novel like this to be too solemn. Often, if we're going into uncharted territory, there's a temptation to crack a few jokes or adopt a comic tone. I wrote the whole thing as a kind of comedy; not a ha ha ha falling about thing, but I saw this whole world as working in a darkly comic way.

Did you discover things, as you perhaps hoped you would, that you felt you were missing by being more controlled?

I think so. At the more superficial levels, I started to evolve a different method of writing. I had the freedom to experiment a bit more technically. This book moves away from straight realism. Up to this book, I'd worked in a more or less traditional way, using suspension of disbelief on the reader in a particular setting, then moving the characters around. I wanted to move away from a recognizably real setting, but you can't then proceed as you did before. If you create an alternative world where alternative rules exist – physical, temporal, behavioural – there has to be a consistency, a new set of rules. You have to figure them out for yourself, because there aren't many models.

Did you follow any literary models?

Kafka is an obvious model once you move away from straight social or psychological realism. Some other countries may have strong non-realistic traditions, but I'm not familiar with them. In the Western tradition you have one-offs, like Kafka and Nabokov.

What about Chekhov for the comedy?

I love Chekhov; his short stories were a big influence on *The Remains of the Day*. But it was partly that I was trying to leave behind, that relatively tranquil atmosphere on the surface with frustrations bubbling underneath. The two writers I ripped off in this case – this is suicide, telling you who influenced me – were Kafka and Dostoevsky. There's a dreamlike quality to Kafka, and Dostoevsky builds up to farce but with serious grand themes. His big four novels are like a Brian Rix low-comedy stage farce, when lots of strands grow to hysterical pitch, then all the characters end up off the stage, screaming away, with doors opening here and there. That tone of hysteria and farce is interesting, and he uses it to very serious ends. I also read Samuel Beckett – mainly the prose.

How exactly does your technique in *The Unconsoled* differ from your previous novels?

In the past I used a method where somebody looked back over his or her life in old age. You built up a picture through flashback of the key points in their life as they tried to assess it. *The Unconsoled* isn't that different, except you have somebody in the midst of their life, with all the attendant confusion. The whole thing is supposed to take place in some strange world, where Ryder appropriates the people he encounters to work out parts of his life and his past. I was using dream as a model. So this is a biography of a person, but instead of using memory and flashback, you have him wandering about in this dream world where he bumps into earlier, or later, versions of himself. They're not literally so. They are to some extent other people, but he gives a reading of their life in such a way that they're memories of how his own childhood was, or projections of how he fears he might end up. I don't want to say literally that Stephan is Ryder when he was young, and Boris was Ryder as a kid, but I wanted to create a world where you could get all these different points in his life. Essentially, you're only dealing with one person. For me, this method gives me a lot of freedom. It's how we use dream. We might dream about the shopkeeper we encountered earlier in the day, but underneath, it's somebody from the past we're trying to work out. I think we do this when we're awake as well. Our view of other people is often shaped by our need to work certain things out about ourselves. We tend to appropriate other people – more than we perhaps care to admit. We perhaps don't see them for what *they* are; they become useful tools.

You've said the book wasn't planned out, but what themes did you start with in your mind?

A central thread is that the book's about a person for whom something has gone wrong way back in his life, and a lot of his energy, the motivation behind his acquiring his expertise and his brilliance as a musician, is his thinking he can fix this thing one day. He has a completely private project of acquiring his prowess to fulfil this inner mission. But by virtue of doing this, people build him up into this messiah figure and he ends up with a huge baggage of responsibility. People who are driven to pursue some hopeless personal agenda accrue expectations from the community at large. So there's a strange discrepancy between his crucial inner agenda and what other people want him to do. A lot of the chaos results from the strain between the two. The novel's essentially about the moment when Ryder realizes he can't fix the things he wanted to fix, that it's too late and, at best, all this brilliance is some compensation, a consolation for something that can never be put right.

Ryder's feeling that something has gone wrong way back in his life that he has to put right, is that connected for you with parents and the fractures within families?

Yes. When we're talking about things that go wrong fundamentally, at the heart of somebody's life, we are often talking about family and things early on – something crucial to do with emotional bereavement or emotional deprivation. This isn't necessarily an overtly psycho-analytic view; I'm not a great subscriber to Freudian theory. It's just my observation of myself and people around me. Oddly enough, as I've got older I've started to feel this more. When you're younger you have a certain strength that comes from the very provisionality of life, you think things are going to shape up eventually. But things seem to catch up on people somewhere after the age of thirty-five, from way back in their past. You start to get a sense of the limit of what you can do, or of what's going to happen to you in life. I don't necessarily mean any huge trauma, though in some people that is the case. It might have been a chronic thing, or something as simple as childhood coming to an end, discovering that the world is more complicated than the world of childhood. It's my feeling that a lot of creative people and those strongly motivated in politics derive a lot of that motivation and drive from something that's out of line way back.

Have you identified something in yourself as part of that pattern?

Possibly. This is a more complex question. The view presented in this book derives from an observation of myself and others like me. After you've spent years sitting alone in some study writing novels, you start to wonder why you do it. You can think of practical justifications, like earning money. But I remember when I had no idea I'd earn anything. There are people out there who give up all their free time, who're prepared to wreck their relationships and marriages because they want to write their novel, or make their film, or campaign for this and that. I became curious about why other people did it. . . . Sometimes it's associated with some horrific thing, like being abused as a child, but often it's not as blatant. It still begs the question of why some people do it and others not.

For you, was the lost equilibrium to do with displacement?

Yes, in my case. I think it is something to do with moving from Japan to England. For me, the creative process has never been about anger or violence, as it is with some people; it's more to do with regret or melancholy. I don't feel I've regretted not having grown up in Japan. That would be absurd. This is the only life I've known. I had a happy childhood, and I've been very happy here. But it's to do with the strong emotional relationships I had in Japan that were suddenly severed at a formative emotional age, particularly with my grandfather. I lived with my grandparents for the first five years of my life; it was a three-generational family, and my father was away for three of my first five years. So my grandfather was the head of the household, the person I looked up to. It's only in the past few years that I've begun to appreciate the importance of what happened then. I've always been aware that there was this other life I might have had – not in terms of being happier in that society. But here was a very important bond. It didn't get severed, because I always thought I was going back, but it faded away. Then he died when I was still in England.

Why did you choose that title?

It's this thing you can't fix – Brodsky talks about a wound. It's something you can't fix or heal; all you can do is caress it. If creative people are driven to writing novels, politicians to leading parties or revolutions, by some inner thing, success is never going to fix it; the most it can be is a consolation for the thing they lost early on. Brodsky thinks late in life that even the love of a woman can only be a consolation, but nevertheless, he thinks it's worth having. These people don't get even that, that's why they're unconsoled.

There's a recurrent theme in your work of self-delusion, people evaluating their life and achievements, and deluding themselves in the process. But for Ryder, there doesn't seem to be the moment of realization that he's evaluated his life wrongly.

In a way, the first three books were each an attempt to rewrite or hone down the material used in the previous one. It was almost three attempts to cover the same territory. With *The Remains of the Day*, I came to the end of that process. This was part of the reason for not using that method; the theme comes with that technique. In those days, I was interested in how people lie to themselves just to make things palatable, to make a sense of yourself bearable. We all dignify our failures a little bit, and make the best of our successes. I was interested in how someone settles on a picture of himself and his life. Ryder's not one of these characters. Although I was interested in self-deception, that method creates a sense of life being ordered, because you're witnessing it at a point of reassessment. You see a shape emerging: that was the point at which a mistake was made, or a key opportunity was let slip. You can misapply your energies or your loyalties. But in those novels, life seems quite orderly; it seems that if you stood back you could reduce your life to these key moments, when you decided to be loyal to this person, or didn't make the break at this point, or didn't declare your true emotions to this person.

But as I got older (I'm forty now) I wanted something that would reflect the uncertainty and chaos I started to feel. Life didn't feel to me like a process whereby episodes came at you and you didn't live up to the moment or you did. It wasn't as clear as that; things seem messier. I wanted to write a book not from the viewpoint of someone looking back and ordering his experience, but of someone in the midst of chaos, being pulled in different directions at once, and not realizing why. Self-deception is dealt with differently in this book. It's absurdly exaggerated. Ryder's always deluding himself. His memory and perception are convenient for him; he censors things, and manages to pinpoint things he emotionally needs and blot out others. He'll forget things from a few minutes before and rewrite things that just happened.

Why did you choose a musician as your central character?

It was convenient. I didn't want him to be a writer . . .

And you'd done the artist . . .

Yes. But here, although he's a musician, music doesn't function in a realistic way. It doesn't play the role in this world that it plays in the real world. Music seems to have taken the role of politics: the question of which kinds of musicians should be celebrated and which demoted is rather like who should be prime minister or president. So *yes*, he's a musician, and he's not a musician. I was working with this metaphor of music standing in for other things which in a realistic book I would have to map out. I wanted a figure people looked towards for cultural and spiritual leadership, and expected much of, and his need to fulfil this role. At least music was something I was vaguely familiar with . . .

That's part of the metaphor, the idea that people don't really understand this music, and Ryder's their interpreter. It's partly to do with control and losing control of life.

Yes, musical forms have got so complex and are deemed absolutely crucial to the quality of life, but people don't understand them any more, they have to look to experts to guide them. This is something I feel, that we're supposed to be democratic citizens, ultimately responsible for the big decisions. I've had the privilege of a good education, but I'm completely ignorant if you ask me questions about economics or industrial or military policy. I could probably give very basic answers. In democracies ultimately, we are responsible if our governments do weird things. The buck has to stop with us. But when you have to worry about your job and looking after your child and going to Tesco, it's difficult to make yourself sufficiently expert on monetary theory or the effect of taxation on the inflation rate. Most of the big questions seem to be so complex it's beyond most of us. We find ourselves expecting these expert leader figures to save us.

When *The Remains of the Day* came out, you said: 'I write out of fear I might try to do things I think are important and later realize they're not as great and useful as I thought. We all live in small worlds.' Is that Ryder's fear, as well as yours?

In the past, I was careful not to write things that only apply to me. I know there's nothing frightfully interesting about the travails of a writer. The only interesting bits are those that are the same for anyone who strives to make something of their lives. With Ryder, I might be going dangerously close to somebody who people don't readily identify with – a celebrity, an artist. The universality might be limited by his special position. That's something that happens when you don't plan, you write instinctively. Perhaps this was a spilling over of an autobiographical concern of mine, as I've started to gain notoriety, and to feel pressures on me. But I've always asked what in my life is relevant to everyone else.

You went back to visit Japan in 1989 for the first time since you left Nagasaki aged six. Do you think you'll ever set something in Japan again?

I might do. It was good, but odd. I was surprisingly big news. As this Japanese who's gone abroad, lost his Japaneseness and won a prize, I was both comforting and the embodiment of their worst fears. It was an official visit organized by the Japan Foundation – the equivalent of the British Council. . . . It was a privileged visit and there was an unreality about it. I was carried around in a bubble. . . . I was cushioned or distracted from the emotions of going back; I went back and I didn't go back. I always knew if I went back, I'd be going somewhere else. So if I ever write about Japan again, I'll probably write about the real Japan, as opposed to the Japan I felt compelled to write about out of my childhood memories.

15

Maxine Hong Kingston

with

Maggie Ann Bowers

This interview with the prominent Chinese American writer Maxine Hong Kingston provides insights into the personal influences and the political inspiration for her work; it also explores the debate amongst Chinese Americans regarding cultural authenticity and approaches to cross-culturalism. Born in 1940 in Stockton, California's Chinatown, Kingston first spoke Chinese and learnt to speak and write English around the age of five. Since the publication in 1976 of her seminal semi-autobiographical work The Woman Warrior: memoirs of a girlhood among ghosts, *Kingston has been the focus of intense critical debate. For many Chinese immigrants of Kingston's generation, access to the United States could only be gained by suppressing facts and constructing an identity and history acceptable to the immigration officials. It was only as recently as 1948 that Chinese Americans were able to become United States citizens. The result of this authorized racism was a feeling amongst Chinese Americans of anger and misrepresentation. Her second novel,* China Men *(1980), is both a history and a memoir of the first Chinese immigrant men who came to America and includes autobiographical details and stories passed down through Hong Kingston's family. The third novel,* Tripmaster Monkey: his fake book *(1990), concerns a new generation of Chinese Americans and is her most stylistically postmodern novel, playing with concepts of the reliability of the narrator and magic realism. Her fourth novel,* The Fifth*

Book of Peace, *was published in 2003 following the loss of the first draft when her house was burnt in the forest fires of 1994.*

Through her cross-cultural and feminist adaptation of Chinese mythology and the use of magic realism, Hong Kingston's work interrogates the notion that there can be an absolutely 'real' Chinese America. She has also written two poetical works, Hawai'i One Summer *(1987) and* To Be the Poet *(2002). In this interview she reveals the personal concerns and sources for her ambivalent attitude towards a prescribed Chinese American identity and her continued commitment to peace and political activism. Kingston's own postscript to this interview in 2004 follows: 'Since we spoke . . . much has happened: I finished* The Fifth Book of Peace, *for which I rewrote the Woman Warrior myth in poetry form. I was able to do that by changing myself into a poet, a process I divulge in* To Be the Poet. *I read the new Woman Warrior come-home-from-war chant at a rally in Washington DC trying to prevent the shock-and-awe of Iraq. I was arrested and went to jail. I have been travelling everywhere saying "Peace Peace Peace", and continue to believe in the power of words to improve the world.'*

Maggie Ann Bowers Some writers are said to be visual, others evoke a mood but I've always felt your writing as loud and audible. There are a lot of songs in it, poetry, shouting and in *Tripmaster Monkey* the ranting of Wittman Ah Sing. What is the importance of sound for you?

Maxine Hong Kingston There are many importances to sound. I write about the struggle to find a voice . . . a personal as well as a political voice. I want my writing to be like music. I heard *China Men* as a symphony. Quite often as I was working on it I heard major and minor movements of the symphony which were very clear to me and then I translated it into sound and words. In the process of writing my work I always read it aloud. I want it to stand up as an oral piece of art and not just text. Perhaps I have been influenced by 'talk story' – I was raised on 'talk story' and I understand that in all human cultures we tell stories to one another before we can write. As a child I listened to and told stories before I could write and I wanted to put over all the strengths of the oral story even though I was writing text: the changeability, the voices. . . . It's interesting that you have picked up on the music of what I do because I think of myself as a very visual person. I paint, but I'm not knowledgeable about music. I don't have a system for recording music and hence I can't remember music. The only way I can remember it is to write it down as a story or a large book with many movements, small themes and rhythm. Another reason why it is important to me for my work to be read aloud – I love it when people tell me they have read my work aloud to children – it's then I think that I am closer to how ancient Chinese poets worked. They not only composed their poetry but they painted it; they did their calligraphy and sang and performed it. So an artist in ancient China was a more integrated and whole person; I think I am aiming for that.

Would you like to move more towards oral storytelling and recording your writing?

I have recorded. There is an abridged *The Woman Warrior* which I recorded but more importantly I'm now enjoying very much reading out loud to audiences and that is performing in a way. Also, *China Men* and *The Woman Warrior* were done as plays so the work is being performed and coming out of text into oral tradition.

Can you see yourself writing a play?

No, because I lived in Hollywood for some years – my husband is an actor – and after reading scripts and hearing that a speech must be no longer than an inch of type, no. I love writing description and you are just not allowed that in a play. I like the speeches and dialogue . . . getting accents and dialects and ways of speaking – I like that but I don't want to write a play.

You spent part of your early school life silent in English and in *The Woman Warrior* you refer to the pain of speaking – are you working through these demons by producing such audible writing in English?

It was so traumatic for me when I realized the language of home was different from the language outside . . . and then it was also such a wonder when I eventually learned English and saw how easy English is. I can write in English. A child can write in English and you can take the phonetic alphabet and write in any other language. You can take sounds into that alphabet and it's so much fun to play with that. Once I have figured out a way to express something, then I find the next thing which is difficult to write, so that I find I am going into things which are more and more subtle and larger and larger in the writing. In speaking I also find I am trying to say things which have not been said before by me or by other people. Sometimes it is very alarming. I think that I have worked through a way of speaking and then I'm struck shy or start to stutter or a situation arises where I can't think of what to say; it happens often. I used to think that if I wrote down a nightmare it would go away or that, as in psychotherapy, they say if you have an insight or see something then your obsessions will go away, but I find that if I learn to say or write something then somehow the stakes get higher and the challenge gets bigger as I go further. It's hard. Every book seems to get longer and it takes me longer. It took three years for *The Woman Warrior*, maybe four years for *China Men* and then eight years for *Tripmaster Monkey*. I hope it doesn't keep going like this!

One thing I am very aware of as a reader is the power of words in your work to both create and to harm – it comes across very strongly. I'm thinking in particular of breaking taboos by speaking out and conversely, of the threat that was put on the community in *The Woman Warrior* by that breaking of taboos. Also you wrote that you thought you would actually wound your father with words. Do

you feel danger and freedom with your use of words? Are you conscious of this when you use them?

I feel both these things and, of course, freedom has its dangers. I am working now on an idea that there are ideas out in the world and there are ideas that humans can invent and we can invest those ideas into a physical reality. The medium of doing that is words. I think of ideas being invisible – that we can make them more manifest so that we can send them to one another. After words . . . there is a next step which is building the physical universe. I am thinking we can make a peaceful world – how can we change the world? First there has to be the idea of peace and community and love, and I am working on the idea that we can't have love without ideas.

I had a similar idea that by using magic realism in particular, you could bring things which don't exist into writing and there they can exist simultaneously as things which are known to be real, that in a sense you talk them into existence?

Yes, yes, that's what I mean! Talking and writing things into existence – a wonderful way to put it. This word 'peace' is a common word but I truly think that most people haven't said it right. We haven't explained it right. . . . I don't quite like the term 'magic realism'. It's about eight years ago that Toni Morrison and Leslie Marmon Silko and I were in China and we were talking about what it is that we do. At that time we were satisfied with the term 'magic realism' but since then I've decided I don't like it. It's because 'magic' means supernatural, instant changes that come out of nowhere, and I believe in a logical scientific sequence of events in which there's an idea, there's finding the words for it, and one word at a time one makes a blueprint and then one puts the posts into the ground, the steel flashing we put into the posts, the two-by-four framework, the plaster and so on; the negotiations, the dialogue – one word at a time between people taking place moment by moment, and each moment causing the next moment, and that's not magic.

Magic is illogical, supernatural, it's not in our hands and that world isn't in our hands.

What I was thinking of just as you were saying that was Brave Orchid, your mother, and the episode in *The Woman Warrior* at the medical school in China where she battles with a ghost and you write a wonderful comment: 'Medical science does not seal the earth, whose nether creatures seep out.' I was wondering if this is a revision of your thoughts when you wrote that?

There is a constant contending with people who think like her – that's not even thinking. That's another state of mind where the supernatural exists. At home I still contend with that. My mother just turned ninety-one and she says she is ninety-two but she refuses to move into my sister's house because she says there are ghosts there to push her down. So now she is living in the backyard in a trailer – it's brand new and so there are no ghosts there. When we were trying to talk our mother to move in with my sister I was thinking: why am I having to talk around these ghosts in the 1990s?

There's a reminder in your writing of the physicality of words and the way in which things can be created in words and also of the very physicality of writing itself. In *The Woman Warrior* the narrator's name sounds like ink, she appears covered in ink and becomes an embodiment of writing. Fa Mu Lan's back in the 'White Tigers' section of the book is carved with words and is a wincingly painful reminder of how words can exist almost as a living presence. What is the connection for you between writing and the body?

After my house burned and my book burned and disappeared, I phoned my mother and she said, 'You've got hands – just build it all again.' Immediately after my hands hurt. After the fire my hands hurt for a long time and I'd wake up in the middle of the night and they'd hurt. They weren't burned in the fire or anything, but what I thought was that it was sheer energy being caught in my hands because I couldn't get started with my writing. I couldn't do it fast enough and I felt once in a while my writing arm hurt; I think it's all of those ideas trying to come out and my not being able to do it fast enough. I have been very inspired by the Buddhist statues and Indian statues of gods with many hands. Sometimes they have thousands or ten thousand hands and each of those hands have hands radiating out and I wished for that, so I could have more than one writing hand. Some of those hands have eyes and I love to imagine that each of my hands has an eye in the middle of it so that I'm more mindful and careful if I touch things, and I know I can see better if I use my hands better. I have often thought that if I couldn't see and didn't have hands I couldn't write any more. That's very scary. It's so strange that writing is to do with the hands. Manuscript – *manu* means hand doesn't it?

Do you feel you could switch to a purely spoken skill?

I've heard of people being able to compose onto a tape recorder but I think it's too slippery, it's too 'un-handlable'.

You said that your house which contained your latest manuscript was recently destroyed in a fire. Originally, when I was thinking about *The Woman Warrior* I thought that by writing an auto-biography, no matter how many fictional elements there are, you are proving your existence and writing down something which is un-erasable. After the fire, do you have a new attitude towards the longevity of the written word, the life of your work; the security of writing?

I'm pretty sure that I've always known that I am not my writing. I'm not the same person as my writing. I have a very full life apart from my writing. A book being lost in a fire . . . When I arrived at the fire and realized that the book was gone I had a series of very interesting experiences. I remember standing there feeling I was 'thingless'. I felt divested and empty. I felt I understood the Buddhist sense of emptiness. Suddenly I felt full of something which I named 'idea'. I could have also named it 'spirit' but I felt it was all around me and maybe it was because I was alive and I wasn't killed in the fire that I could feel this life energy, but I thought, 'I know what this is, it's "idea" and it was the book before and after it was in words.' The manuscript that I wrote still existed – it was an idea that was all around me and inside me too.

You are now working on a continuation of the book that was burned. You call it *The Fifth Book of Peace*, which refers to a series of lost books in China called 'The Three Books of Peace'. The fourth book refers to the book lost in the fire and the fifth is the book you are now writing. This idea of lost books is particularly interesting and ties in with the impression I have that each one of your books fills in a gap in history which has been untold, denied or ignored. I was wondering if you consciously recreate history in your work?

I did know that I was writing history and I felt that I needed to give readers some background in order for them to understand stories in the foreground. That had been a problem for me as a young writer because I wanted to write more simple present-time stories and I didn't want to spend a lot of work on expository information, and yet I had to do it. So, I was always working out ways to educate the reader in history. I hadn't realized until you just said it that I am working in a sequence of history, that I am filling in gaps even into telling the history of the 1960s as well as the time of Genghis Khan. I noticed at one time that I was working on a whole series of wars throughout the ages. I didn't realize until you just said it that what I have done is actually quite ordered.

You mentioned war – you have a concern for the Vietnam War. I know your brother Joe was involved in the war but could you explain why this event in history has a particular interest for you?

I'm surprised that more people don't feel the way I do because the Vietnam War was so long. I noticed that in *The Odyssey* they call the Trojan War 'The Long War' and that is what we could call the Vietnam War. It took up so many years of our lives. I've always been aware of the wars in my life and I don't understand how people can say, 'Oh, I didn't know there were concentration camps', because I was a baby during World War II and I was perfectly aware that the Japanese were being taken away [to be interned by the United States government]. I was aware when they came back and all those Japanese American children were coming into kindergarten with me. I remember the blackouts and I knew there was a war from the very moment there was consciousness. For most of my youth there was the Vietnam War. I was very much part of it. I tried to stop it and in that way I was engaged and personally involved. I felt not just that it was happening but that it was my responsibility to do something about it. Even if it was not my responsibility to fight it, it would still be my responsibility to stop it. So I have referred to it as 'my war'.

Considering Vietnam and the problems you face as a woman from a minority group in the United States – one which has received not only racist but anti-communist prejudice as well – what is your attitude towards your nation the United States and its authorities? Did any negative feeling you might have felt towards the United States push you towards the emotional connection with China, evident in the *The Woman Warrior*?

Of course my feelings of being an American are very complex and constantly changing. There were times during the Vietnam War when I just wanted to leave – but then, where do you go? There was a vague thought of leaving for Japan because they have a non-military constitution but then I got as far as Hawai'i which gives another interesting feeling about the US. Living in California, being born and raised in California, you feel you are at the edge of the United States, but then going to Hawai'i brings you to another kind of United States. Then, finding that while Hawai'i has so many races, it is one great military base . . . But there are good feelings about being an American. One good thing is the Bill of Rights. I see the Bill of Rights as saying, 'Practise free speech! Just go out there and talk and write and practise assembly!'

You toured China with Toni Morrison and Leslie Marmon Silko. It seems to me that your writing is very similar, not so much in style as in the issues which you are all working with – memory, oral storytelling, the magic and the real.

These are exactly similar images. Working in the sugar cane, ceremonies, communities, storytelling. We all feel that we have inherited stories from the ancestors – the ancestors that can fly! I see exact correspondences.

One way in which all of your writing is similar is that you all write from a female perspective but go beyond your gendered experience. You have all written feminist books with male protagonists. *Tripmaster Monkey*, with the very engaging male protagonist Wittman Ah Sing, reminds me very strongly of *Wise Children* [1991] by Angela Carter, but I can't imagine *Wise Children* with a male protagonist. Is this a continuation of the same feminist stance you had when you wrote *The Woman Warrior* or is *Tripmaster Monkey* representative of a new direction?

I feel that a mature . . . human being first understands oneself and then considers the other. First there is compassion for oneself and then, for it to be true compassion, it has to go out to one who is not the same as oneself. I see my work going from a self-centred narcissistic world into a larger world. I think there's always a struggle in people to break out of narcissism, to feel the emotions of others. I think a great writer has to be empathetic to people who are seen to be different. In my work I work through an understanding of myself. When I was very young I thought only women and girls had feelings and I was sure that men and boys did not because I saw no evidence that they had any. They never cried, they were able to fight and hurt each other as though they enjoyed it, so obviously they had no feelings. I had the idea that feeling in men and boys was something that I conferred on them with my empathy. I feel it is a philosophical stance that I am going to assume they have feelings and I have to treat them that way and write them that way.

I know you wrote the passages set in China in *The Woman Warrior* before you had visited China; you were writing an imaginary China. Walter Abish in *How German Is It?* [1980] wrote an experiment of the imagination to see how closely he could imagine Germany without having visited. There is a question about whether his accurate descriptions of contemporary Germany are stereotypical or whether he has accentuated key elements of German society. I know we've said before that stereotypes can seem very close to real people, but could you be in danger of stereotyping when you imagine things which you have not seen?

I guess people seem stereotypical if one doesn't look deeply enough inside them. I have a sense that I don't describe how people look, but I write about what they are thinking and feeling and in that sense we get beyond appearances – which is what stereotypes are – they are just appearances without essence and depth. I imagined China before going to China; the first long trip through China was with Toni and Leslie. At that time *The Woman Warrior* and *China Men* had already been written and I was fearful and curious to see whether the China I had imagined would be similar to, or invalidated by, the China I saw in real life. It turned out to be very similar in detail and in feeling. Of course, I felt glad that my powers of imagination were affirmed by 'reality'. I was thinking that a strong imagination imagines the truth. But then, that brings up another philosophical question about perception; am I so imprisoned in my way of seeing that when I get over there I am not able to see through my preconceptions to what reality is, and how does one do it? I tried to be mindful of whatever I was looking at, looking for something new, something to surprise me and actually looking for things to contradict what I knew. I saw how people live so close to one another. However, there were essential human truths that were borne out by the journey. I only found details which would tell so much; I wish I had had them because it would have made my work even more real and physical. . . . If anything, in China everything I saw affirmed what I wrote in detail.

16

George Lamming

with

Caryl Phillips

George Lamming was born on the former sugar estate of Carrington Village, Barbados. He was educated on a scholarship at Combermere School and in 1946 moved to Trinidad, where he worked as a teacher. In 1950 he emigrated to England. There he became the host of a book review programme for the BBC West Indian Service in London. Lamming published his first novel, In the Castle of My Skin, *in 1953. The book, which earned him the Somerset Maugham Award in 1957, reads as both a memoir of an individual's childhood and the collective biography of a West Indian village during the decline of the plantation system. Lamming's work ranges in tone from the despair of* The Emigrants *(1954) to the powerfully hopeful* Season of Adventure *(1960), and he explores the complexity of the West Indian experience as affected by the process of decolonization and national reconstruction. In* Of Age and Innocence *(1958) Lamming cites the immigrant experience in Britain as a catalyst for social and political change back in the Caribbean, and the non-fiction essays in his collection* The Pleasures of Exile *(1960) describe the experience of a writer moving from the Caribbean to a metropolitan culture.*

Lamming is deeply committed to West Indian politics, and during a period of literary silence from 1960 to 1972 he remained involved in political developments. In 1965 and 1967 he was co-editor of the Barbados and Guyana issues of New World Quarterly, *and in 1967 he spent a year* as writer-in-residence at the University of the West Indies in Kingston, Jamaica. In 1972 he published two books within the same year, Water with Berries and the historical novel Natives of My Person. In 1974 he edited the anthology Canon Shot and Glass Beads. Since then he has continued to be a political organizer and has lectured and taught in the Caribbean and overseas. In 1976 he received a British Commonwealth Foundation Grant, which enabled him to travel to major universities in India and Australia. Lamming has been the recipient of several awards and fellowships, including a Guggenheim Fellowship in 1954. He is interviewed here by Caryl Phillips, now a distinguished novelist, dramatist and critic who 'followed on'.

Caryl Phillips You won a scholarship to one of the three grammar schools in Barbados, where your English master was Frank Collymore, editor of the literary magazine *BIM*. I wondered how important it was to you, as a boy from a relatively poor background, to have received this scholarship, and how important it was for you to have found yourself with Frank Collymore?

George Lamming It was of immense importance because first of all education within that context was the only means of escape from the system and if I didn't get the scholarship, it's almost certain that I would not have gone to that kind of school. And that school functioned in an interesting way: while it increased your advantage it also cultivated in you a tendency to remove yourself from where you had started. So, when much later I started to read about class and class stratification, I discovered that I had really lived this long before I had encountered it in texts, that to grow up via education within a colonial context was in fact to grow away from where you had started. So, whatever the disadvantages of that kind of dislocation – and I think that is rendered in various ways in *In the Castle of My Skin* – there was certainly the advantage of meeting Collymore, whom I would not have met in the social context of Barbados had it not been for the school. What he did for me was to create in me a sense of the book – not so much as a source of instruction; he was very unorthodox in that way – but a book as a unique window on the world. And the book has remained with me to this day in that particular kind of function, that through the book you enter an immense terrain of life and culture, people whom you were not likely to bear direct witness to.

Were there any books in particular that, for you, opened windows onto another world?

Collymore was trouble for me at school because as a scholarship winner I was supposed to do well; in fact after the first or the second year I stopped doing well. The reason was that he had allowed me to come to his house and use the library. In those days he had what I would have considered an immense library. I remember taking out H. G. Wells's *The Outline of History* [1920]. This is the book that really did something to my head, because we had grown up with a notion of history as our relation to England. And then one discovered through Wells – in that very sophisticated, popularized way that *The Outline of History* is – that there was a world of Egypt, that there was an extraordinary world of the Mediterranean, that there were these what we now call 'diasporic' adventures taking place among a variety of cultures, and so on. And although I haven't looked at *The Outline of History* for a long time, there are very, very strong echoes of that book in my head. I think it had something to do with cultivating in me a certain intellectual curiosity about unknown places and unknown people.

In 1950 you sailed to England on the same ship as Sam Selvon. You once described yourself as 'an ordinary immigrant going to see if I could make it'. However, London was the literary mecca at that time, and I wonder how you balanced this feeling in yourself of being an 'ordinary immigrant' with your obvious hopes and desires for a literary life in London? And, what was the atmosphere like on the ship?

I have told a lot of that in *The Emigrants*, particularly in the first part. Now what I meant was that, irrespective of background or education, everybody on the ship in 1950 was a person who was travelling towards an expectation. . . . So, by 'ordinary immigrant', I mean that everybody was looking for a better break. Everybody was in search of an expectation, and because of what they would now call your 'socialization', because you had lived so much with the idea of England as facilitator, everybody was more or less sure that England would come to their rescue.

Did you talk to Sam Selvon on the ship? Did you speculate about the writing life you might have in England?

I don't think we talked much about the writing life. What happened in the case of people like myself and Selvon and like, say, the man who was going to be a plumber or a technician of some kind, is that we had already been in touch with England through *Caribbean Voices*. There was a man called Henry Swanzy who was a very important figure as a contributor to the evolution, really, of the literature of the Caribbean, who edited *Caribbean Voices*. We would have written to Swanzy. Everybody who had seen themselves as writers in Trinidad or Jamaica, whoever was going to England, would have written to Swanzy. And Swanzy would have been expecting you. And he understood also the economics of your situation and so on, and he would arrange for help – I mean, most of us had no money, there probably was enough for rent for a month or something, and I don't think that I would have been able to write *In the Castle of My Skin* had it not been for the income, small as it was, coming from readings and so on with *Caribbean Voices*. So that was very critical. And I think that would have applied to Selvon, and to Mittelholzer; that would have applied to almost every Caribbean writer who came to be known, arriving at that period in the late 1940s and early 1950s.

You wrote *In the Castle of My Skin* entirely in England.

Yes.

I'm interested in how you managed to penetrate English literary life, and eventually sign a contract with Michael Joseph. That cannot have been a very easy proposition for a young writer from the Caribbean.

It was very, very astonishing, and I don't think it has any precedent. I had started to write, shortly after I got there, what turned out to be *In the Castle of My Skin*. There used to be two or three English critics invited to give views on our work. And the fiction critic was a man called Arthur Calder-Marshall, who was up to the 1950s a very prominent, leading sort of novelist – he belonged to the generation of Isherwood (Isherwood, Calder-Marshall and Greene) and I don't know what the relation with Swanzy was but Calder-Marshall used to come once a month or so and do that fiction review. Roy Fuller did the poetry review and on two or three occasions, Stephen Spender. So once I had probably three chapters or something, I asked Calder-Marshall what he would suggest, that I would like to send them to a publisher. And he said (I think I may have read one extract from these in the *Caribbean Voices*) I could try; from what he had heard he thought there was something there. Then we got on to publishers – who would be the right kind of publisher. He had experience in that; his advice was extraordinarily sound. He said, 'Well, for you, the best publisher going at the moment, for literature, for the book as literature, is Michael Joseph. It is not one of the large things, it is not that small. And their retained reader is first-class.' The retained reader was Walter Allen. And so I took this plunge, and I sent – I think there were probably three or four chapters, not even half the book – I sent it to Michael Joseph. I think it was a matter of about ten or twelve days, I had a letter from Joseph asking me would I come to see them. I went, and to my astonishment they read me Allen's report, and his advice that they should not lose this. And I signed the contract there and then, the same afternoon. As I say, it is probably unique and it may not have had a very good effect, because from then on that's why I never thought I needed an agent. It's only much later –

You just dealt with the publisher?

I dealt directly – I mean after that, there was no question of who will be the publisher, there was no question of whether it would come, it would simply be the strategy of should they bring it in this year, or the next year, and that went on . . . right through *The Pleasures of Exile*, *Season of Adventure*, in fact all the books I've done, except *Natives of My Person* and *Water with Berries*, by which time they too had got incorporated and sucked into larger publishing houses, and collapsed. But that was the story of *In the Castle of My Skin*.

At this time in the 1950s, there was Mittelholzer, Selvon, Roger Mais, and others living in England. There was a kind of Caribbean literary community. You've already mentioned Stephen Spender and Roy Fuller as representative of the English literary community. I know that you briefly met Dylan Thomas. What constituted your literary community? Was it the Caribbean community, or was it the white English community, or was it a mixture of the two?

Mine was a mixture. It took this form: there was, as you would say, a very small West Indian formation. There was Mittelholzer, but Mittelholzer was never quite a part of that, Mittelholzer kept a strategic distance from being identified with any West Indian group; there was Selvon; and there was a man who for the next forty years or so had assumed the role of holding people together, this was the late Andrew Salkey. He was very much the centre you met around; Andrew Salkey, wherever he was living. So you had that group. And later there was Roger Mais. . . . So the BBC with its adjoining pubs . . . each section of the BBC had a peculiar topography, at the time. There was the Third Programme, and those people drank in one place, and the Home Service people drank in some other place. And then there was the Overseas Service . . .

Was that in Bush House?

No, it wasn't there yet. *Caribbean Voices* was on Oxford Street – 200 Oxford Street is really what Bush House became, and 200 Oxford Street had its own pub. This is where the connection began, because off 200 Oxford Street, leading down into Soho, there would also be the famous Magdala Club, where one would run into McNeice, who was a producer, R. D. Smith . . . I've forgotten some of their names. Barker, the poet . . .

George Barker?

Yes, George Barker. This was the Bohemian heart of London. Today it strikes me as a curious anachronism. I was in and out of that world; I found English writers were not too inclined to discuss literature. They talked money, but there was not literary discussion. I found out much later that if you went to Paris, you couldn't sit down for five minutes in a cafe and not be involved in the most intense kind of discourse, on a great variety of matters, connected to or going beyond literature. I never thought of that at all among the English people I knew and that I discovered.

You received a Guggenheim Award, a Somerset Maugham Award, both of which enabled you to travel. You travelled back to the Caribbean, to Africa and of course to Paris. You seem, almost immediately having established a literary reputation in Britain, to have become restless with Britain. Was it something to do with the prevalent anti-intellectualism, perhaps a growing discomfort with Britain in the 1950s, that led you to go beyond Britain? Or was it the allure of what you imagined might be 'beyond' Britain which dragged you away from the place where you had made your reputation?

The reputation was swift, and remember that, unlike today, there would not have been very many of us. So if you were looking for a figure representing a particular terrain or some strain of interest, there was A or B or B or A. There weren't a lot. I'm extremely grateful to London for providing me with the opportunity of multiple encounters. You see, in 1950, London was still a major political capital. There was a gradual dissolution of empire, but its voice was still very potent and very influential. It meant, therefore, that the entire colonial world – because up to 1950, apart from India, there was no other independent territory; none south of the Sahara – we tend to forget the speed of this change – but all colonial radical groups met in London. So apart from the literary side of the pub and the BBC, I became increasingly conscious of the political continuities between the Caribbean, and the kinds of discussion taking place among Ghanaians and Nigerians at the West African Students' Union house, which was in Chelsea – and by the way, you may be interested to know it was right next door to where Carlyle had lived, and I always wondered what he would have thought about these niggers making all of this noise in the house next door! [*laughter*] So the visit to Ghana, even before the Somerset Maugham Award and so on, already the seeds of that visit were planted, because I was meeting Africa in person. Not the landscape, but in person – having friends, discussing the politics of Africa.

So London became a kind of crucible in which you could see yourself not only as a West Indian national, but you could also begin to see yourself as a writer in an international context.

Very much in an international context. This brings us to the importance of the Paris Conference of Negro Intellectuals in 1956. An international context that was held together by more or less the same strategies over that very long period of time. I think it must have been the first meeting of its kind, that meeting of the Negro Intellectuals in Paris. It was an occasion in which you learnt, too, the different ways in which the imperial power had influenced the colonized. For example, nearly all of the French-speaking delegates – that is, whether they came from Africa, whether it was Senegal or Guinea, whether they came from Angola, Portugal or Haiti – what was very striking was that the French had, in a way, transmitted to the colonial intelligentsia a feature of French intellectual life which was the fusion of the man of letters and the man of public affairs. That is, nearly all the Haitians present, or the Martinicans and so on, were not only poets, as in the case of Cesaire and Senghor, they were actually political people. They either held office, or if they didn't a lot of their time was engaged in political discourse. Fanon, for example, was not just a writer. It's very difficult to find that equivalent in England. If you take a parallel situation, I don't know of any comparable English novelist or poet who had anything to do or say about the Kikuyu uprising at all. Kenya was not a matter on their agenda in the way Algeria was a matter on the agenda of the French intelligentsia.

A critic recently spoke of the themes which inform your work in the following manner: 'Chief among his concerns are the cultural orphanage engendered by slavery and colonialism and the attendant crises of alienation, exile and reconnection.' What I find fascinating about your work is not just your subject matter, which is eloquently spoken to here, but the restless concern with form. It seems to me to be as important for you how you say something as what you're saying. Would that be a fair summary?

That's very accurate. ... There is a sense in which nearly all of my novels are dramatic poems. And I still write very much, first of all, with the ear – so much so that if anyone is reading back a page, I can spot immediately if a definite article has been omitted. It is not about meaning; it is something about the rhythm of the sentence that is disrupted. There is a sense in which that need for pattern, and what you call form, remains. I've therefore never been too happy with the novel in its traditional sense, and in most of my work you will notice that there is a breaking up, really, of the forms, an attempt to fuse a number of different genres into that.

There is, to my mind, a particularly brilliant section of *The Emigrants*, when they're arriving in England.

The arrival, yes. By the way, Cyril Connolly reviewing it in the *Sunday Times* said he couldn't make head nor tail of it.

I detect in there echoes not only of drama, I detect echoes of Eliot's *The Waste Land* [1922] – the section in *The Waste Land* where the voice says, 'Time, ladies and gentlemen, please'. It reoccurs time and time again, this idea of voices off stage. Then again, during your arrival sequence, there is a wonderfully eloquent, lyrical hymn to England. There are so many different narrative positions within this sequence. There are influences from other authors, there are influences from other disciplines and in that sense I understand not only as a reader, but also as a fellow author, when you describe your work in terms of dramatic construction. I'm interested also in your use of the play *The Tempest*. I was looking again at *Water with Berries* and I was once again very taken by your use of *The Tempest*. You used it for the first time, really, in *The Pleasures of Exile*. Recently I listened to Kamau Brathwaite literally and metaphorically referring to *The Tempest*. I wondered if you could say a few words about this play, which seems to have become a kind of master-text of imperialist discourse for your generation of Caribbean writers.

I think 1960 was probably the first time in our hemisphere that this was attempted, and seen as a kind of paradigm for that colonial enterprise. That gave rise to a lot of rethinking of *The Tempest* among critics and theatre producers and so on. And I'm not finished with it. Brathwaite's reference to the killing of Prospero is preoccupied with that. What I am very concerned about, really, is what one might call the persistence of the metaphor of Prospero. I would go so far as to say that I am not interested in killing Prospero, because Prospero cannot be killed. I'm going to return to *The Tempest* because if you then see Prospero as being synonymous with the phenomenon of the modern, and modernity, there is no part of the planet – I don't care how remote you are, in Africa or Asia or Australasia – there is no part of the planet that can now escape the triumph of modernity. What each culture has to try and do is to find how it incorporates modernity into whatever it imagines to be its specific destiny. But modernity, and modernization, can be seen as a metaphorical extension of Prospero. And there can be no question about killing this off, this simply cannot be killed off. The great challenge is how that is to be incorporated in what you conceive to be your specific and special cultural space. So Prospero is not simply the old imperialist. In fact, he comes up now, if you take the technological society, in new and more sinister forms, because technological society threatens to be the most absolute of all the dictatorships we have known.

When you say you're writing about this, and that you haven't finished with Prospero or *The Tempest* as a metaphor, what type of writing are you doing?

I have gone back – I've never really left it – to that format of the 'Ceremony of Souls' which you found in *Pleasures* and which is used the strongest in *Season of Adventure*. I'm using that ceremony to look at the meaning of Columbus from the other side. I started again what is a kind of drama but moves into prose, moves into poetry, moves into his own text, to bring them all, and us, on trial. That is, in the 'Ceremony of Souls' the dead return to engage the living in arguments that were left unresolved when the dead left us. So I have worked that format out, in which Columbus comes back. All those key figures – Columbus, Oviedo, Las Casas, the men who were engaged in argument about the rightness and wrongness of what they were doing. Columbus comes back to say what it is he was doing, and how he was thinking. And they are all cross-examined, as in the Ceremony, by the Mambo. In the Haitian cosmology, there is either Hougan or the Mambo in the role of priest. . . . I'm somewhat sympathetic to Columbus. I don't share this view of the unique murderer. I see him as an example of the classic outsider. Here was a man who is put in charge of a crew who see him as a foreigner. The crew is Spanish, and he's supposed to be Italian. Here is a man who doesn't have any money, he's a relatively poor man, but on this crew are people who have invested in this voyage. He has to deal with that disparity of financial influence. Here is a man without any formal education having to argue before the products of Salamanca University, the people advising the queen, the leading scholars of the day . . . always on the margin of the world with which he is dealing, which is really how I am seeing him all the time. And hence the secretiveness: Columbus never lets anybody know the half about him, and this is the figure whose severity of punishments and so on have to do with the felt insecurity that you could not take your authority for granted because you know that the others were questioning and you had to impose it from time to time. And also – I don't play with this too much, but throw it in – if you think of the timing: Columbus's journey is going to begin just a matter of six months after the expulsion of all Jews from Spain. There is always in the minds of some of the crew the suspicion that he's also Jewish, that there's some Jewish element. All these peculiar kinds of spoken or unspoken negatives, he has to deal with.

I think you have an admirable detachment from the vagaries of the publishing industry. I noticed the change in your pattern of publishing in the early 1970s, when you were probably the first Caribbean author who had established a reputation in Britain to suddenly publish first in the United States and then in Britain. In other words, with *Natives of My Person* you switched your allegiance from the English publishing industry to the American. America came first. Would you say that today New York is the literary mecca that London was in 1950? In other words, has it become

more important for a Caribbean writer to have a reputation, and a publishing contract, in North America, rather than in England?

I have some difficulty with that because there is, I think, still some resistance in North America to the literature of the Caribbean region; I don't think that has yet penetrated, even within the African American context. There's a marginalized quality to that Caribbean literature. Whereas, in a curious kind of way, in spite of all those changes that have come with postcolonial societies, a curious bond and constituency remains between the Caribbean and London. What I expect will happen, and is beginning to happen very slowly, is the formation of small publishing houses within the Caribbean. I think that people are realizing that it may not be necessary to go outside, also because going outside is not quite so prestigious, perhaps, as it once was. But when you speak of 'mecca', in the 1970s, from about 1975, 1976, what I thought and had argued was that Havana would become the cultural, intellectual and publishing centre of the Caribbean region, through Casa de las Americas. It's a very, very remarkable thing that Casa de las Americas extended that prize to the French- and English-speaking Caribbean ... And what to me was very important then about that, apart from these ideological questions and so on, was that Havana was the gateway to Latin America. It was in Havana that I met all the major Latin American writers: García Marquez, Cortazar, Benedetti, Juan Bosch, a whole lot, I mean anyone you name. That was the meeting place and that was the critical connection which was a blank as far as the English-speaking Caribbean was concerned.

So you would say that there is perhaps a more sympathetic and receptive literary community in London than there is in New York?

That is my impression, yes. I think so. And as I say, what could probably happen is that, in time, that may become even more so with the developing curiosity about the black British looking into origins and their formations. . . . I think that will happen, that you might find a second or third generation of black British becoming much more interested. This often happens in the United States, that the first-generation Americans of Italian origin don't bother much with Italy; it's when you get to the second or the third that they start making enquiries into this original root. Fascination with the past is heightened by your remoteness from it, and a desire to reclaim it.

What are your observations of these individuals who didn't exist when you first came to Britain; the black British people? What characteristics differentiate them from West Indians?

The first difference that I notice looking at them is that I thought they were in many respects closer to the black youth in the urban centres of the United States than they were to any Jamaican or Barbadian of my generation. And the reason for that is that they were, in fact, the products of an urban culture – the products of a very atomized kind of urban life. My generation came out of strong community living, strong village living. And also in the Caribbean, because of the size of islands, and particularly small islands, you really did not have a strong sense of any great distinction between country and town. Everybody was within striking distance of the centre of civilization; in some cases, you walked to town from the remotest corners. And that was the difference. I saw them as closer to the black Americans. . . . My generation walked very softly. We wanted to be there, but we didn't want to make too much noise about being there. On the other hand, there's now an element of aggression . . . a very different relation to institutions. For example, I was never, in England, afraid of police. As a matter of fact, if I was walking – I lived in Chiswick at one time – at night, I was always very relieved if I saw a police officer. The police did not signify, for me, a moment of menace. That is the very opposite today. . . . I have the sense of a people marginalized in spite of that authority, and the great affirmation of 'me' and the me-ness of me and the we-ness of we is to me some evidence of a continuing insecurity about the relation they have to the landscape in which they live. There is an unresolved problem of whether they are going to be of the society, as distinct from simply being in the society. ... That ambivalence, and that uncertainty of direction, is a difference. My generation were in England and had no particular quarrel with not being of it, for the simple reason that we never broke our deepest sentimental links with where we had come from, that the Caribbean remained alive in you in England. And when you speak of 'home', that was home, even after thirty or forty years. That remained home, and also carried with it the fantasies of being buried at home. West Indians would tell you the one thing I don't want is for my bones to be laid here in this place. I can't be sure of it, but I doubt very much that that young British black has a comparable sense of home.

17

Rohinton Mistry

with

Robert Mclay

Rohinton Mistry is the author of three novels and several short stories set amidst the closely knit and isolated Parsi community in Bombay. His first collection of stories, Tales from Firozsha Baag *(1987), explores the position of the Parsi in postcolonial India as well as pointing to a sense of unease created in the figures from this community who chose to emigrate. As the protagonist says in 'Lend Me Your Light' – one of the stories – 'I am guilty of the sin of hubris for seeking emigration out of the land of my birth, and paying the price in burnt out eyes: I, Tiresias, blind and throbbing between two lives, the one in Bombay and the one to come in Toronto.' Mistry's first novel,* Such a Long Journey *(1991), is set during the period of the Indo-Pakistan war which led to the liberation of Bangladesh and was shortlisted for the Booker Prize.* A Fine Balance, *published in March 1996 when this interview took place in London, extended the range and scope of Mistry's Indian setting to include an imaginative landscape which was deliberately unspecified. Mistry's most recent novel,* Family Matters *(2002), concentrates on illness and mortality in a setting familiar to his other works, the Bombay-based, modern-day Parsi family living in an overcrowded apartment block. Mistry left Bombay at the age of twenty-three to migrate to Canada.*

Robert Mclay There is a point in your latest novel, *A Fine Balance*, where the young Parsi student Maneck Kohlah first comes to the city and meets the allergic proofreader Vasantrao Valmik LLB on the train. He asks him about his past. Valmik replies that it is a long story, whereupon Maneck replies that they have 'such a long journey', echoing of course the title of your first novel. Do you think that storytelling is itself a journey?

Rohinton Mistry Well yes. That was a little treat for anyone who had read the earlier novel. I think journeys are themselves stories and vice versa but without some sense of core values it is difficult to know if and in what direction you are moving. I suppose that if we consider families, which are very important in India – as they are everywhere – then the whole extended family, especially the grandmother and the grandfather, is the source of storytelling and it gives the individual a very good sense of where they come from. Relating this specifically to myself now, I left Bombay for Canada at the age of twenty-three, and assumed before I got there that it would be no new thing for me. It would be a new land but I felt sure I knew the language, that I would understand the culture and the society because that was the way I had been brought up in India; my language was English, my literature was what I had studied at school and college and so on. And yet it was all so very different. . . . The English I spoke was not the English they spoke. I mean there were so many different Englishes. We were separated by a common language and yet I found I was able to make my way with some confidence. It was strange and new but it was navigable. It was fortunate that I emigrated when I did because this meant I had been fully formed by my own culture and my own family. At one time I thought this was the culture of the West but I now know it was something different. It was the Indian version of the West and it was mine. Despite, or maybe because of, having lived in Bombay for my twenty-three years I felt something in me was incomplete. Because the music and the literature I learned came from the West I felt that if I went there there would be a wholeness to my being. That was not the case and it was in fact quite jarring; jarring, but as I said navigable. I can only assume that if I had left at say twelve or thirteen I would not have felt this way. However, having arrived in the West, this sense of incompleteness turned around and I became aware of the loss of my home.

This reminds me of a passage in *A Fine Balance* where Dukhi returns to his village 'slumped in the bullock cart, barely aware of the wheels jouncing over the ruts and bumps jarring his bones'. Simultaneously, as you put it, 'he felt crazy surges of energy that made him want to hop out of the cart and run'. He seems in part sustained both by tradition and the past but has a compulsion to strike out on his own. This also seems to be a continuing preoccupation in your other writings.

Yes, there is a great difference between remembering the past, which is creative and life-enhancing, and trying to preserve it, which is detrimental and debilitating. I am thinking of Sohrab's collection of butterflies in *Such a Long Journey*, Jehangir's stamp collection in *Tales from Firozsha Baag* and Rustom's violin in *A Fine Balance*. All these things become useless through lack of use and loving attention, which after all is what memory is. And also it is sometimes very difficult not to be compelled to preserve the past, especially when the present is so painful. Dina draws great comfort from her memories of her dead husband Rustom and following his death carries on a kind of secret ritual; that way madness lies. It is only after the nephews skip through and reinvent the empty rooms that Dina can see them as they are and remember properly and lovingly. We cannot rely on our forebears' victories to sustain us. In *A Fine Balance* each generation tries to inhibit the following from achieving their own successes and Gustad too in *Such a Long Journey* must learn to let Sohrab win his own struggles.

There is a great sense of loss in the novel. In the physical sense each character has lost their home and family surroundings

through leaving their villages and going to the city. Do you think their sense of family values has been retained or in fact transformed and deepened by their experiences in the city?

Well, each of them undergoes a separation and perhaps digressing slightly, I think loss is part of the human condition. We all undergo a separation and of course the first separation is from our mothers' wombs and that is the commencement of the journey. So in a sense we are all migrants in the broad sense that we are leaving our first place and going somewhere else. But when Maneck and the tailors, Ishvar and Omprakesh, come to the city they have not forgotten who they are. They remember how they used to live, how to live and what is important in life and that is what makes that little family crystallize in the apartment, despite their suspicions – their doubts and their mutual differences. The other thing within the core of their being – their families – is stronger and it eventually resurfaces throughout their lives. On the other hand they also need each other to survive in difficult circumstances. We see Dina go through these self-doubts and feelings of self-hatred. The tailors seem so good to her, so concerned about her well-being and yet is she keeping them there on her veranda because she wants to feel tied to them or is it because she needs them for their labour? She has been told by the export company and her friend Zenobia to differentiate rigidly her life as an employer from theirs as employees and to draw a line between them or she will not be respected. But she cannot maintain that line and eventually she must cross it, and it is her need to love as well as to be loved which makes her become a family and give in to what is inevitable. I think that means that all such lines are artificial and there are stronger forces at work and if such a line is made to persist it will lead to chaos or lead to even more problems. Partition was just such a line and history has amply shown this.

Another aspect of journeying or moving away is that you leave behind the comfort of simple everyday things: for example Maneck

dwells metonymically on his father's giant tea cup. You cannot take all these things with you ... but then what matters are the ideas, the empathies you can carry, even through the reconstruction of simple routines.

There is a bit in the novel that describes the 'family' at rest, a quiet before the storm, where Maneck takes comfort in their communal activities: cooking, planning and especially making the quilt which gives meaning to their lives. And writing too can, in a strange and particular way, be a communal and comforting activity. Just as God is in the detail, comfort within the family is in the routine, the small details of family life.

Edward Said saw a key aspect of modernism as residing in the move from filiation to affiliation, the new as against the traditional, but your view is that new affiliations are determined by and reflect core values?

Yes ... again it is part of the extended family I mentioned earlier. When the brothers were small their father [Ishvar and Omprakesh's father, Narayan] took them to the Muslim tailor and he said, 'Ashraf, he is like my brother so you must call him uncle, you must call him Ashraf chacha', and once they start believing that and living with that, that he is their father's brother, it doesn't matter that he is a Muslim; they would do for him what they would do for their own father because in the Hindu extended family, the father's brother is as good as the father.

In his book on Baudelaire, Walter Benjamin speaks of the city poet's special concern with ragpickers, beggars and suicide victims or heroes. This points to some interesting continuities with modernism in your work. He also spoke of the Arcades project as bringing together the interior and exterior lives of Parisians in complicated ways. Do you think your treatment of the extended family revisits these arguments, making them interesting and fresh again?

I hope so. But going back to the family idea; especially in *Tales from Firozsha Baag*, where the entire Baag is a family or at least the individual blocks are families, we have to keep in mind that the people who live there sometimes find the proximity too much and the exterior intruding. I use the word deliberately because it can become utterly overbearing. There is a yearning at times just to be alone without anyone watching or knowing what you are doing. And of course the entire street is occupied with families and people. I tried to show how the smallest plot of land can be occupied in the city and how difficult it is not to become aware of their plight and difficulties. In the city everything can become everything else – homes, hostels, workplaces, prisons, doorways, streets, whatever. In this sense the city helps to inhibit line drawing.

Walter Benjamin also suggests that the modern city, because it atomizes its inhabitants – makes everyone a detective, so to speak, so individuals are perpetually driven to both hiding and discovering secrets – that this in fact generates the detective story. In *A Fine Balance* there are both unsolved murders and discovered secrets. Was this deliberate?

In the novel the two tailors are the source of a lot of anecdotes and stories just because of who they are and what they are up to in the city. They are looking for accommodation and they are looking for work and in the course of their innumerable journeys, things happen to them which they relate to the waiter at their favourite tea stop, the Vishram Vegetarian Hotel. In a sense, they are sharing their secrets with the waiter, who is always happy to see them because he loves their stories. Also, Rajaram the hair collector – later the family-planning motivator – has a big secret to tell about what happened to him one night while working as a hairdresser. The beggar Worm/Shankar has a dark secret, as does his mother, Nosey, and indeed Beggarmaster himself. But the tailors claim it has nothing to do with them; it is the city itself that provides them with fodder for these stories. 'It is a great story factory.' So in a sense the city does create secrets which, when revealed, become little and sometimes big stories.

The Vishram, the *jhopadpatti*, Dina's apartment and the student's hostel are all sites where secrets are hidden or divulged; is it this that transforms them into homes?

Yes, that's a good point. I was just thinking that the only secret that is not revealed is Maneck's encounter in the hostel and Maneck is the only one who is finally unable to maintain the balance and commits suicide which is the real tragedy. But Dina's quilt is also a secret in a way because it is coded. Someone says – Ishvar I think – that they should take it to the Vishram Hotel because the waiter would enjoy it because all their stories are there, and Omprakesh points out that he wouldn't understand the quilt because it is in their own secret language and only they know what the patches and scraps mean. Maneck says he could translate for him.

Are there any other secrets about the novel you would like to divulge?

Well not a secret perhaps but something I would like to share is that after writing my first two books, I became aware that they were stories about a very particular and special kind of city and even then I had focused only on a very small part of it – the Parsi community. I made a conscious decision in this book to include more than this, mainly because in India seventy-five per cent of Indians live in villages and I wanted to embrace more of the social reality of India. So I made the tailors come from a small village and Maneck come from a hill station in the North. While the city is certainly important I wanted to give a strong sense of the different locales and I wanted to root the reader in those places so that he or she has a very clear sense of where these people are coming from and what their difficulties are now.

In the novel you have suggested how individuals can achieve a sense of balance in their lives through making connections and affinities, but how much of the book is also about the complete lack of checks and balances in the body politic brought on by administrative and political chaos?

There was the chaos in the city but there was also chaos as regards the caste system in the village. For example when Ishvar's father is still young, the upper-caste Brahmins talk of two-headed calves being born when the Chamaar caste has newborn sons and really they have only daughters. This is the result of chaos in the universe brought on by some transgression in this world of the natural social order. They then talk of increased vigilance and a more rigorous adherence to the caste system, which obviously means more floggings and beatings, which is the real chaos.

You wrote this book in 1995, some twenty years after the Emergency. Do you think the geographical and temporal distance helped you look at it more objectively?

Yes, I think it was an advantage. Distance makes things clearer. It is almost as if time helps the inessential things to wither, revealing what is at the centre of things. It would also have been intimidating, even downright dangerous to write about these things in India at the time they were happening. Certainly for a journalist the consequences would have been quite terrible. The press of course was heavily censored and anyone making the least sort of progress would have been severely dealt with – probably like Avinash.

Unlike other cameo figures which reappear in the novel, Avinash, who is 'officially' murdered, does not. He remains a brooding presence throughout the novel. Would you agree?

Yes. He has affected Maneck deeply and it is through him that we feel his presence throughout.

A final question. Following their disastrous and forced sterilization, the tailors are reduced to beggardom and we are left with the image of Omprakesh guiding and pushing Ishvar, who has lost his legs but is supported by the now unravelling quilt. So in a way their stories and secrets still sustain them. Have you felt that your stories and secrets have sustained you since you left India?

Well I once read, and I think it was by Camus, that one can redeem oneself by writing and that has stayed with me. I think that is why I began to write. I wasn't sure how redemption would come through writing but I'm still writing.

18

Keri Hulme

with

Rima Alicia Bartlett

Keri Hulme is the author of The Bone People *(1984), a novel which won the Booker Prize in 1985, and a collection of short stories* Te Kaihau/The Windeater *(1986). Among her other publications are two collections of poetry:* The Silences Between/Moeraki Conversations *(1982) and* Strands *(1992). Rima Alicia Bartlett interviewed her at her home in Okarito, in the South Island of New Zealand: 'A letter, a plane, a train, a bus and there she was at a fork in the road. We drove for miles down the hill until we reached the place of the lagoons and the sea. I found myself in a quiet land, suffused with soft light, a land where the greenstone trails wind through the mountainous backbone of the land, a land called Te Wahi Pounamu; Pounamu can be interpreted as greenstone or jade, a sacred stone to Maori people; wahi can mean place. As I walked over the shingles of this beach of many currents, where the winds and waters meet, I bent and picked up the grey stones, pressure moulded and water woven. The sky was bundled with clouds, the birds flew low above the pale ocean, the trees were a dark blend of rimu and manuka and many others I don't recognize. Hulme took me to a collection of houses that look like they are perched there temporarily. One of them was hers, a house she built herself.'*

Keri Hulme completed a new novel, Bait, *in 1999 and began work on* Shadowlands. *Her work continues to be eclectic as it is stringent: she composed a libretto, 'Ahua: a Story of Moki' in November 2000. Her paper*

for the Royal Society of New Zealand entitled 'Mystic Fires of Tamaatea'
(2002) attempts, as she has said, 'to creatively rewrite New Zealand's cul-
tural and tectonic past'. Speaking of her literary influences she has said
that 'people and life and love and misfortune and death inform every word
sent out into the world. I celebrate these when I can, mourn them when I
must.'

Rima Alicia Bartlett When I first met you at a New Zealand writers'
conference in London a couple of years ago, I was stunned at the
way you, jerkined, sandalled and *tokotoko* [a *tokotoko* looks and
acts like a walking stick, but it is also a talking stick which was
used to aid genealogical recitation in the old days], seemed to
bring the spirit of New Zealand with you. It hit me with almost a
physical force. What effect does the place where you live have on
your work?

Keri Hulme I've described myself as a 'quintessential dweller on
strands'. It's what makes me me. I was conceived by a beach, grew up
on beaches, I've lived on beaches literally all my life, I'm continually
reduced to wonder at all forms of life, isopods, marine life, mammals.
The beaches here are unusually rich and full of flotsam: whales, dead
bodies, tools . . . The world is always changing, humans are temporary,
and when you live on a beach you recognize that. Especially here, in this
house built over a river bank. Okarito being twenty kilometres to the
crack between the Austronesian crust plate and the New Zealand one. It
is a world of transition and being here makes me know that. When I'm
in mountains I look for the nearest escape route. Everything closes in. If
you put me in the mountains, this rather substantial body [points to
herself] would wither. This is where I've made my life, I'm at ease here
and able to be productive. There's something very physical, obvious
and omnipresent about beaches, maybe it's the sound of the sea,
knowing it's there. Besides, the fishing is good!

Where do you get your inspiration from?

Tihe Mauriora! They were the first words ever spoken by the first created human being, a female. According to *Ngai Tahu* [Maori tribe of the South Island to which Hulme belongs through her mother] tradition she's saluting *Tane* [a major god] who's given her life. Then there are dreams, fantasies, words themselves.

How do you access it?

That's sort of like asking, 'How do you breathe?' I walk on the beach a lot, and the beach is always changing. The other day I watched a tree stump, which was covered with barnacles, thousands upon thousands of them. Then the sun came out and they put out little feather-like filaments as they were dying. Quite extraordinary. Things like that make you wonder about all sorts of things.

How about the world or worlds you create partly from your dreams?

My dreams are very rich and fascinating. I have a dream dictionary and have been checking my dreams for about thirty-five years. I get recurrent themes and ideas. As an example, I quite frequently dream about finding caches of jewels and weaponry, which I filch, but I know I shouldn't. I have that dream about three or four times a year.

The Bone People **is very much a product of a particular place-in-space, this place, Okarito and Moeraki. What does Okarito mean in Maori?**

Two things. Okarito is the name of a former chief. *Karito* means somebody who's blond, like flax. It also means the young edible shoots of the *raupo* plant [a kind of swamp rush]. *Raupo* is found underwater and within the lagoon. The place's vibration is the gross note of water in many forms. The colours here are quite extraordinary; for instance there's a broad range of colours all contained in the colour grey.

That's fascinating. What does the darkness mean to you?

Excellent question. It's the beginning. It must contain everything. According to the *Ngai Tahu* the darkness was pierced by a song, and the song itself was of the darkness. I've always found that a very satisfying idea.

I notice you obviously love playing with the imagery of light in your work. I used to live in Wanaka [a town a couple of hundred miles to the south] where the light is very bright, almost crystalline in quality. I notice the light here is particularly soft, almost watery. How does that affect you?

There are thousands of shades of grey. Grey is the colour of the sand, of the sky, of the sea. It's a very soft colour, very beautiful, not sad at all. I love colours. I don't know whether they represent anything, but they're one of the joys of life, like food. Colour is like music, part of what makes life so enormously attractive. The other meaning of light I want to talk about is a light presence. I've been here when the whole sea lights up, moonlight in water, a completely non-dangerous light. This happens all over the world, but here the whole surfline goes like that, in a big sweep.

As an outsider, another thing that seems to be special about this place is that it's really windy. I noticed you called your volume of short stories *Te Kaihau*, or *The Windeater*. What does the wind mean to you?

Te Hau. Hau is the particular kind of breath that animates humans. It's the most lively element I know in weather terms. Winds are as various as creatures: boisterous, aggressive, gentle, comforting. On the other hand the one element that really gives me the heebies is the wind. I like the water, can deal with fire, the earth, even when it shakes [a reference to the number of earthquakes in New Zealand]. Tawhirimatea [the god of winds] is the permanent enemy of humans because he opposed his brother Tane in the action of separating their parents – Papatuanuku the earth and Ranginui the sky. The wind off the sea can be enormously draining.

I believe one of the strengths of your work is that you don't state things directly; but in many ways you imply that the answer is in the relative and unchanging. You have been described as part Maori, yet I suspect your Maoriness is your essence, running through you like a deep vein in a greenstone, although its expression may glint in the light in different ways. What would you say to that?

Yes. I wish I could just answer with that word. If you separate me out, this part is Maori, that part is *pakeha* [white], it's not right. Wherever you come from you're still one person, you don't war, you don't fight, at least you don't in my family group. Maori culture is what we do. And we do it in varying intensities. When my neighbour died, my last words to him were a *karanga* [Maori call]. I've rarely been involved with what you're involved with, a Maori culture group, but I've taught the people here how to do a *hangi* [traditional feast of food baked in the ground]. One of the things that have sustained me is finding out the background history about the Maori side of my family. *Hui* [gatherings], *marae* [meeting houses], reading, listening, thinking about things. I speak Maori, but I'd love to become really fluent in our dialect. There's only one *Kai Tahu* speaker left.

[As Hulme has told *Wasafiri*, this situation has changed since the interview took place in 1997. There has been a successful programme to increase fluency in the *Kai Tahu* dialect.]

I notice that in many of your writings you seem to associate stones with indigenous knowledge. For instance in *Strands* you write, 'I have a stone that once swam / strange, warm ancient seas'. Do you really?

Yes, definitely. There are some proverbs, including numerous exemplars about how *Te Wahi Pounamu* got its name, to do with minerals. To this day when Maori say 'stone' we generally mean *pounamu*, almost none of us is without it. We all wear it, secretly or obviously [points to a greenstone armband under her shirt].

You have such beautiful descriptions of *pounamu* in your book. The other descriptions that particularly strike me are to do with the moon. Distant Simon is covered with 'moonshimmer hair', Kerewin's shadow is a 'moonshadow', moonwater of emotion flows. According to many traditions the moon is associated with unconscious knowledge. Does the moon represent conscious or unconscious knowledge to you?

The Maori don't actually separate the two.

Good point. I have a question on a slightly different subject: how did you learn Maori?

When I was seven I began writing down Maori words, and making my own 'dictionary'. At school it was reported that I wanted to learn Maori instead of French – *not* done in those days. Now I have sixteen Maori dictionaries so I can check as far as possible the meanings of words.

I had the same problem at school. I wanted to learn 'Polynesian' (I thought it was one language), instead of French. On a different note: what advice would you give to aspiring writers?

Be bloody-minded. Believe in yourself. Unless you're writing just for money, ignore the market. You're the one doing the writing, doing the work. You have to have the bloody-minded determination to see it gets out in the world. I've been writing for myself since I was seven, and I wasn't published until 1975 when I was twenty-eight. There are several kinds of writing. There's writing as therapy, writing as self-entertainment (my drawer is full of a sci-fi monstrosity), writing as exploration, where you do acrobatics with language, and writing as communication, which needs to reach readers. But we limit ourselves if we think readers only respond to the communication category, just because that's what publishers respond to. You need to get out there. *The Bone People* was first published by a feminist collective, although after the book won the Booker, other publishing companies came up to me and offered to publish it.

What were you doing when you heard *The Bone People* had won the Booker Prize? How did you feel?

I was sitting in a hotel in Salt Lake City. . . . I'd been having lunch with my mother when I was called to the phone. There was someone very pleasant from the BBC who said: 'I've got the Booker result and I'd like a comment'. I was just getting ready to make the appropriate comments on Peter Carey's *Illywhacker* – I thought it had won – when the lady came back and said: 'It's you. You've won the Booker.' I said: 'Bloody hell.' I just didn't believe it. When I didn't come back after half an hour Mum realized what was going on and was absolutely delighted. Utah's a dry state and she got half a bottle of champagne and brought it back in a brown paper bag. She was so delighted, not least because I'd bet her half of the prize money that I wouldn't win. So she got half of the 34,000 dollars. That was a really weird night.

One of the best things about winning the Booker must have been that it put Maori writing 'on the map' for many people all over the world. How do you feel about that?

It's good for New Zealand writing. I can imagine the ghost of Katherine Mansfield leaping up and down somewhere in France, the same with Janet Frame. The Maori writer Apirana Taylor was published two months later in America as a result. I think it showed that people in this country could really write. It was not just English-speaking countries which showed an interest. *The Bone People* was, and is, very popular in Germany, the Scandinavian bloc and Holland.

It was once said by a critic, Paul Sharrad, that the Eurocentric propensity is 'to look to definitive lines rather than what they enclose or how they interconnect'. Do you think we need to judge novels by a Eurocentric yardstick?

What a revolting thought! The novel is not a European invention. I would think a native of Japan would be mortified if their extremely long tradition of novel-making was judged by ideas that came from a European canon. Nations develop their own traditions. When I wrote *The Bone People* I didn't think it would go outside the country. All you can do is judge a New Zealand novel by a New Zealand tradition.

Doesn't that seem to contradict your winning the Booker Prize?

Yes. Very good point.

Eurocentric critics say the form of the novel is very new, very radical. What do you have to say?

The Bone People is a *purakau* or fantasy story, part of an old Maori tradition of 'tales told in winter'. Irehapeti Ramsden said it reminded her of being in her meeting house in Rapaki. She'd wake up and hear people chanting in the corner, then go to sleep and wake up again. There were ongoing conversations on all kinds of levels within the *marae*. The merging of oral traditions and written forms was likely to take place in a country like this. It's a kind of realist writing, playful albeit. The only person I know who writes about similar traditions is the Niuean writer John Pule, author of *The Shark Who Ate the Sun*, a wonderful book which deserves to be better known.

How would you feel if you were, like the hostages recently in the Lebanon, confined to a cell for many years, with no possibility of writing?

The dependency would be the worst thing, but I have a perfectly wonderful fantasy life. The biggest frustration is I'm quite meticulous about checking words, I have one hundred and twenty-seven dictionaries. I'm not frustrated if I can't write things down as I have an extremely good memory. I can fix words to the pictures in my mind and remember them, like learning a chant.

Albert Wendt said in an interview that he doesn't like set systems of thought and set systems of belief. Is this true for you too?

In a word, yes. A set of beliefs is good as a starting point, but if you wholly absorb them you will amputate what being a human is all about. What you believe literally determines what you see.

It is night when I leave Keri Hulme's house. I felt the rush of a bird's flight through the spotting rain and the darkness. I thought I caught a glimpse of it.

19

Amit Chaudhuri
with
Fernando Galvàn

Born in Calcutta in 1962, Amit Chaudhuri was brought up in Bombay. He came to Britain to study at University College London and then at Balliol College, Oxford. His first novel, A Strange and Sublime Address, *was published in 1991 and his second,* Afternoon Raag, *in 1993. He has received a number of awards, including the Commonwealth Writers Prize, the Betty Trask Prize, the Encore Award, the Los Angeles Times Book Prize and the Sahitya Akademi Award. When this interview took place, at the University of Alcala, Spain, he had just published* Freedom Song *(1998), set in Calcutta during the winter of 1992–3 against the backdrop of growing political tension between Hindus and Muslims; so it is interesting that he discusses how the profound and often intimate differences which define cultures cohabit in and influence his work. Since 1998 he has written* A New World *(2000) and a collection of short stories,* Real Time *(2002). Chaudhuri's latest work is* D. H. Lawrence and Difference: the poetry of the present *(2003), in which he looks at Lawrence's position as a 'foreigner' in the English canon – an ongoing critical project.*

Fernando Galvàn You were born in Calcutta in 1962, and lived in Bombay during your childhood. What have these different cities meant to you? Reading *A Strange and Sublime Address* I had the impression that Calcutta was a city of the mind, like Dublin was for Stephen Dedalus.

Amit Chaudhuri Calcutta is identified in my mind with my family on my mother's side, because my father is an only child, like me. My father worked in a corporate firm, so I grew up in corporate Bombay, with high buildings; it was a kind of existence outside of any community. To go back and visit Calcutta was to go back to houses which were nearer the street level. Streets in south Calcutta had their own particular noises; with me was my maternal uncle's family, and my cousins. . . . I identified Calcutta as a place that was home. Home was interwoven with the Bengali language, my mother tongue . . . which was hardly spoken out of my immediate home. In school I spoke only English, so to go back to Calcutta was to re-enter the Bengali language. . . . I've written a piece about that, 'Beyond Translation', published in 1997, about me as a child reading books in English and my cousins sitting next to me in Calcutta reading the Bengali books. It was a house to which all kinds of people would come and vanish again, relatives from different parts of Eastern India, because all these relatives actually belonged to East Bengal and Sylhet, all had been displaced by Partition. . . . So Bombay represented to me the English language, the medium of instruction, examinations, of school.

Did you also want to be a writer, at that time in Calcutta, like Sandeep in *A Strange and Sublime Address*, or is that completely fictitious?

No, it is not absolutely fictitious. I did want to be a writer, because I liked writing stories and poems; but I had no idea what it meant to be a writer. Then I genuinely thought that writing suspense stories, horror novels, was to be a writer.

But in your story 'Portrait of an Artist' you present a different picture, that of a boy who feels captivated by his master and the

intellectual surroundings, and wants to become a writer. Didn't you
have that sort of experience, of discovering Bengali literature and
then wanting to write?

Well, the story in 'Portrait of an Artist' is based on real experience and
characters. It's very true; I mean, I don't think I made up a single word
in that story. So, yes, I was that sort of boy.

Did you suffer any kind of discrimination when you came to Britain?
Other postcolonial writers have referred to that experience of
coming to the metropolis and feeling rejected by the British.

I came to London as an undergraduate student to UCL but also to start
publishing poetry. I'd been before, but it was still a shock to me. That is
not so much to do with the issue of discrimination as just the complete
difference in the way of life, the climate, and the absence of sunlight.
The issue of discrimination I didn't feel very much. By the time I
graduated I didn't feel it at all, just the opposite. But that doesn't mean
I was not miserable. I was extremely miserable, those three years in
London. I had encountered the issue of discrimination as a child when
I came to London in the 1970s. But that was partly because England
was in a state of economic recession, and it was going through a pretty
bad time: the National Front was pretty awful.

Your three novels seem to be different steps in the construction of a
Bildungsroman. Did you intend to write a postcolonial *Bildungsroman*: the experience of a young boy who grows up either in his own
country or abroad but who is always fighting against the dilemma of
belonging or not belonging?

The structures and the narratives I chose would not lend themselves to
a traditional *Bildungsroman*, or even a trilogy which would cover that
kind of subject. In the first novel I was really writing about a boy's
discovery of Calcutta and of an extended family. In the second I was

writing about the narrator's estrangement from both cultures; and in the third I was writing about the family afflicted, or changed, by old age. The younger people in the family were either absent or gone to some other part of the world, or other parts of India; the young people who had stayed on are doing all kinds of things that were perceived as idiosyncratic. Calcutta, and India itself, were on the brink of change.

Most critics have described the first two novels as the works of a miniaturist. They have praised the style; at the same time as they praise the evocative power of your language, they complain about them not being true novels in the sense that there is no development of characters, that they seem to be autobiographical essays in a poetic mood, etc. What do you think about that criticism?

I suppose they are right; it is especially true of a novel like *Afternoon Raag*. With *A Strange and Sublime Address*, the short novel, I think that it is quite self-contained. It's true that it is not exactly a conventional novel. The third novel has quite an unfinished quality about it, although it's longer than the first or the second. I think somehow that if I returned to that work, I'd write about those characters again. I began to write novels by accident. I began as a poet, and found that my poetic impulses needed the space of something larger, so they express themselves best in a more architectural space where I could talk about lives, and spaces, and all kinds of things interacting with each other. At the same time there is a poetic impulse, in which I want to let things remain unsaid, or not finish things completely, so maybe that goes against the grain of what the novel should be all about.

A Strange and Sublime Address **is a rather a typical case as a novel, since there is a main narration, divided into fourteen chapters, and then a second part, constituted by nine short stories, each with a title, and all of them independent. In a recent paperback edition of the book, there's a subtitle: 'A Novel in Nine Stories'. Can you explain this?**

Well, it's really a novel and nine stories. All the stories are intertextual and set in Calcutta, so they can be taken as a larger work. It was said in the hardback that it is a short novel and nine stories, but when the book was republished I said, 'Could you put a subtitle saying that it's a novel and nine stories?', and the editor on the telephone heard me saying 'a novel in nine stories'.

Could this book be called autobiographical?

Well, it's actually based on characters I've seen in my own life, places I've been to – but I am not interested in myself in the novel. I mean, I suppose that's one of the reasons why when I began to write that novel, I veered away from the tragic to the comic, because the tragic for me is identified with the self, with one person. Comedy is dispersed into all kinds of areas, all kinds of languages clashing with each other, so this is to a certain extent a novel about joy, about different things coming into contact with each other, and as I wrote it after spending time in England, it's also a novel about spaces, streets, sounds, the auditory background with which an Indian lives, which is completely absent in England, and which is actually, you might almost say, synonymous with the Indian subconscious. Something is always happening elsewhere, life is happening elsewhere, something's going on.

The way you write about those experiences sometimes evokes the Modernist style. Did you try to do something like Joyce in his *Portrait* . . . **perhaps?**

I grew up with Bengali and Bombay culture, which was a mishmash of Western culture and the local culture. Temperamentally I suppose I was always interested in modernism, the image side of modernism, the psychology of sensation, of impressions, but that doesn't mean that it had not been there before. You can find it in ancient literature, in poetry as well. . . . I was not interested in that side of modernism which dealt with bewailing the disintegration of European culture, which is what T. S. Eliot is always doing. It's funny because he was an American, and much of what has been written about the disintegration of Europe and European culture has actually been done by Americans. That was one side I was a bit uncomfortable with, because it wasn't temperamentally close to me, this sense of despondency and this sense of tragedy. I admired poets like Eliot or someone very different from him, Larkin, for a long time. I tried to write poetry like them until I moved to a suburb in Bombay, and I realized that this was not really what I was interested in. What I was interested in is the sort of drift and flow of street life. . . . I am not interested in the disintegration of self . . . but I'm interested in the dispersal of culture from the self, and that for me is a joyful thing, in contrast to the dispersal of some unified self through terror or pressure.

This notion of the dispersal of identities, as well as the title of the first novel is also very Joycean, isn't it? The presentation of the young man who wants to become an artist, etc. I don't mean it was particularly intended, but was not the *Portrait* at the back of your mind when you wrote it?

Well, it wasn't actually. You know, I'd read *A Portrait of the Artist as a Young Man* when I was seventeen years old, and I hated it at that time. Then I read it later, when I had written this novel and I was revising it and loved . . . the second rereading. I saw an affinity there, but when I was writing this book Joyce was not in my mind. Again as to *A Strange and Sublime Address* being a portrait of an artist, I wasn't conscious of doing that. I realize that there are certain parts in the novel where I talk about him wanting to write, but at the same time I said he wanted to write horror stories, so I sort of undercut that association; I wasn't consciously interested in Sandeep as a character. Sandeep was just there, but to me the city of Calcutta, and Chhotomama, and that house, those were what interested me.

So that focus on the city, on the background, on the physical details, maybe makes your characters on many occasions more aware of the outside life than of their own inner lives. That impression is created, for instance, in your second novel, *Afternoon Raag*. Are characters not very important to you perhaps?

I think my characters are very important, the psychology of the characters, or their inner lives, as you use the phrase – I don't think I look for those things. Quite often, to use Isherwood's phrase, I just behave like a camera, I just follow them about, eavesdrop on their conversations and see what they're doing. So there's almost a child-like sight, that is the child who wants to spy, to overhear, without being noticed himself. So at the end of *A Strange and Sublime Address* I talk about ghosts who have the ability to go back to the world they once lived in, to see without themselves being seen; and to me that seemed like a privilege.

You describe objects, noises . . . rather than people. The impression sometimes is that the reader doesn't get a picture of the characters, not only from the inside but also from the outside. What are some characters like, for instance?

You're talking about *Afternoon Raag*, yes. I think in *Freedom Song* characters are described in their physicality, the colour of their skin, the kind of eyes a particular character has. When I talk of Mini, the friend of the old woman Khuku, I described how, because she is a spinster, she has no marks on her belly, while Khuku has the marks of the caesarean operation on her belly. . . . With *Afternoon Raag*, although I do describe details, they cease to be recognizable. I was really concerned with Oxford and India, and the fact that Oxford is not what it seemed to be, it's a place of transition, it is an ancient university, but it's a place where no one belongs, because people are moving through. Every three years the faces are renewed. I suddenly realized what a strange place this is . . . and the more I saw it as a local culture rather than some place called England, the more I saw differences within England. It's a very unreal place, quite different from any other small town, quite different from London. So that maybe was what I was trying to get at, that's why I dwell on details, because everything is strange. Even when going back to India – although this is home – I'm talking about the way things are not fixed, things are not as they seem.

You once wrote about Rohinton Mistry's *Such a Long Journey* [1991]:

> In the West, because of the climate, people get to know each other in rooms. Relationships form. So do characters. In India, the human face, being part of a river of faces, refuses to lend itself to characterization, disappears, like a hint, soon after appearing, remains ghostly, without inwardness. . . . Subject to the more occidental practice of 'characterization', his protagonists tend to be unconvincing. [*London Review of Books*]

Is this then the way you look at your characters, the reasons for this peculiarity in the creation of characters we are talking about?

Well, it's partly true. When I am writing about my family or people I know well, that is not true. I find the concern with characterization such a boring and obsessive thing. . . . When I read nineteenth-century novels I think of rooms, of closed spaces. All the interaction takes place through social interaction. In India there are very clearly demarcated social spaces, even perhaps more so than in the West: social events like festivals, weddings, funerals, other things – at the same time you come into contact incompletely with many more characters. You come into contact with millions and millions of people in your lifetime in India whom you actually don't know very well. That forms quite a profound constituent of your consciousness, of humanity, so it's not just that one-to-one, or three-to-four psychological interaction which occurs in the West. In India it's quite different. There is that, but there is something else as well, and so you have a real sense of humanity, but it need not be connected with this existential sense of self which, I believe, exists because of the closed spaces of the West. In India those closed spaces are always being undermined, firstly because the window is left open. . . . So how can you have that kind of single character? You are a composite of interruptions, smells, sights, what you've overheard, memories, ambitions, all kinds of things. That well-rounded thing is not given a chance to exist.

Space is a fascinating aspect in your novels. Readers may wonder whether the confrontation between the closed and open spaces (rooms, windows, streets, etc., in *Afternoon Raag*, for instance) responds to a sort of image of the confrontation or confusion of identity – that is, that you're fighting within yourself between a sense of belonging to Britain and at the same time to India. Do you feel that sort of confusion?

That's very interesting. I'd never thought of it in that way. As far as the question of belonging is concerned, I think I belong to India but the moment I say that it becomes much more problematic, because I don't know exactly which India I belong to. Bengali culture is a profoundly middle-class culture. So you have a society of mainly old people and children, the people who have stayed on are like Bhaskar in *Freedom Song,* who has joined the Communist Party because he is not good for anything else. So the Bengal I grew up with, with its own language and its own culture, and which I consider psychologically to be home, no longer exists. Bombay, although I grew up there, I don't feel at home in, because I grew up in a corporate world, which is opposite to what you associate with home. So I feel I belong to India and in some ways I suppose I belong to England as well, having lived there for so many years.

Do you see yourself as a postcolonial writer? When you wrote that review of Rohinton Mistry's *Such a Long Journey* you commented on the condition of postcolonial writers. You said: 'Like most

postcolonial writers in English, he is something of an accident, the fortuitous meeting-place of a local sensibility and a foreign lan- guage. He is a writer who sings of his land but has no mother tongue with which to sing of it.' Then you mentioned that this writer living in Canada, and talking about his own country in a language that was not his homeland language. Do you see yourself similarly, when writing in England and in English about those memories of your homeland?

As I listened to you, I realized that my own views have changed, because I don't think English is a foreign language. But at the same time I don't think, as many people say, it's – in any sort of unproblematic way – an Indian language. Yes, it is a language used in India, it's an Indian lan- guage to me for all kinds of purposes, and yet it's not obviously an Indian language in the way Bengali or Sanskrit are Indian languages. The fact that we write in English, and we write in Bengali as well, has everything to do with colonialism. But why only call it colonialism? It is the condition of modernity, of industrialization.

Would you suggest another label?

No, because it's a very, very complicated area. One of the words, a very simple word, which we can use about late nineteenth-century or early twentieth-century Indian – or maybe Bengali – consciousness would be the adjective 'modern'. Another term for more recent movements in culture is the word 'post-independence', because there are marked dif- ferences in what it means to be an Indian, and part of the Indian nation state, after independence. . . . There is such a thing as Indian history quite independent of coloniality.

In some of your reviews you criticize the ignorance many West- erners have of India and the kind of clichés – the Orientalist views described by Said – that are applied to the East, because they offer stereotypes and false pictures of the reality of India. In your fiction

you present a view of India which is extremely lyrical, evocative. So isn't that to a certain extent the traditional view all of us in the West have of India?

There's a big difference, because at the same time I am quite unhappy about postcolonial theory, as far as that is applied to Indian culture. My problem with traditional Western ideas about India is that they never realize, and still don't realize, that India had a middle class; that India had a history, that in the nineteenth century and late eighteenth century, a middle class began to grow, and that these people were looking back at their own history, trying to make sense of it, and coming to terms with modernity. So India is ahistorical, the middle class is sort of elided, in that Western version of history. There are only fantastic things happening in India; India becomes a version of a myth or a fairy tale. I don't think Saidian criticism addresses the fact that India is not in every sense of the word just different from the West, and that that difference is just misunderstood by the West and misrepresented. In many ways India has a middle class which is very like the Western middle class, and that middle class has its own forms of oppression and its own 'others' within India.

Is your style influenced by Bengali literature, and particularly by Tagore's poetry? To what extent do you feel the Bengali influence is more important than the European heritage, because your writing seems to owe a lot to writers like Proust, in its dealing with memories, for instance?

I was never competent enough in Bengali to read much. But I have read Tagore's poetry; another poet who means a lot to me is a Bengali poet called Jibanananda Das. Ray's films meant a lot to me, and later on the writer Bibhuti Bhusan Bandyopadhyay, from whose novel *Pather Panchali* [1929] Satayajit Ray created his first film in 1955. That writer has meant a lot to me and I read him in Bengali and in translation. In his writing you find the very things you are talking about, the presence of memory and going backwards and forwards in time. I suppose among the English writers, or rather among writers in English, Katherine Mansfield and James Joyce.

Do you perceive a difference in the way the English literary establishment has read your novels and the Indian reception? One cannot possibly escape the 'Rushdie effect' in England after the 1980s, can one? Do you feel that you are being read as 'another' reflection of Indian writing in English?

The English literary establishment is not the only villain, they have their virtues as well, because while they are open to exotic representations of India, they are also open to the literary dimension of the work, the way a certain world has been transformed imaginatively into a work of fiction. Especially in post-independent India you have a pretty sententious Indian upper middle class, who are always claiming that they represent India; for me, they are a slightly more pernicious establishment than the British literary establishment. It's not that Rushdie's kind of writing has only been taken up by the British. I've met many people in England who have tired of that sort of work. But it's being taken up in a big way by the Indian upper middle class. I think that the Indian upper middle class who belong to Delhi, or Bombay or whatever, feel the need for a Rushdie all the time, because it speaks more to them, the historical narrative of Indian Independence, children at midnight, Partition, etc. Bengali writing has its own modern tradition, it's quite different. I feel that there are some members of the Indian upper middle class who feel slightly distant from my writing because it doesn't address those sub-Rushdiesque themes. So when I'm talking about India I'm talking about a particular, sort of subset Indian upper middle class, English-speaking. If I were to talk about the Bengali middle class, and Bengalis generally, I would say that their response has been less postcolonial-inflected and more literary.

Indian writing, and particularly Indian novels, have become popular in the West, and that is a consequence of that Rushdie influence, don't you think?

I don't think that the Indian novel has much of a space in the West; the Indian novel in English does, and the Indian novel in English after Rushdie. But as a writer friend of mine was saying the other day, 'The moment one door opens ten other doors close.' So you have one kind of Indian writer being made a fuss about, and you have ten other kinds of Indian writers who might be very good and who are not known. I think the most sophisticated, the most interesting writing in India has been done in the Indian languages. But no one knows about that writing over here. Perhaps gradually they will.

20

David Dabydeen

with

Mark Stein

David Dabydeen first became known for his prize-winning collection of Creole poems, Slave Song *(1984), which he had written as a student in Cambridge. He has since made his name not only as a poet but also as a novelist and author of many academic books. Dabydeen belongs to a generation of writers such as Grace Nichols, Fred D'Aguiar and Caryl Phillips who were born in the Caribbean but have spent the greater part of their lives abroad, writers who come between the generation of George Lamming, Wilson Harris and V. S. Naipaul, and younger British-born writers such as Zadie Smith and Diran Adebayo. His long poem* Turner *(1994) revisits J. M. W. Turner's painting* The Slave Ship, *and* A Harlot's Progress *(1999), his third novel, is in dialogue with Hogarth's title-giving series of prints. His books therefore write across time and genre, but they also cross geographies, as does his most recent novel* Our Lady of Demerara, *which is set in Ireland, Coventry and Guyana. Currently Dabydeen is co-editing the* Oxford Companion to Black British History.*

The dialogue which follows took place in June 1998, when the fiftieth anniversary of the arrival of the SS Empire Windrush *was celebrated in Britain. Landing at Tilbury in 1948, the ship had carried almost five hundred West Indian migrants and became the symbol for the beginning of large-scale post-war migration to Britain. This interview raises questions*

about the anniversary celebrations as well as the literature written in the
wake of Windrush.

Mark Stein All over Britain there are uncounted events to celebrate the *Windrush* jubilee. The BBC is doing a lot and there are the
books by Mike and Trevor Phillips [*Windrush: The Irresistible Rise
of Multi-Racial Britain*, 1998], Tony Sewell [*Keep on Moving*, 1988]
and Onyekachi Wambu [editor of *Empire Windrush: Fifty Years of
Writing About Black Britain*, 1998] . . .

David Dabydeen And a special issue of *Kunapipi*.

. . . Special issue of *Kunapipi*, edited by yourself. That's right! And
there are the readings, festivals, the processions, exhibitions, you
name it. The black weekly *New Nation* expresses fears of 'cash-ins'
on this important date. So that's one position. On the other hand,
however, there are complaints that the celebrations are actually
inadequate; that, for example, the exhibition *Windrush – Sea
Change* at the Museum of London is lacking in scope. People go
there and respond: 'It's too small. It's ridiculous. I've come all the
way from Birmingham to see it; to find out about my parents. And
it's so small!' How do you feel about it? What is your position on the
celebrations?

Well, West Indians always mutter, moan and complain. So it doesn't
matter what you put on, we are going to find some point of criticism. I
don't think that it's sad. My own understanding of what's been going
on is that there's been tremendous coverage of the *Windrush* anniversary. The BBC has really highlighted the *Windrush*, the television
and radio programmes; the publications. Now people know about the
Empire Windrush in general; who would've even known there was a
fiftieth anniversary before the celebrations started? Now more or less
the whole nation knows. The whole nation knows to such an extent
that I get race hate mail. Yesterday I received a 'nigger-coon' set of

cartoons with a leaflet from the French National Front and the German fascists, and a calling card from the British fascists.

That came through the post?

It arrived in the post addressed to: Dr Dabydeen, Warwick University. That indicates that at least the events surrounding the *Windrush*, and the *Windrush* itself, have actually become embedded in the consciousness of the people. So therefore, we can't moan and complain. To say that people are cashing in is absolute nonsense. You know black people don't have much commercial value in the society. What, people are gonna buy our T-shirts? Or, are they gonna make a boat called the *Windrush* and sail to the Caribbean? It's just inevitable carping.

What is the meaning of the *Windrush* today? Five decades ago it stood for the beginning of large-scale post-World War II migration. What does it mean in 1998? What is the status of the *SS Empire Windrush* in the political unconscious of Britain today?

Thinking about the past thirty years that I have lived in Britain, I can say with some conviction that there is a much greater awareness now of people of West Indian origin as full citizens of the country deserving of the benefits as well as responsibilities of citizenship. For example, the word 'repatriation' is no longer part of the political vocabulary. When I was growing up in the 1970s in Britain, repatriation was the buzz term, the Powellite term. Now it's totally dead. It's impossible to talk about repatriation. So the fiftieth anniversary of the *Windrush* has really just acknowledged that we are now third- or fourth-generation people. As John Agard says facetiously, 'I like grey, / I'm here to stay.'

It's interesting, that point, because in their book *The Irresistible Rise of Multi-Racial Britain*, Mike and Trevor Phillips feel somewhat uneasy about the *Windrush* as a myth. The arrival of the *Windrush* can either mean, like you said, 'We're here to stay'. But Mike and

Trevor Phillips are saying there is a danger, with the celebration as well, that by remembering the arrival one emphasizes the fact that British Caribbean citizens actually first had to arrive. British Caribbean citizens are thus being relegated to the status of arrivants even when they constitute a second, third or even a fourth generation of black Britons. So is the celebration of the arrival not a double-edged thing?

Well it's not double-edged at all. I think these are some nice points. But the fact is we did arrive. There was an arrival. We may have been in the country since Roman times, dotted here and there, a few thousands, but the fact is we arrived really in 1948 in large numbers. So why not mark the arrival? And of course I am an arrivant. I have no problem in calling myself an immigrant. Even though I'm settled here, I was once an immigrant. The modern condition is one of migrancy. We are here to stay but we are also here to move on if necessary, and emigrate and go back to the Caribbean and go anywhere else, with our British passports. So, I think those kinds of criticisms are a kind of carping. I see nothing wrong in saying we are immigrants: we were immigrants. Many of us are still immigrants. Intellectually or imaginatively we have not settled in the country. I remember Roy Heath, the Guyanese novelist, saying that although he has been in Britain for forty-five years he still dreams about Guyana and writes about Guyana and he can't write about England. Not because England is unworthy of description in that sense. But because imaginatively he is still a migrant.

Is that the same for you?

Yeah, as a writer, sure.

But also in terms of the memories of Guyana? Is that something that has remained more vivid?

Yes. I think of Guyana constantly. I've just come back from Guyana.

The first ten, twelve years of your life are the formative years. I spent thirteen years there. Those are the experiences that form your character. Some people say writing is just about explorations and re-explorations of childhood experiences. So in a sense: yes, I feel Guyanese. . . . The non-writing part of me, the restrained part of me is Britain. The imaginative part of me is Guyana. But then one can't have these easy dichotomies either; but you know what I mean, there are grey areas as well.

But in your fiction and poetry you do write about Britain and you've done that since *Coolie Odyssey* [1988] and *The Intended* [1991].

Well, the novel I've just finished is called *A Harlot's Progress*, which is based on the Hogarth painting. It is set in eighteenth-century London but it's also set in an imagined Africa. I could not just write about England. It has to be England in relation to Africa, India or the Caribbean.

You're always transcending Britain?

Well it's not transcending. It's a kind of double-consciousness, isn't it? We're all doubled-over. Either in the dockyards, lifting all that heavy stuff, or Caliban doubled over by the log. Now we're doubled over in terms of an imaginative life.

You're influenced by V. S. Naipaul; for example your novel *Disappearance* [1993] writes back to his *The Enigma of Arrival* [1987]. Is there a general point one could make about the influence of the *Windrush* writers on the second and third generation of writers such as Caryl Phillips, Fred D'Aguiar or Grace Nichols?

I can say it in one simple word: they achieved. Forget their themes or forget their concerns. The very fact that they achieved meant that it was relatively easier for us to publish because there was already Derek

Walcott, there was already George Lamming, there was already Sam
Selvon, there was especially V. S. Naipaul. However much we criticize
Naipaul, let's not forget that he opened up a lot of doors, indirectly, to
people like myself. So, you had a sense that there was a body of writing
to which you had a certain responsibility and which also presented a
challenge. I mean how can you write the sea in the way that Walcott
writes it? Or how can you write the Guyana landscape in a better way,
or with more excellence than the way Wilson Harris does it? In a sense
we are a poor generation of writers. When you're following Walcott
and when you're following Lamming, certainly when you're following
Naipaul, how can you achieve excellence? Our literary ancestors really
sit on our shoulders. How do you follow T. S. Eliot, you know? Sometimes I think we're just marking ground for another Renaissance in the
next millennium. In other words, the presence of these writers who
were excellent must breed a certain modesty in us. I hate blurbs now.
When I was younger, I liked to have lovely blurbs that said 'what an
excellent writer'. But now I think some of these blurbs are tremen-
dously embarrassing. When I see things like 'a great literary giant' in
relation to some of my friends or, in relation to me, 'a powerful Caribbean lyrical voice', I think: 'No! No! No! Come on!' These things are
nonsensical compared to Walcott. Compared to Naipaul we are still . . .
We've only just written four, five novels. Two, three books of poems.
These judgements should only come at the end of one's career.

**But isn't this kind of promotion and hype, which may in fact only be
partly justified, resulting from quite a big interest in black British,
and in Caribbean writing?**

We must not overstate the achievement of it; some of it is very bad. I
mean there is stuff that I've written, that I certainly would not have
written. And so therefore it's literature in the making and should be
acknowledged as that rather than lauded as part of a major contribution to a major tradition of English. It has its beauties and it has its
tremendous failures. We have to be honest enough to cast a cold eye, a

critical eye on what is being written, rather than adopting a kind of adulatory or valorizing attitude towards it.

From which perspective can we do that? With reference to the 'first generation' one could say: 'That is the standard by which the literature that is following has to be measured.' But this is only one of the traditions being pursued. You are writing in Britain, within the context of British writing; you are writing within a context of black British literature; but then you're writing after Caribbean writers too.

Yes, but you can read a Russian novel, you can read *The Brothers Karamazov* and still read it sensitively and intelligently, although it is set in Russia in a time span that is different from yours. I can't come up with a critical aesthetic on the spot. I'm arguing for a close reading of texts, really. And the same sensitivity and critical faculties that have brought to bear on other literatures should also be applied to ours. There can be an over-sensitivity to what we write. And a critical reticence based on the grievances of history. You know: 'This is black stuff, so let's leave it alone in case we offend people.' I have to say for some reason I've been exempt from this 'care'. I get some severe lashings by these white people. Sometimes I just wish that they would just shut up and go away.

Are you retreating from a postcolonial framework of reading when advocating close readings as opposed to a 'special interest'?

Well is it moving away? It is actually trying to say that one can still read the literature within postcolonial frames. Though it's best not to impose any kind of frame onto readings. But a postcolonial frame can give a very rich, politically astute reading of the writing. I'm not arguing against that. What I'm arguing for, really, is the end of kid gloves. Let's have a bloody fight now. Let us now engage in combat. Because before I was winning all the time. Because of history you have made some space for me to win. Let's engage in serious dialogue, critical, intellectual, literary dialogue. And then, you see, we are then properly tested and assessed.

Do you want to say something about new poetry and also about your new novel? You said it's just been accepted by Cape and could you maybe just say what it's about?

The new novel is set in England in the eighteenth century and it's a rewriting, if that's the word, of a Hogarth painting. A very famous Hogarth painting, the first English painting to represent the lives of the common people in paint rather than in print. At a time when paint was for the depiction of aristocratic life and religious subjects, Hogarth painted prostitutes and lepers, blacks and Jews. [The painting] has an anti-Semitic slant, so I take this up in the novel and explore the Jewish character. But basically it is a rewriting of the scenes of *A Harlot's Progress*; a reconfiguration of them, rather than rewriting. It has a black character as the narrator, so it's England from eighteenth-century black eyes. But of course it has resonances of today; it's eighteenth century only in form.

What's the text's relationship to Equiano's *Interesting Narrative* [1789]?

Well, very important! The writer who has really influenced me emotionally, has been Equiano. Equiano is somebody who has definitely entered into my writing, almost like a posthumous spirit or a posthumous presence. So it's a novel by Equiano, of course. A novel about writing, a novel about arriving at the state of writing in the way that Equiano had to in the eighteenth century.

21

Jackie Kay

with

Richard Dyer

Poet, playwright and novelist Jackie Kay was born in 1961, in Edinburgh, Scotland. Her mother was Scottish and her father Nigerian. She was adopted by a white couple and brought up in Glasgow. Having studied at the Royal Scottish Academy of Music and Drama and Stirling University, where she read English, she later moved to London and eventually to Manchester. The experience of being adopted by and growing up within a white family inspired her first collection of poetry, The Adoption Papers *(1991). The poems deal with an adopted child's search for a cultural identity and are told through three different voices: an adoptive mother, a birth mother and a daughter. The collection won a Scottish Arts Council Book Award and a commendation by the Forward Poetry Prize judges in 1992. The poems in her second collection,* Other Lovers *(1993), explore the role and power of language, inspired and influenced by the history of Afro-Caribbean people, the story of a search for identity grounded in the experience of slavery. The collection includes a sequence of poems about the blues singer Bessie Smith.*

Kay's poems have appeared in many anthologies and she has written widely for stage and television. Twice Through the Heart *(1997) was a poetry documentary for BBC2 and became an English National Opera song cycle. Her first novel,* Trumpet, *published in 1998, was awarded the Guardian Fiction Prize. Inspired by the life of musician Billy Tipton, the novel tells the story of Scottish jazz trumpeter Joss Moody, whose death revealed that he was, in fact, a woman. Kay's most recent book,* Why Don't You Stop Talking *(2002), is a collection of short stories. She has also published a novel for children,* Strawgirl *(2002), and a new poetry collection,* New and Selected Poems, *is due in 2004. This interview centres on her 1998 collection of poetry,* Off Colour, *which explores themes of sickness, health and disease through personal experience and metaphor.*

Richard Dyer Have you been 'keeping by' the poems in the collection for some time, because they seem to work as a coherent whole?

Jackie Kay Yes. I've been working on *Off Colour* for about four years and I had a concept of what I wanted to do in the book so that each poem would relate to each other and they would all relate to the general theme which I had loosely in my head as illness.

I like the use of the title *Off Colour* as it refers not only to not feeling well, but possibly also to being of mixed race.

No, I hadn't thought of that. What I did think of was 'of colour', that the book also concerned colour and race. I didn't think of it being to do with the actual hue of mixed-race people.

I was looking at Alastair Niven's comments on the back of the collection and wondered how you felt about terms like 'black poet', 'Scottish poet', 'feminist poet'. Do you think it is possible to construct yourself outside of those terms, or are they always constricting, confining and defining?

They do ultimately become very dull, those terms, because they tend to box you in and give people an expectation of you. It's liberating to define yourself if you are the one that's doing the defining, but when other people are constantly doing the defining and when all they ever do is define the Other in society, the black person, the gay person, the woman, then they assume that the white heterosexual man is the norm and everybody else deviates from that. You don't get the likes of Ted Hughes or Andrew Motion being described as white, male, middle-class and heterosexual. And if every time they were written about they had to face these terms it would really be a pain in the arse for them, so why should I have to put up with it?

Even when people use it positively, in the sense that Alastair was, it's still constraining in a way, because you write about the things you write about because they are what concern you and some things happen to be about race or whatever, but they don't have to be.

No, they don't have to be. I do think that black writers have it much tougher than white writers in the sense that there are expectations as to what their subject matter should be. So it means that if a black writer writes a negative black character then they get accused of negative racial stereotyping, whereas if a white writer writes a negative white character they don't get accused of the same thing. It does become very difficult. You have to really clear your mind of all that and write what you really want to write and let absolutely nobody tell you what you can or can't write.

So you aren't writing for anyone or for any agenda?

No. I write for myself. I mean if other people get something from it and are moved by it or think about their own lives then that's great because I think that when we read, reading is just a search for ourselves and when we really like a book it's because something in the book seems to have understood us, or seems to have known our secrets. But I don't have a sort of 'I want all black people to read my books' or 'I want all women to read my books'. I don't mind who my readers are. I mean of course it's great if you do have lots of black readers but I don't write aiming at a particular sector of the community in that way.

Because for you it would be a very false position.

It would be because it wouldn't come naturally to me. Perhaps if I'd been brought up in a black community with a black language, it would be easier. You know like Toni Morrison says, for instance, that she writes for black people, if other people get something from it, fair enough. I admire that.

When you said we like a book because it seems to have understood us, to have been where we have been, I had that feeling with one of the poems you wrote about your mother, 'Lucozade'. There are three poems about mother figures: 'Bed', 'From Stranraer, South', but particularly in 'Lucozade' you've gone right inside the experience, you've not held back. Did you find it very difficult to write?

Well, it was a strange mixture. 'Lucozade' is a personal poem, an autobiographical poem in a sense, because my mother was frequently ill throughout my childhood and that created a different set of imaginings, fearful imaginings. And 'Bed' and 'From Stranraer, South' are both fictional poems on the same theme and taken from things that I know, but not specifically autobiographical. The mother in that ['Bed'] is more like my gran, more like a particular kind of Scottish woman who thrives on being a martyr, and on being hard done by, and that character really interests me as a writer.

I wonder if there's something about the fact that 'Lucozade' is closely based on personal experience and the other two poems about mothers are not, that has something to do with the intensity of the poem, even though on the surface it seems to be about a much more slight subject matter, in fact it's much more powerful.

When you write about things that are completely true to you you can write more powerfully, but also the opposite is true. You can write very badly when things are true to you because you are no longer objective and you want to get the whole memory in; it doesn't matter if it happened or if it didn't happen, what matters is the poem, and the poem has its own memory and its own set of circumstances, so when you do write about your own life you've got to be able to transcend those local details and find a way back into the memory that isn't too specific but is detailed enough to make it moving.

You were saying earlier about writing the collection at the same time as *Trumpet*. Many of the poems in *Off Colour* are about death and illness, as is *Trumpet*. It seems to me that *Trumpet* is more about death, rather than crossing gender barriers, which is a very interesting theme in itself. But most of the writing in the novel seemed to be exploring death and bereavement, and that's from a non-autobiographical perspective, whereas a lot of the poems are autobiographical. Do you think it's because in poetry exploring personal situations is more possible, whereas in the novel it's excluded or it's not legitimate?

There are certain things that I could never dream of doing in a piece of fiction that I could do in a poem and vice versa. I think there are different intimacies that you can get from each and different revelations. But certainly I would be more comfortable revealing almost straightforward autobiographical things in poetry than I would in fiction. In a novel it would always be much more fictionalized; even if I was using my own life nobody would know except for little tricks that I might play on the reader! Like Colman [the son of the jazz trumpeter in *Trumpet*] has the same details as my own adoption. I think that we are all not that different really; I think any fears, or dreams, or hopes or anxieties I might have, you might also have. So I always write from the knowledge that we share a very common humanity with other people.

Was it very difficult, switching from the sort of feeling you had when you were writing the poems, to then writing the novel? Did different

ideas present themselves as being expressible either as a poem or as fiction?

I don't usually have an idea and think, 'Well how will I do this?' *Trumpet* had to be a novel and *Off Colour* had to be a book of poems and I already knew that, it kind of comes fully clothed and it's already got a walk and a gender, a colour. It's already got a shape.

Do you think it's possible to write about something without actually having experienced it? Like the way you write about death and bereavement. I presume you haven't personally experienced all the things that you write about in these poems?

I suppose you can write about something even when you haven't experienced it. I've never actually experienced bereavement in a big way. I mean I had my gran die when I was wee, and my grandpa, but I've not had a very close lover or a very close friend die, touch wood! I think that writing is a curious mixture of what you experience yourself first and then what you glean from other people's experiences. One quality I do think you need to have as a writer is empathy, and then you can write about bereavement even if you haven't experienced it.

When you articulate the experience and histories of black figures from Britain's past, such as in 'Hottentot Venus', 'Christian Sanderson' and 'Gambia', do you feel it's like an act of reparation, a reimbursement of dignity?

Yes, that's a good way to put it. I think the history that children are taught in schools, British history, doesn't really include black people, and yet black people have been part of this country's history long, long before the *Windrush*. I did a lot of research into various black people that lived in Britain and I found it quite exciting, liberating in fact, to find knowledge of these people. And I thought how sad that these people appear for a moment, and usually they appear because they are connected with someone who is famous or because they have committed some crime, then they disappear from the records once they have been transported to Australia. You catch a glimpse of them, and what I wanted to do in writing those poems was capture that glimpse so that that person would stay and wouldn't disappear, and anybody else that is interested in black British history could read those poems and find out more about those people so they don't become part of the vast disappeared, the black people throughout history in fact who have just disappeared without trace or record of themselves, in the way that working people disappear. Whose history gets recorded?

It's very selective, history, I mean what's called history.

Yes, middle-class history, so I think it is very important to bring people to life as a writer and that's one of the things that I'm interested in doing.

How did you find out about Christian Sanderson, and who is she?

Through this Edinburgh historian who was going through the records of people that had been deported, it said 'Christian Sanderson' and it said 'Mulatto' next to the record, the details in the poem were true – that she was sent to Australia for seven years for stealing sixteen shillings. There are a few people that always get trotted out, like Olaudah Equiano, and Ignatius Sancho, but this historian was finding people that were unknown. I was particularly interested in Christian Sanderson because she was from Edinburgh and I was born in Edinburgh and I was trying to think of how she would have spoken. So writing about her is in a way writing about myself only it's a different time-period.

How did you actually evolve the concept of the virus poems, which break into the text intermittently and infect the other poems with their own lines, and it seems, with their own ideas as well, bleeding into the preceding and following poem?

Well that was in my original idea for the book. In fact I wanted to write a book of poems that would be about viruses; mental, physical, spiritual, societal and historical. I'm very interested in the way that sicknesses change shape and evolve. Even now, we have various forms of bacteria that outwit medical science, so I wanted to find a structure that would reflect that, how illness changes people's identity, how viruses go in and literally eat from the blood, so the virus actually sucks from one poem and then leads on to the other. It's just the same as if you were infected by the common cold and you pass it on to someone through sneezing or snogging or whatever. So the virus in the poems is a way of doing that. One poem snogging another!

Do you think that writing poems about illness, madness and death is a way of exorcizing those states of terror and dread, a way of neutralizing memories or fears?

When you're frightened of death it's quite interesting to write about it. I did feel quite superstitious when I was writing the whole book. You know sometimes you get paranoid and you think that you've got illnesses, the whole mood of the book did affect how I felt myself, it just began to make me feel quite ill!

In 'The Black Chair' you bring out certain aspects of a visit to the dentist – the sensuality and the eroticism that is part of the enforced intimacy of that situation. Is that something that has come out of personal experience, or were you just . . . trying it on for size?

That's really funny, but no it didn't come out of personal experience except that I met a dentist on an Arvon course. She was talking about how dentists are maligned and how it just feels awful to be a dentist and she was thinking of giving it up altogether because she felt so hated by everybody and that gave me a wonderful idea. And I thought, well you could write a love poem to a dentist and what would that be like? I'm also very interested in teeth because they tell us so much about ourselves. We do have a journey of life, from milk teeth to teeth now, and then middle age teeth and false teeth.

There are quite a few poems about teeth. I'm thinking of the Joy Gardner one, which uses teeth as a fulcrum point to talk about racism, as do other poems like 'Race, Racist, Racism'. Do you think racism is a fact of society, or do you think it's something that can be eliminated or reduced by education?

It really feels very sad to be going into the next millennium with something like the Stephen Lawrence case having just happened and living in a country where the police still are very racist, where black people are being murdered and victimized. You *can* educate and change people's attitudes towards things, as we have done in the past, and things have changed so we mustn't be totally pessimistic, but I don't know that you can completely get rid of racism. You would think that after fascism and after the guilt that there would be no young Nazi movement possible in Germany and yet they are thriving at the moment, so it is horrendous how history has cycles as well, like illnesses and viruses. You would need every single country in the world, from the roots of the country upwards, in its institutions, laws, images, advertising, media and its arts and culture, to have an awareness of the destructiveness of racism, and we don't have that. I don't think children are instinctively racist. They just learn those things from their parents.

You mentioned earlier about a strange poem, 'Somebody Else', which at first appears to be quite humorous but then reading it over and over, I found there was something in it that was much deeper. There's that line, 'I have been somebody else all my life'.

It is a sad poem, it is really about being adopted in a sense. When you are adopted you always have this possibility of having been somebody else. Literally, you are born with a different name and with a different set of parents, so really it's about the fact that you would have had a different fate altogether. Sometimes you know what fate you would have had if you trace your biological parents. In any case it would have been somebody else, some other life, some other name. I don't think I would have been a writer if I hadn't been adopted. I think about it quite a lot. I'm very positive about being adopted and I'm really glad that I was. The other me is just behind me or just to the side of me. I think lots of people (adopted or not) have a sense of this other self that they could have been. People who are gay for instance and are not openly gay live their life as somebody else all the time.

When I read your poems I've always got your voice in my head because I've heard you read many times, but sometimes it suddenly exaggerates when you are taking on the voice of certain characters, usually from the older generation, from Glasgow, that particular brogue, and the way you have of writing particular words and at first one thinks 'What is that word?', then it suddenly becomes obvious. Is there intended to be an element of humour there or is that something to do with an English ear misreading it because the Glasgow accent is always seen as comical by the English?

Yes, for me it's meant to be funny. Often I use it for emphasis or because I want to give a certain sense of a particular character. I think that the language that you choose for any given poem is really important. In *Off Colour* there is Ma Broon, who does actually speak like that, that's the language from the Broons [a well-known Scottish cartoon family]. It's almost like a kind of pastiche. The Scottish folk have done it to themselves.

What do you think of the concept of moving a poem over to a completely different medium – as happened with your epic poem 'Sabbath', which was made into a television feature film? – When one has an actor reading it can sound dreadful because they do this terrible 'actor thing' to it.

I think it's better to have the poet's voice, but I also like the idea that poetry can be read by actors or performed on television or made into news. I think there's lots of potential for poetry to be seen and merged with other mediums. The six o'clock news in poetry. It would be nice if it really entered the fabric of people's lives in the way that say, initiatives like Poetry on the Underground does, rather than just being something that one or two people read in small magazines. I like the idea that you write but other people can do something else with it afterwards. I like the idea of it having more than one life. I think poems should have more than one life, about as many as cats!

I was very struck by 'Pride', the last poem in the collection, where the black man on the train recognizes that you are part Ibo, and you use that very potent metaphor of the map: 'There was a moment when my whole face turned into a map, / and the stranger on the train / located even the name / of my village in Nigeria / in the lower part of my jaw'. Are you interested in tracing your birth parents, in discovering aspects of your African ancestry?

I'm interested in writing about it. I don't know that I'm interested in actually doing it, and I like the idea that your face is a map. Just like you can trace maps you can trace faces. I liked writing a poem about strangers on a train. . . . It did actually happen to me and sometimes when things happen to you, you know you have got to find a way to write them. I mean there's all sorts of things that we take out, like when he offered me some of his meat pattie I said, 'No, I'm vegetarian', but I couldn't put that in the poem! If you are adopted you do have a curiosity about your original parents and some day I might trace my birth father but I don't know. I'd need to get on and do it quite soon before everybody dies. I don't know if I could be doing with the upheaval of it all, the disruption of your life. It's like what we were talking about earlier, with this other life. If you trace, then you go into this other life and you are not meant to be in that life, you're in this one. I think that is why people find it so traumatic when they do trace because then they are trying to have two lives simultaneously as one, and they can't merge them. In fact that's explained it to me, why I haven't traced. It's funny how I didn't really know that.

And in that same poem you have a sort of epiphany where you envisage yourself going back to your village, and you are welcomed by the old people of the village, you start to dance: 'I danced a dance I never knew I knew / Words and sounds fell out of my mouth like seeds.' Again, following on from birth parents and whether or not to trace them, is it the same thing with your African heritage, I mean is it something that is desired or not? Do you feel any link – would you ever go to Africa for that reason?

I think if I went to Africa I would definitely feel a link and I think there must be things in me that are definitely African that I don't even know about, and definitely Nigerian. Probably I would find things about myself that would surprise me but I don't know that I would set off to do that deliberately. It would be great if it happened by accident rather than by design, because there is a kind of difficulty in being black and British or being African-Scottish or whatever, however you want to put it, in that you are born here, you are brought up here, then you call Africa your roots, but how much of it is your roots when you've never been there and you don't know its traditions, culture and language and you could be rejected by its people?

You can't say that you're half-Scottish and half-African, because you are much more Scottish than you are African, in terms of culture.

That's right, and it seems to me that we get encouraged to do this because of racism, because of all these forces around us that make us cling to something that we see as positive.

But in a way it's a false process, because there are lots of people who were born in Britain of African decent who feel that they are missing something, a notional idea of 'African roots'.

That's right, I've become very wary of it because how much is that authentically and genuinely you? I could go there and find lots of things that were genuinely me, or I could go there and find nothing, but either way, I wouldn't say that I had to do it in order to know myself because I feel I already do.

22

Michael Ondaatje
with
Maya Jaggi

Michael Ondaatje was born in 1943 in Colombo, and moved to England at eleven, then to Canada at nineteen. His novel The English Patient *(1992) co-won the Booker Prize and in 1996 became a Hollywood film, which won nine Oscars. He has written ten volumes of poetry, and among his prose works are* The Collected Works of Billy the Kid *(1970),* Coming Through Slaughter *(1976),* Running in the Family *(1982), and* In the Skin of a Lion *(1987). He edited* The Faber Book of Contemporary Canadian Short Stories *(1990) and* The Brick Reader *(1991). His latest novel,* Anil's Ghost *(2000), is set amid the Sri Lankan War between the mid-1980s and early 1990s. Anil Tissera, a Sri Lankan-born, US-based forensic anthropologist, gathers evidence for an international human rights body to identify an exhumed skeleton, dubbed 'Sailor', as a victim of government 'counter-terror' – a 'representative of all those lost voices' amid a 'casual sense of massacre', where truth is 'a flame against a sleeping lake of petrol'. She works with the archaeologist Sarath; his brother Gamini, who is a doctor at the war front; and the gem-miner and Buddhist eye-painter Ananda, who is grieving for his wife.*

Maya Jaggi *Anil's Ghost* is your first novel set in Sri Lanka. You've described the experience of *The English Patient* as a 'gift'. Did that gift give you the freedom to write this new novel?

Michael Ondaatje It was a gift. I don't know how many writers have this chance given to them, of being able to write without worrying. I would have written this book anyway, but whereas people expected me to write a romance set somewhere else, it allowed me to write exactly what I wanted. Once you become that public, everyone has an opinion about what you should do, what you *could* do, even. So you become secretive, and do something not expected. *Anil's Ghost* was the only thing I could have done, only I didn't know how to do it; I had no idea how to write this book.

What made you tackle Sri Lanka's civil war?

I've always been aware of the conflict. Part of the problem is that I'm well known in the West, and not many Sri Lankan novelists are. What worried me is that this book would get taken as representative; I do backflips to avoid that. There's a tendency with us in Canada to say, this is a book 'about Sri Lanka'. But it isn't a statement about the war, as though this is the 'true and only story'. It's my individual take on four or five characters, a personal tunnelling.

It wasn't that you felt a sense of responsibility, as the best-known Sri Lankan writer, to make the country's plight better known?

No, because that would seem didactic; that 'Hey, now I've got you, I'm going to make you listen to a lecture'. But I remember reading the Indian myth, 'The King and the Corpse'. It's a strange, nightmarish tale about a king who ends up with a body round his neck that he has to be responsible for. I quote it briefly in the book. The king keeps burying the body, but he wakes up the next morning and it's round his neck again. Without making too many parallels about trying to save a community, it hit me that Anil has that same kind of obsession with the skeleton – not letting go of it.

You've said your prose begins with fragments of images or facts. How did *Anil's Ghost* begin?

When I finished *The English Patient*, I wanted to write poetry again; I hadn't for a long time. So I began with *Handwriting* [1998], and the tradition of Buddhist statues being stolen and buried, and moved around and reburied, and it seemed a strange parallel to what was going on politically. *Anil's Ghost* began slowly, through an archaeological angle and the idea of unburials. I've always been interested in archaeology. There were also a couple of characters I worked on. I wanted to write a poem about a man – Ananda – and a wife who are separated by violence. *Anil's Ghost* has Ananda at a later stage in his life, as opposed to his courtship. It was almost through the poems that I found a situation. But there was no one image like the plane crash in *The English Patient*. Perhaps it was the Anil character, too – the idea of somebody coming back to a country.

Though when *Handwriting* came out, you said you didn't want to do the novel of a Sri Lankan who goes back 'home'.

I didn't want *Handwriting* to be a book about myself. *Handwriting* was very important to me as a book; it and *Anil's Ghost* go hand in hand. But what I didn't want was a sequence of autobiographical poems where I returned and rewrote Sri Lanka. The few poems that are personal, such as one about the woman who looks like my mother on the plane, come intentionally quite late in the book. They grow up in a historical world. I don't think *Anil's Ghost* is an autobiographical book. It's quite a personal book. Anil's return is ironic, because she doesn't really know the country very well; she has to relearn it.

Is that what you were doing with *Handwriting* – relearning Sri Lanka with its ancient calligraphy, Buddhist statues and sacred eye-painting?

Yes, I was relearning an awareness of a deeper historical portrait of the place, not just the contemporary snapshot we get in the West.

Anil's Ghost spells out the dangers of political tourism: 'the history of the past 200 years of Western political writing – go home, write a book, hit the circuit'. How does a writer from abroad safeguard against that kind of literary tourism?

I don't know, it's a real problem. I'm sure I'm just as guilty as anyone. That's why I didn't want to make assured judgements about what should be done – which is often incendiary and facile. I think there was a responsibility. It was easier to write *Running in the Family* because it was about my family; I could be jokey and outrageous. But that side of my writing wasn't in this book. I was very careful to try and avoid the easy solutions.

You consciously don't end with Anil leaving on a plane to the US; we stay with Ananda and the country Anil has left.

Yes, I really didn't want to have that kind of ending. We stay with what she's left behind. I think that remark by John Berger, 'Never again will a single story be told as though it were the only one', is a crucial remark. I was therefore trying to work against that tone of voice, of the 'returner'.

Your early novels took subjects – *Billy the Kid*, for example, and the cornet player Buddy Bolden – where there were few historical facts, so you could invent them. But here there are public events, such as the suicide bomb that mirrors the 1993 assassination of President Premedasa. Why?

There is a still a lot of invention. I wasn't trying to write a formal document. It is still very much a fictional world. I wanted to write the situation of the individual in a country like this. I was more interested in how people live: how fear affects you, and denial. In many ways, the book isn't just about Sri Lanka; it could be Guatemala or Bosnia or Ireland. Such stories are very familiar in other parts of the world.

Did you go on specific research trips?

To a certain extent. It was more a case of listening and talking to people; being passive in the way I listened, which I tend to do with a book, rather than going out and trying to grab 'the truth', as we do in the West, as though we know how we can solve the dilemma; as if we would know how to fix it. Most of the book takes place in private. The public events are very brief, and there is a huge gap between the public and the private.

You've said fiction is always the unofficial story, and that you're interested in 'unhistorical lives'.

I still believe that. The morality comes with what you decide to write about, as opposed to what your judgements are; you decide to write about individuals who are working as doctors, rather than about New York society or Hollywood, or the presidential race. Our newspapers are full of official stories, and what the novelist is responsible for is something unhistorical, unofficial – what goes on in private. That's what interests me. I was thinking, what do I like most about *Anil's Ghost*? It was a scene when Gamini doesn't want to embrace Sarath's wife because she'd discover how thin he is. For me, that is a heartbreaking moment, light years away from the official stories.

Your characters tend to love their work. What's your interest in this?

One of the dangers of being a fiction writer is, if you invent, you want to take off from something firm. To write about doctors in an abstract way means you end up with something fanciful. I think we are governed as characters physically by what we do. I am a writer. I sit down four or five hours alone every day, and it makes me a certain kind of personality – and I don't think writers are any better than doctors or archaeologists or trumpet players. What people do is *a way* of getting close to how they think. Rather than having a third-person narrator telling us what Gamini thinks, we can see what he's like, though he's so exhausted he is not even thinking; he's slipping into dreams. So when I'm writing, there is a process of learning. Rather than going into a book knowing what I am going to do, which would bore the hell out of me, I want to know how a doctor works, or how a musician works. So you try and find out how bridges are built in Toronto in 1920, and it's quite difficult because the people who do that are often not very verbal. But that doesn't matter because this isn't drama; you often get one image from a small gesture and can build a whole book from that.

Anil, who is Sinhalese, is reunited with her Tamil ayah, and there's a sense in the novel of fractricide, of a family at war. Do you think your own mixed Tamil, Sinhalese and Dutch ancestry has shaped your view of the conflict?

Sure; my background is a real mixed salad, so it's difficult to know what I am. I think it is kind of true. Though I don't know if I have more validity because I'm more of a mixture. I'm also seeing it from the Western point of view. I certainly don't think there is one side to the story; there's no easy right or wrong. The tragedy is that it's a country that is completely multicultural and multi-religious, but rather than celebrating that these splits happen.

The archeologist Palipana says, 'there has always been slaughter in passion', and Anil stabs her lover to break free of him. Was there an analogy with political separatism?

Yes, though it was something that hit me later, of course! To start to have a bird's eye view of *Anil's Ghost* now, after writing it, is strange. But I think one of the things I did almost subconsciously recognize was that everything in the book becomes about one thing: separation. It's almost as though love has disappeared; it's a very celibate book. I wanted to call one chapter 'Celibacy'; everything was in the past or repressed. It's strange: you spend eight years doing something and find you have only used three or four colours; you don't step into other spectrums. This is not a conscious thing. If I planned a book too carefully, I know that it would have been too loaded, or heavy-handed. As a reader, I would be aware of the preparations. That is why I write not sure where the novel's going. Themes take care of themselves. I am much more interested in how a scene works. The focus is more on the emotional element of the story, as opposed to a thematic line.

You've said the Anil figure is not autobiographical. But there's a point when she refers to Sri Lankans as 'us'. Was there such a moment of identification for you?

I definitely had that identification with Sri Lanka; I don't feel I'm solely North American. Sri Lanka's a place I still feel very much a part of. No book survives in a vacuum: the context for this book is all the other books. Obviously, they are part of the same person; there are habits. But to me, the voice in this book is very different from the other books; it's a different vocabulary at work.

In your family memoir *Running in the Family* you talk of 'running to Asia', saying: 'In my mid-thirties I realized I had slipped past a childhood I had ignored and not understood.' Why had you, and what was the trigger for going back?

It wasn't so much ignoring it, as surviving in the West. I was eleven when I came to England, and it was more a case of having to adapt very fast to a different way of life, having to deal with what was around you. Then, when I went to Canada, I literally couldn't afford to go back to Sri Lanka. It was quite a long time before I could. It was very present in me at that time, but far away too. Then later I'd made a film about a theatre company in Canada, with a director friend, Paul Thompson, who grew up in a farming community in Ontario. He went back there with actors, and they made a play about it. I made a documentary called *The Clinton Special* [1972] about the process. Paul had in effect made a regional memoir, and there are those regional writers I love and envy, like William Faulkner or Alice Munro. A lot of writers like us who are nomadic don't have those deep regional roots, those wells, and you envy that. I decided I also wanted to do something like that; it was a test, a new discovery.

Your parents separated when you were five. Was yours a 'wonderful childhood', or what your sister called a 'nightmare'?

It was an easier childhood for me being the youngest. I remember very vividly feeling 'solitary'; not so much feeling alone, but scattered with uncles and aunts. I guess I had lost my childhood. I suppose in *Running in the Family* I was really reinventing it; maybe that has something to do with nostalgia. But going back to places jolts your memory; they become the source of memory in a strange way.

One critic called your view of character 'forensic'.

I don't like novels where the author seems to know the characters completely. I like novels where, when they're off stage, they're off stage and we don't know what happens to them. The ending isn't a closed door. I love the idea of characters having lives outside the book, grow-ing in the scenes where they're not there. It makes such characters equal to the writer, and to the reader as well. Books where you can sense the author talking down to the characters like puppets don't interest me. In all the books there are mysteries that are not fully told; everyone has secrets from the other characters, and also from the author and the reader.

While you were writing *Running in the Family* you went through a divorce. Did that affect the book?

You write books when you need to write them. I had already started writing *Running in the Family*, but it was very light, with comedy and verse. Then there was a pause and I realized that if I was going to go further, I had to write about the darker nature of my father. Why do people write about family when there is a break-up? There's a need, I guess.

You've said you inherited a sense of drama and storytelling from your mother but your father's secrecy and reclusiveness.

I'm secretive but not a recluse; only in the sense that if I'm working, I'm on my own for most of the day. I love privacy. And it's strange to be a private person and also to be a writer; it seems an odd conflict. That's why it would be difficult for me to write a book if I felt the characters were autobiographical; my characters are mostly invented. Most of the time I have a costume on.

There's a line in *Anil's Ghost* about the 'usual suspects in any Asian library'. When did you become aware that there was another version of history to the one in English books?

You go into any bookshop in Sri Lanka you'll see every one of P. G. Wodehouse's books; that quirky tradition of wit has become part of the culture. English readers in Sri Lanka would read Paul Scott, John Masters, Agatha Christie, Wodehouse and Jane Austen's *Pride and Prejudice*. But I think the postcolonial perspective was something I discovered much later on.

How did you feel coming to England at eleven, and going to board at Dulwich College?

It was a radical change; you were suddenly dressed strangely. You had to wear a tie; I'd never seen a tie before. It was confusing, getting used to a new set of rules. I was at a school which, in retrospect, should have been a haven for young writers. There was a tradition of writers who had gone there – P. G. Wodehouse, Raymond Chandler, David Thomson, Graham Swift. But we had no knowledge of them then. I was only interested in cricket and swimming at the time.

Was it less welcoming than Canada?

There was a kind of romance of England among people who returned to Sri Lanka after going to school or university in England. That was real nostalgia! But one of the things I have to work out is, was I responding to England as a weird, tough time because I was a teenager? Every teenager is lost and at war, so that's probably how I responded. In Canada I felt you could do anything. I'm sure I wouldn't have become a writer if I'd stayed in Sri Lanka, or in England. When I came to Canada I met young writers who worked on little magazines and worked at small presses, so I thought I could try this. I started writing poetry. I didn't feel that I shouldn't do this because of John Donne and Sir Philip Sidney. When I was in England, it was in the 1950s, before the Beatles and before hell broke loose. It felt repressive.

Why were your first two prose books, *The Collected Works of Billy the Kid* and *Coming Through Slaughter*, about aspects of US culture?

It grew out of my childhood fantasies, wanting to be a cowboy. At the end of *Billy the Kid* is a picture of me as a boy in Sri Lanka dressed as one. I wanted to make a movie about him, but I couldn't, so I wrote a book. But it was my completely unofficial version of the life – invented, improvised. All I took was the fact that he died at twenty-one having killed twenty-one people. I wanted to write something that was completely ominous and anarchic and fresh, so that he became dangerous. I'd been a poet until that time and I was also switching from poetry to prose. I had learned how to make a documentary film for three years, and here were seventy-five scenes I had to rearrange to make a story. I was mixing up genres – old photographs, drawings and white space, prose and poetry and fictional interviews and songs. It was partly because I'd worked with small presses and knew the possibilities of the form; I've always been interested in how a book is actually made.

You've said jazz is the ultimate art form.

It's the one I envy the most. If I could be Fats Waller I wouldn't be writing. What I love is its communal form, how it's completely free and improvisational and still everything is held together. It's made by a group as opposed to an individual and this really interests me. I believe books are communal acts. That's how you escape into something that is not just you when you are writing. It is when you can become more than yourself and speak from a different perspective. That's why it's always a learning process for me.

You've also said Herodotus' sense of history is yours.

Herodotus is supposedly either the father of history or the father of lies. His method of research was essentially to listen to everybody and then write most of it down; some of it was true and some not believed and then later on was discovered to be true. I hadn't read Herodotus when I was writing *Running in the Family*, but it seems similar to the way I listened to everybody and 'believed' them, receiving stories and then structuring them into a shape. The story about my grandmother takes twenty-odd pages, though I hardly knew her. I vaguely remember her; I was pretty small. But I talked to people who told me anecdotes and fragments. The writing, the fiction, came in the structuring of it: how one concentrated on certain things, found echoes, exaggerated certain qualities and habits.

With *In the Skin of a Lion* you chose, you've said, to write about European immigrants to Canada at the beginning of the twentieth century, rather than Asian post-war immigrants. Why?

I'd just finished *Running in the Family*, and if I'd written a novel about immigrants and they were Asian, it would have been taken as auto-biographical. I really didn't want that. One of the pleasures of writing fiction is to step into somebody else's shoes. There was also a wish not to get labelled. I was interested in the building of the city – the histor-ical moment of Toronto – and in saying immigration is not just a contemporary issue; it's how the whole country was developed. Immi-grant families, with that wonderful variety of values, are hopefully the saving grace of any culture. It seemed to me that that story was much more heroic and important than most traditionally heroic stories. I wanted to celebrate someone coming to a new country, and having to learn the language and bringing up a family and working in rough circumstances. That goes back to choosing what you want to write about, what's important.

While you were born into wealth – though your mother hit hard times in London – *In the Skin of a Lion* **is scathing about the rich. Where did that perspective come from?**

Well, even in *Running in the Family* my family was on the edge of hard times. But what one is as a child, or where one comes from, doesn't necessarily mean you are going to be locked into that perspective for-ever. I guess the perspective comes from having a postcolonial take on the world around you. It also grows out of the characters you choose to write about. What's interesting about fiction is that you as a writer grow into a knowledge you didn't have before. If you are writing about someone like Caravaggio, who is pissed off at anyone who has prop-erty, or the English patient, who has a perspective about nations, you learn things as you delve into the characters. In some cases you did not know these things before you began writing. It was about three years into that book when I started to write from the perspective of the English patient himself; he had been this silent mystery when I began the book. I was not quite speaking in tongues but I was writing from a different angle.

**You say your view comes partly from a postcolonial perspective –
from migration?**

Yes, I think moving does affect you; you learn twice as much. Starting
anew can double you, like living three or four lives. I hope I have a
double perspective. That's a gift I've been given. In a way, writers themselves are immigrants; every time you write a new novel you're coming
to another place – unless all your books use exactly the same landscape,
or the same narrators. There's a sense of going to a new value system
and discovering it. There is a similar parallel to being an immigrant. It's
exciting and also terrifying: you're in a new land, with a new language
and new rules. And sometimes possibly a new genre. Hopefully, every
book will be different, not just in story and location but in the way I
write it.

**What was the experience of *The English Patient* like, with the
Booker and then the film?**

It happened very fast. I arrived in England the day the book was published and the same day it was shortlisted. With the film it was odd,
very surreal. I liked the people I worked with, the director Anthony
Minghella and the producer Saul Zaentz; they're both avid readers, not
just people who make movies. When they first read the script and we
talked, I was quite unguarded. I wasn't trying to protect the book
because the script altered it in terms of dramatic structure, and I was
excited about that: it wasn't just an illustration of the book. So I threw
in some ideas. I also learned a lot about structure, about the craft of
film – though film is a form I don't think I could work in at all; it's so
strict. Everything is governed by time.

Though you did make films – documentaries.

Yes, but they were always too long. Films don't like repetition; you can't
have the same thing happening to two people. Everything has to be

chronological; you can't have too many flashbacks – which was a problem in *The English Patient* because everyone was having flashbacks; it
was like a way of life. Someone said, 'No one will know what the hell is
going on.' I loved the craft of film, specifically the editing process: how
you can shift a scene from one point to another. Similarly when I
worked in theatre I was more interested in the blocking than the words.
You always learn by witnessing a different genre. In the temple art in Sri
Lanka, the panels combine key moments along a wall, almost like little
trailers. It's a completely different art form from anything you have in
the West. There are so many interesting forms available to us. Fiction
tends to be staid in the way it tells a story; it's the most conservative of
genres, compared to music or art. We tend to be handcuffed to realism.
But I'm interested in forms of art which have a different structure. So in
film what interests me is how someone like Minghella, within that
conservative structure, can make these radical leaps back and forward
in time. It's not radical for a novelist, but it is for a movie.

**The novel is revisionist history, contesting the official view of the
Second World War?**

I was very conscious that all the mythology of the war I'd grown up
with was English. When I came to England I was reading all these war
novels. The movies of that time were all Second World War movies,
and it seemed utterly, completely white. You were either an Englishman, or a Frenchman with an accent, or American; those were the
allies. But the population of Indian soldiers who were massacred was
very much part of the war; they weren't just background figures. It was
a very one-sided view. If you look at an English film such as *The Dam
Busters* about the bombing of the German bridges, you see no reference
to any damage done, or people killed. I wanted to step back from that
kind of hero–heroine, allies-and-enemy, portrait. Americans are continually making movies about Pearl Harbor. Now why is that? To justify
Hiroshima? Hiroshima is one of the major events in our history, but it
hardly gets acknowledged in American history.

The novel's also about a historical shift in 1945, from the colonial to the postcolonial.

It is a historical moment; that's how I see it. There are historical moments that remap the world and that was one of them. The balance shifted from the colonial to a different kind of world, where people like Kip see themselves as empowered.

The shift is from the English patient and Caravaggio towards both Kip and Hana: Asia and the New World?

I hadn't thought about that in symbolic terms, but certainly that exists. The shift is towards the younger characters, from the old humanism of the patient to Kip, who is of the new age. There's also a shift from the main character in *Anil's Ghost* to others, like Ananda; there are structures one stays with.

So how did you feel about Kip's becoming less central in the film, and the absence of the scene where he hears news of Hiroshima?

That was the sad part for me, and I suppose for Anthony Minghella too, because all the scenes around Kip were written and shot. In the end, partly because of the structure, the Hiroshima sequence didn't work. I saw it on one of their versions and it didn't work at all. It looked like a scene from another film. So there was a loss. And I still wish there had been more of Kip in the film. The irony is that in a film a personal death becomes more important than a huge war crime. A book can do incredible things. You can bring in someone in the last few chapters which makes all this stuff look ironic. But in a film it looks like some-one put in the wrong reel. I think that's one of the weaknesses of film; one of the things it cannot do is come out of one story and go somewhere else. It can't turn 180 degrees; it can tell only one story. The book can be more of a debate, a meditation between characters and with the author. In a film if you have a debate between the patient and

Caravaggio, and the patient is the lead actor, suddenly the author's point of view is linked to his. But in a book that isn't the issue: in a book you have three people talking and arguing, not just one giving a speech. The problems with films are not just to do with the people who make them but the media, the posters; all these things govern our perceptions. Having said all that, I really missed Kip in the film. It could have been another half an hour longer, and included him; it was a pity.

23

Zadie Smith

with

Gretchen Holbrook Gerzina

On 9 June 2000 Gretchen Holbrook Gerzina interviewed Zadie Smith about her then newly released novel, White Teeth. *Gerzina is host of the* Book Show, *a radio programme that airs nationally in the United States and is recorded at WAMC in Albany, New York. A young author who had achieved sudden fame, and was surprised by all the attention, Smith was making her first American book tour, with back-to-back media interviews. Smith's first novel addresses the contemporary realities and history of multicultural Britain, its diversity and the condition of postmodernity; her second novel,* Autograph Man *(2002), delves into the hollow centre of celebrity. Born in 1975 to a Jamaican mother and an English father, Zadie Smith grew up in Willesden Green, North London, where much of her first novel, which won the Guardian First Book Award, is set. Since this interview took place,* White Teeth *has been translated into over twenty languages and was adapted for Channel 4 television in 2002. Zadie Smith has also edited an anthology of erotic stories,* Piece of Flesh *(2001), and was nominated as one of the best of young British novelists by* Granta *magazine in 2003. She is currently a Fellow at Harvard University in the US.*

Gretchen Holbrook Gerzina The moment I opened this book *White Teeth*, I was struck by the confidence of its writing. I thought we might begin by your saying something about your decision to write a novel at all, especially one that isn't autobiographical, while you were still at university, and perhaps something about the characters you've created.

Zadie Smith I didn't write it at university. I wrote the beginning of it at university and . . . it wasn't a decision not to write an autobiographical book. It's just fiction, and . . . there's a long tradition of young novelists writing fiction. So it wasn't a conscious decision; I just always wanted to write a novel – it was fiction and the characters in it are . . .

Well, there are many characters in it.

Yeah, I mean there are a whole load of characters, but I don't know why there are so many. I had quite a few things to say so I needed quite a few characters to say them, I guess.

So, what are the things you were trying to say, that you needed so many people to say?

You've read the book so you know it's not really one thing; it's lots of different things. They're probably best expressed by the book itself, because otherwise you would just write a Ph.D. or something. But I did want to write about England, post-war . . . and so that's really what I did.

Although you yourself have a multi-racial background, you exhibit in this . . .

It's not so 'multi-', it's just one black parent and one white! I think those words kind of . . . sound very strange to me, because I never thought of it as anything other than my family.

Well, I just . . .

My mother is Jamaican and my father is English, but yeah, there are characters like that in the book.

But what I was going to get at is that in the book you exhibit an astonishing knowledge of histories that are not your own and not your own family's . . .

There's not that much astonishing history in it. People keep on talking about the historical background in the book, but if you look at the Second World War section, the actual information contained in that section is, like, one tank, one date and one country [*laughs*]. That's not a huge amount of historical research; that's, like, two hours in a book, or, you know, half an hour on the Internet. That's not historical research. I think the gift of the novel is that it makes people think that whoever's written it must be so brilliant because it's a world unto itself. But, for all the historical research in that book – I mean, you could count it on one hand. It really isn't that extensive. I don't do a lot of research, and I don't enjoy doing research, because I like writing fiction.

But the parts perhaps about . . . South Asia, or the . . . background of other families not your own, were really brought to life.

But my family doesn't appear anywhere in the book, and I know – in terms of the Jamaican stuff in the book – people have assumed that I must know that because I have a Jamaican mother, but I don't have any contact with the rest of my Jamaican family, so it's as alien to me as anything else in the book. As for the kind of Asian . . . do you mean the Indian Mutiny stuff?

Yeah.

That was literally an afternoon in a library. I'd heard that story – the story in the book about a guy called Mangal Pande who started the

Indian Mutiny . . . but that's kind of it! Novels are a huge con job, because it's not like academic work; you don't have to prove anything. You just have to mention something and everybody's convinced that you must know everything about it and that's not the case.

Perhaps one of the reasons you're so convincing is that you use a number of local English dialects – London dialects in particular – very well, which give the book a real sense of panorama, even though it's mostly in one city, and the dialects I think help to bring it all to life.

Sometimes I'm asked about the research that goes into portraying a Bengali family but I don't know what kind of research you would do for that. I mean, you can't walk into a Bengali family's house and say, 'Hey! Here I am. I just wanted to nose around.' I just made the assumption that people are people and their race was kind of irrelevant to me, to be honest. I mean, that's just the truth. . . . I really didn't care what Bengali people do or don't do or. . . . I'm not interested in representing people in that way. I'm interested in making characters.

I was actually speaking about Archie's accent.

Archie's accent is just a product of watching a whole load of British television, because I don't think many people actually talk like Archie. I really think . . . some of the language – 'I should cocoa' and that kind of stuff . . . I think a certain generation did, but I'm quite interested in showing the language of a generation who were kind of . . . alienated from themselves. The people who are kind of Archie's age, in their mid-seventies, who were young during the Second World War.

So?

The way they speak, certain ideas they have, seem completely anachronistic now, but they're still around, and I think that's a very funny experience – to be living in an age where a lot of the things you do seem irrelevant to people but it's not irrelevant to you because, you're living it.

Right.

And Archie finds that very hard in the book because he's you know, he's still around. He's not part of the past, no matter how much everybody else might want to forget about that period of history. He's still here, hanging around, and so he's kind of out of place and out of touch, but I think, I mean, in Archie's case, he has . . . quite an adorable way of dealing with that.

Archie – for our readers and listeners – is a character who is white, who is forty-seven, I think, when the book opens in 1975.

Yeah, I think he's forty-seven at the beginning, yes.

And he has not had a greatly successful life; he makes decisions by flipping coins rather than measured, careful thought. Yet, a lot of the reviews say that this is a novel about history and cultural dislocation – about people who try to make sense of the past by manipulating the present and the future.

Yeah.

Do you agree with that take on the book?

Yeah, I would. I think it is about ordering the past. I wrote a book which was very much kind of fascinated with the past. It's not something that . . . I think about from a very personal point of view; it's something I had to get done, if you know what I mean.

What do you mean?

In order to move on with other stuff that I'd like to write. I just had to put the past in order. Not really my personal past, but the past of the place I'm from and ... maybe even of England, and on a larger scale English literature, just to kind of shake free of some of my influences and move on, so ... It is a book about the past. I think it's strange for that reason.

But I also found it a book very much about the future.

It's optimistic, I think.

Well, optimistic, and also people's attempts to manipulate the future ...

I was interested in religious ideas of the future, spiritual ideas of the future like fate, and scientific ideas of the future like how it's possible to interfere with nature, and the dividing line between nature and nurture which people think of as quite scientific but depending on which side you fall, it's also like a faith, it's a belief, because you can't know really what influences someone, whether it is in their nature, in their genetic make-up or how they're brought up and how they're conditioned. There's a very thin line between these two things and you can't know, but it tends to be that the people who believe one thing fiercely and the people who believe the other fiercely ... those ideas are based on some kind of faith. People who believe it is nurture believe it wholeheartedly and won't hear a word for the science, and vice versa, so I'm just quite interested in showing people who have those very extreme beliefs. The Chalfens family who are the scientists in the book are so sure of themselves and so sure of their science that in the logic of *White Teeth* they kind of, they come bad. Anybody who's completely sure of themselves in *White Teeth* doesn't do very well.

I think that's right, that's a good way to put it because at the end of the book you've got someone who's become a very political radical, someone who's a scientist and, also, a group of people who are very strongly religious all of them confronting each other, no one listening to the others.

I'm kind of fascinated by religion and I like to be around religious people actually, and I'm very envious of the faith that religious people have. What I have a problem with is certainty, and I did want to show that the atheists in the book, the supposed rationalists, the scientists are more certain and more kind of fundamental than any of the religious people really. They're much much worse. Take Samed – he's a Muslim but he's in constant doubts, he's always worried he has the right relationship with his god, whether he's behaving correctly. He's never certain if he's taken the right path. The Chalfens on the other hand are always one hundred per cent certain and they make bad decisions because of that. They don't leave any space to listen to other people.

Do you find a certain arrogance in that kind of certainty?

Yeah, it kind of drives me insane.

In real life?

Yes, but I don't think there's anything wrong with for instance genetic science per se – well, I do think there are plenty of things wrong with it, but I think it's something that we have to discuss. Scientists have to talk to the public, and information has to be spread, and we have to know what we're eating and what we're putting into our bodies; just information, just awareness that there are other people in the world and you have to deal with them, and you can't just go along your own path doing whatever you like to do, without paying attention to them.

People have compared you to Rushdie, and I can think of lots of reasons for that . . .

Can you? I can't.

One of the reasons I noticed was your use of twin sons.

Yeah, this is a funny thing. Firstly, I hadn't read Rushdie until I'd finished the book. There are twins, but then I've noticed in lots of other writers – my peers, English writers – there are twins as well, or double fathers – which is what happens in my book. I don't want to give the end away, but to a certain extent there are two fathers to one child, and I've seen that in two other books by my peers, and I think it's . . . to do with indeterminacy . . . a generation obsessed with things which are indeterminate where you can't be certain of things, and that it's – I mean, I can't pin it down – but there's some relation in that image because more than one person has used it. And with twins – I think it's again the nature/nurture issue, because twins are one of the most succinct ways you can discover whether it is nature or nurture, because . . . if you separate twins from birth, put them in opposite places, and see how they go; that's a very stark way of seeing that development, and in *White Teeth* it's kind of satirized because the kid who's sent to Bangladesh to become a Muslim comes back, you know, a typical Englishman and the kid who's left here becomes a fundamentalist Muslim. So . . . I'm interested in those ideas of development. That's maybe why twins appear in both our books, but it's a more general influence because I hadn't read Rushdie when I wrote *White Teeth*.

I think that's great. I'm glad you hadn't read him. I'm actually fascinated by what you've said about your peers and the ways in which they used twins or double fathers . . .

I think that in about ten or fifteen years there'll be a good Ph.D. in it for somebody, but it's something which you start to notice – and it's very freaky – because you think of yourself as someone who's sitting in a room, writing completely independently of everybody else in the world. Then you start reading other books and think, 'My God!' You do write as a generation and you do write under the influence of some of the same things, and one of the main things we're influenced by is the idea of a network, so instead of centres and . . . roots – things . . . that Rushdie's generation were maybe more concerned with – my gener-ation thinks of things as networks and having many different causes and effects, of being far more complex maybe, and you can see that in the work of people like Foster Wallace.

Or even Richard Mason, who had similar things to say about twinning and doubling when his book came out last year.

Yes, it's a funny thing.

I'm going to ask you one last question about the novel and we can move on to some other things. I just want to ask you about Irie, who is Archie and Clara's daughter, because she's my favourite character.

Really?

She tries so hard. She's overweight. She loses her hair when she tries to get it straightened to impress Millat, and I was wondering what it is about the Chalfen family, this group of liberal intel-lectuals, also the genetic engineering scientists, who slot people into categories in disturbing ways, but yet they appeal so much to Irie. What is it about them that grabs her?

The same thing when the English went to India or when they went to Jamaica. One of the reactions was horror – look at these people coming to take us over. But the other one was to be charmed. Colonialism is like a love affair between two countries; it's not just one country going to subdue another; it's two countries becoming fixated on each other. And that's what happens with Irie and the Chalfens. They have come to kind of control her and educate her and in some ways maybe repress her, but they're also charming, funny, educated, witty, with a beautiful culture around them in their house, pictures on the wall, artwork; and she falls for that. The Indians fell for the English, and the Jamaicans fell for them too. That's how it works.

But it's a class issue as well.

It is. But colonialism is all about class. The middle classes are irresistible ... to a lot of people and it's only later that you start to realize the problems with that.

Right. You've called this a 'baggy novel'. I don't remember where I read that, but I remember distinctly that you used the term 'baggy novel'. What did you mean by that?

It's just, you know, it's big like *Tristram Shandy* is big, like Dickens's books are big, like Rushdie is big. They're all big novels – nothing wrong with them, and I've read a lot of those kind of books for a long time and I also think there's another kind of book ... which is tighter, shorter, which I also admire. I'd like to try writing one of those.

But in a sense it's a tour de force to make a 'baggy' novel come together. It's like –

It's a show-off. It's a form for show-offs and I've done enough of that now.

Is that what you feel you've done?

Yeah.

I also read somewhere that you felt that you've made plenty of money now on this book and you'd like to go on and think about some other things; that someone gave you a handbag, I think, to carry around.

My mother was very angry when I said that. She said it was an outrageous thing to say.

About the handbag or the money?

The money. All I was trying to say is that people constantly ask me about money and seem vaguely fixated on it and it's not that I have more money than I can use . . . or whatever, I don't need any more. That's not true. I haven't even paid my damn mortgage.

What were your ambitions?

To do something worth doing. Sometimes you look at these people earning millions and millions, and I just want to say, you do realize you're going to shuffle off the planet; you get that right, you get that you're going to leave with everybody else, there's nothing you can do to stop it, and no amount of money is going to stop that. Maybe that's an adolescent attitude but I find it incomprehensible people make like forty million dollars. What the hell for? What for?

I'm sure that the reason people ask you about money is simply because you had so much success so quickly and so young . . .

Hmm.

. . . and they're wondering in what ways this affects a person in youth.

Well, the answer is, it's different. Some people go out and buy a Rolls

Royce with their name on it and, you know, a golf course, I don't know. I didn't earn money that way. The money people say I got is hugely exaggerated on the first hand, and secondly there's always the taxman and . . . I don't know, I don't know what to say to that. I feel like it's a kind of weird voyeurism on the part of other people, and I feel a kind of responsibility to try and step on it.

I actually have no idea how much money you've made.

But the best thing for me personally – I'm sure it's different for everybody but the best thing for me personally is to ignore it and get on with what I do.

Which is to write another novel?

Yeah.

How has the big success of this book and now the Channel 4 television series . . . affected your life? Does it affect your life in the sense that it makes you want to sit down and do the next thing?

It affects my life in that I have to talk about myself more than I've ever had to before in my life to a kind of *ad nauseam*, and that's difficult, because it has a bad effect on you as a person, I think, and on your writing because a writer isn't good at repetition . . . and suddenly you have to repeat yourself maybe eight times a day . . . and that's tough. So that is the main thing, and the amount of time it takes, but . . . it doesn't have any influence on how I write the second book. It's something I'm determined to do.

Now, we've got a minute or so left, so what I would really like to hear from you is the direction that you see the young writers in England going now. You said earlier that you were sitting in a room,

not really paying attention, and then it turns out in your work that you're dealing with similar issues and themes.

It's all about – for Americans and the English writers – it's all about facing the complexity of the world with something equally complex. And people who don't like that – in Britain they have a real problem with intellectual writing. Well, they're going to have to . . . wake up and smell the coffee! Because the world is incredibly complex, more than it ever has been. Even in a war – it's not about one country against another – it's about incredibly intricate civil wars, different factions, different people involved, companies, governments. Everything, every area of life you choose to look at is now incredibly layered and it's the writer's responsibility to meet that with a complexity of their own, and the people who whine about the complexity of somebody like Pynchon or whatever don't get it. To be a writer you need more than just a sense of like – it's not Keats any more, it's not about truth and beauty – though that is part of it, but you also need to know a fair amount about science, about technology, about all kinds of things, you need both sides of your brain working, and there are some very exciting writers who do have both sides of their brain working, and who are able to . . . have a lot of empathy for their characters, and to talk of the street and people's lives on an intimate level, and are also able to . . . move out, like – I don't know what you call it – come out of focus and look at the larger picture and see the web of networks and competing power structures and all kinds of things. Those writers are the ones who will still be read in fifty, a hundred years. I don't have that kind of ability myself. I don't know as much as I should do, but it's a long career, writing, and you can learn as you go along.

24

Bernardine Evaristo

with

Alastair Niven

Bernardine Evaristo was born in London to a Nigerian father and an English mother. She has been critically acclaimed as one of Britain's most original and exciting authors. Her first novel-in-verse, Lara (1997), traces the two ancestral strands of the eponymous Lara, a mixed-race Nigerian/British woman who grows up in London in the 1960s and 1970s. It travels from nineteenth-century Brazil to colonial Lagos in Nigeria, from Ireland at the turn of the twentieth century to 'Little Italy' in Islington in the 1920s. The narrative unfolds through the multiple poetic voices of ancestors, friends, family and Lara herself. The Emperor's Babe (2001), her second novel-in-verse, was inspired by the little-known historical fact that black people lived in London in the third century AD, *and began life as a few poems written during Evaristo's Poetry Society residency at the Museum of London in 1999. It is a humorous dig at British history, a poetic excavation and reimagination of Roman London, working with fact and fiction, myth and contemporary culture, tragedy and comedy. The story follows the adventures of a young girl of Sudanese parentage who grows up in Roman London eighteen hundred years ago, recreating Roman London through her eyes.*

In addition to her two novels, Evaristo has also written drama for theatre and radio, won several prestigious literary awards and participated in several international tours and residencies. In 2004 she has been elected a Fellow of the Royal Society of Literature.

Alastair Niven I was very struck by your final remark in *The Emperor's Babe*, as you were giving some late acknowledgements, when you say that Peter Fryer's history *Staying Power* [1984] was an influence over you and it was there that you really discovered that black people existed in Roman Britain. When did you read the book?

Bernardine Evaristo I read it in the late 1980s. It was the first time I realized that there had been a black presence in Britain well before the 1940s. Growing up as I did in the 1960s and 1970s we were led to believe that black people came to England post-1948. And this is what we are still led to believe in this country. Fryer touches very briefly on the Roman period and talks about Septimius Severus – who is in my book – and the legion of Moors stationed at Hadrian's Wall in AD 211. That was a real revelation for me. It is important because it is an aspect of British history that hasn't been fully recognized and that is still invisible to most people.

And do you think people like Peter Fryer and Ron Ramdin, historians of the black experience of Britain, are themselves unacknowledged and should be better known?

I think so, yes. I would say that the majority of the British population haven't heard of Peter Fryer and I think that it is important that these books are brought to light and that we re-examine British history from this perspective.

Was that really your motive in writing this book?

Yes, and I was also really inspired by a writer called Ivan Van Sertima's *African Presence in Early Europe* [1985] and an American Jamaican,

J. A. Rogers, who published in the 1930s and 1940s. He wrote lots of books about the hidden aspects of European and American history and he also examines racial mixing in European history going back through the centuries.

But why did you choose the Roman period and not, say, the Tudor period or one of the other periods that you could have explored?

I had a Poetry Society residency at the Museum of London. I decided that I would explore the black history of London during this residency and write some poems about the different periods. I thought I would start with pre-history and work my way up to the present day so that I could create poems based on different periods of British history. But then I went to the Roman gallery in the museum, a fantastic gallery where they have recreated Roman rooms and a Roman kitchen and lots of aspects of Roman London, and I was inspired because I had forgotten how contemporary in many ways Roman society was in Britain, so I started writing some poems about the Roman period and the book began to evolve.

You mentioned that like most kids you *did* the Romans at school, but do you really know much about that period? Or did you before you researched the material for *The Emperor's Babe*?

I forgot most of what I learnt at school, basically. But I had been to Italy and Rome a few times and I did a lot of research whilst I was writing the book. I had studied Latin for five years; I could then research Latin and use it. The Latin that I have chosen to use in the book resembles contemporary English, so even if you haven't studied Latin you will be able to understand it.

You seem to find the Romans quite attractive as people, whereas a lot of people, despite the popularity of *Gladiator* as a film, feel they were pretty brutal and in some ways rather remote historically.

In the novel I try to see the Romans as I see people today, thus creating characters that could exist in our contemporary world. Hopefully that makes them very accessible. But I also see the people as very barbaric. Zuleika was married at the age of eleven. They used to watch people killing each other for sport.

You have talked of Zuleika not being a victim but someone who despite dying at the end of a short life should be seen as victorious. In what way is she victorious?

In the way that she lived her life. Even though she is married off and she is virtually imprisoned in her husband's house and has a terrible relationship with him she actually makes the most of her life. She ends up having this amazing short-lived affair with the Roman emperor. In the sense of her personality being very strong and feisty, she makes the most out of her situation and that's how I see her as being victorious. What's interesting is that when people read about the book they always presume she is a slave, which I find fascinating because she isn't a slave and there are no references to her being a slave. But at certain moments of history, black people are seen as victims, as downtrodden and enslaved.

She may not technically be a slave but she is virtually sold to Felix. Were you trying to explore the threshold of sexuality, leaving aside all the historical and multicultural aspects that people immediately think of when they think of *The Emperor's Babe*, were you interested in talking about the awakening of sexuality?

I don't think that was my intention but this is what emerges. For Zuleika sex becomes a symbol of her oppressive relationship with her husband. And it also becomes a symbol of her empowerment when she has her relationship with Severus. The way she takes control of her relationship with Severus is through her sexuality, which in a sense is the only way that is open to her.

She is also fulfilled to some extent by Severus. She enjoys the sex.

Yes, even though the relationship only lasts a summer it awakens deeper feelings in her that have lain dormant since childhood. Also the gladiator scene is quite instrumental in her sexual awakening.

But I felt that the key relationships were not entirely with Felix or with Severus, but with her girlfriends. There was a sense of camaraderie between her and her friend, so the book becomes in one part a celebration of female friendship.

And very much like contemporary female friendships today. Young women talking and sparring with each other. But I also wanted to show where a character like Alba really does take control of her life as much as she can and is very much somebody who refuses to be imprisoned by her situation.

Can we go back to the historical dimensions of the book? I was interested that you prefaced the novel with Oscar Wilde's aphorism, 'The one duty we owe to history is to rewrite it.' In this particular case it is not so much a rewriting of history but the writing of it for the first time.

It's creating a new version of history.

But in writing the history of Zuleika and reminding us of that period you are also clearly making a statement about what it is like to be living in a multicultural Britain of the twenty-first century.

There are lots of parallels with what is happening today. For me it was also about having a lot of fun with history and being quite satirical about aspects of contemporary British society.

Let me come to the format of the book. You've made the decision to write a novel in verse. There has been a very mini fashion for this: Vikram Seth's *The Golden Gate* [1986] and other recent examples by people like Ranjit Bolt and the classical pedigree from Pushkin. But it is not a genre that has been much used over the centuries and one wonders why one would have been attracted to it. Could you not have made the same points in prose?

Possibly, but my background is in poetry. And when I wrote for theatre I always wrote choreopoems, dramatic poems. I have always found it very hard to get away from writing poetry and in the past ten years I have been increasingly interested in telling a story through poetry. So the form has chosen me.

You are of course a very experienced reader/performer of your own poems and you have a theatrical training. I was lucky enough to hear parts of this book at a very early stage and I was very struck by its orality.

Quite a lot of my writing is performative. That is not always intentional but I do have a theatrical background which comes through and I tend to create characters that come alive off the page. I don't like using the word 'performing' in terms of my work because I am not a performance poet and I would hate to be lumped together with performance poets. But my writing does have an oral dramatic quality.

But prose poetry is a risky genre in terms of selling books. The fact that the book is accessible and that most of the reviewers have commented on that probably in itself is not enough to make the average reader approach it with relish. Until they have read it they probably think of it as something that is impenetrable.

Even though it is a form that I find easy I do make things difficult for myself by writing in verse. But people tend to approach it in spite of themselves. They think they are not going to enjoy it and then actually find that they do.

Let's explore what lay before *The Emperor's Babe*. You'd written one novel, *Lara*. *Lara* had quite a lot of success. It sticks around and is mentioned quite a lot. The British Council took you up on the basis of that one book and sent you to many different parts of the world. Has that been an educational and constructive opportunity?

Combining work and travel is just a dream come true. I did a lot of readings with *Lara* and that was because it was my only marketing tool for the book. One of the things that I discovered through giving lots of readings abroad for the British Council was that it is a book that travels. For example, whether I'm reading in Capetown to communities of so-called 'coloured' people or in Australia or Sweden there is something about the book that travels to these places.

I found that on accompanying you on some of these travels you were often asked the same questions in different parts of the world and people were always interested in your particular odyssey. In particular your ethnic, racial background.

Lara is a mixture of fact and fiction. It is not autobiography but it does draw on my family history. On my father's side there is Nigerian with a Brazilian heritage and on my mother's side English with Irish and a little bit of German thrown in. But essentially I am mixed-race, one side English and one side Nigerian.

So the coming together of Severus and Zuleika, to get back to *The Emperor's Babe*, is the coming together of two races. You are still exploring the theme of cultural identity.

Well, the thing about Severus is, what did he really look like? From the images I have seen of him on a coin he actually looks Arabic, like a brown-skinned Arab. So Zuleika's parents come from Africa and Severus comes from Africa. I don't see their relationship as an inter-racial one. I see them as coming from the same place.

Really? Well that doesn't strike the reader.

That's because there is a lot of doubt over what Severus actually looked like. He came from a place that we now know as Libya, then called Lepcis Magna. Libya is in the African continent.

There has been a lot of speculation about this. I mean, for example, was Cleopatra black? Increasingly I think black people from central Africa migrated north and colonized Egypt and it may well be that they spread further into North Africa and eventually into the Roman Empire.

Rome was a multicultural city state. There were people there from all over the empire.

People of different races would have been very aware of each other. Or, if you were from somewhere quite remote you would certainly have stuck out and been recognized.

That's the whole point about Zuleika. She is one of the few black people in my version of Roman London and she is noticed because of her colour but she is not discriminated against because of it. The Romans did not practise anti-black racism.

Although later on in the history of black Britain they [black people] encounter that racism repeatedly. Let me think to the future. You have obviously had great success with this book. Are you going to

stay with historical subjects or are you going to move into a new sphere?

I am working on a new book and I don't really want to say too much about it, except that it is about two people who decide to drive to Australia. But along the route they dip into the black history of southern Europe.

Let's just open up the discussion for a moment because I think people would be interested to know your perspective on black writing in Britain. Should we be calling it black writing in Britain any more? Do you feel the scene is too inter-racial and too conglomerate to really pigeon-hole writers in these racial categories any longer? Should we just stop it altogether and just talk about British writing in poetry, fiction and playwriting and forget about this tendency to talk about things in terms of these national or racial labels?

In an ideal world that would be the most desirable thing, not to have some kind of racial labelling, which in effect ghettoizes you. But it is also useful for people to know that if they are interested in poetry or fiction by black writers that they can identify it easily in a bookshop. For example, in America black authors are in the black section but they are also in the general section as well. What happens in the UK is that you go into a bookshop and unless your book has been heavily successful or won lots of awards, a black book will be in the black section but it won't cross over into the general section. This ghettoizes it. I think what happens in this country is that people can't see beyond race. If you are a black writer you are deemed to be writing about black subjects and that is generally perceived to be for a black audience.

But some of the major names in this field writing in this country, like Caryl Phillips and Salman Rushdie and Ben Okri, would fiercely resist this categorization, being described as black, Asian, Indian or whatever. They just want to be thought of as writers. And I am reminded of Nadime Gordimer a few years ago when asked if she accepted the label 'woman writer' or 'feminist writer' – said that writers are androgynous. They are in a sense without gender. Do you feel in espousing a black history and not resisting the labelling according to the answer you have just given that you run the risk of not being grouped with the Rushdies and the Phillipses?

You have to deal with the reality and the reality is that I am seen as a black writer no matter what I may think of that personally. And of course I would like to be thought of as a writer full stop. But the reality is that I am pigeon-holed as a black female writer. So that is something that I have to deal with, as much as I might protest about it. I have given lots of interviews for *The Emperor's Babe* and generally people want to talk about race. In actual fact the book is about many things.

Do they not want to talk about the unusualness of the form?

A little bit. But the focus is all on Zuleika being a black person and whether she encounters racism or not. That was the starting point for the book but it is not solely what the book is about.

That's interesting because there are many examples of central characters who are outsiders, in works of literature, who come in from an outsider community and disrupt it in some way, but they are not always described racially. Do you feel that for a black writer this is unavoidable?

Yes. A writer might for example be called a 'very talented black writer' rather than a talented writer.

Is that still true with Rushdie and Ishiguro?

No, but I think that is also because of where you are in the literary pecking order and what you write about. Ishiguro became famous because of a book about an English butler. Hanif Kureishi's recent books have not really been about mixed Asian and English culture. Rushdie transcended everything through being so famous and originally winning the Booker. Zadie Smith has perhaps transcended it. Although she too is seen as multicultural.

She is seen as a kind of composite. Where do you think the scene in Britain is going in terms of multicultural literature? Do you see evidence that these labels are going to evolve?

We are moving towards it. If you think of the past ten years with the growth of black British literature, and by that label I mean writers who are born in Britain and write from that perspective and who are also reaching into the mainstream with their works, then the signs are saying that eventually those labels won't carry so much weight as they do at the moment. The thing is if you are a writer and you are black and you are exploring an aspect of black culture, or society, or history that shouldn't mean that you should be labelled a black writer any more than a white writer who is labelled as such.

Nadime Gordimer would be called a white writer –

In South Africa, but not here.

So you still have this label slapped on you when the majority are not black. But does it matter much? Such labels can be a way of introducing people. They are not necessarily derogatory.

I think if it marginalizes your work then that is definitely a negative thing.

What about the devil's argument that it does the opposite of that and instead pushes you into the limelight?

Well I don't think it does. There are always the exceptions. A lot of the novels published by writers who are black and British haven't received a lot of attention.

There are about six thousand new novels published each year and only a fraction of those get any attention at all. So what you describe actually happens to white writers as well. It is fated that most writers are overlooked.

But I think it is worse for black writers.

You yourself have actually received a lot of publicity with *The Emperor's Babe*.

Yes, and that's great, but I think it is perhaps the exception. I am not talking about myself. I am talking generally.

I suppose what I am suggesting is that there has been change and that this book could be a kind of watershed for writers in the future. Especially with this novel's format, which could so easily have been marginalized.

I think things have changed enormously. I have a very positive attitude about what has happened for writers over the past ten years or so. Ten years ago it would have been impossible to get *The Emperor's Babe* published, certainly not by a fiction publisher and certainly not by someone who is committed to promoting the book in the way that it has been. That would not have happened five years ago. The book is also a comment on multicultural Britain, certainly multicultural London. I guess one of my arguments has always been that we are all mixed racially and culturally.

It makes a nonsense of those politicians who talk about ethnic purity.

For example, it is estimated there were about twenty thousand black people living in London in the eighteenth century. Obviously their genes went into the local population.

This is one of the studies of the future; they are embedded in the language we speak every day.

There is a lot of history still to be uncovered. For example, Africans who were living in the islands of Scotland in the fourteenth and fifteenth century. This is an amazing discovery. It only enriches British history.

It can work the other way around. There was the story of a mass grave in China in which the people appear to be Celts wearing tartan.

This is one of the points I wanted to make. The Romans were travelling all over the place and they were also going backwards and forwards so why is it so difficult for people to think that black people could be in London two thousand years ago?

The idea that distance was a barrier. The knowledge that all kinds of Europeans went to America long before Columbus is just one example of that.

I am committed to exploding the myth of Britain as monocultural and 'racially' pure until 1948. There are so many layers of British history to be peeled back.

25

Ama Ata Aidoo

with

Nana Wilson-Tagoe

Since the publication of her first play The Dilemma of a Ghost *in 1964, Ama Ata Aidoo has been an important and vocal figure in the struggle for Ghanaian national liberation and self-determination in the context of colonialism and neo-colonialism, as well as the broader pan-Africanist struggles against imperialism and racism. At the same time she has been an outspoken proponent of women's liberation in national and international contexts and an avid critic of the corruption and hypocrisy of the national bourgeoisie in post-independence Ghana. She has likewise made influential contributions to both the development of African literature and literary criticism both as a writer and as a scholar. Born in 1940 in the central region of Ghana, Aidoo was the daughter of a chief in the town of Abeadzi Kyiakor and grew up in the royal household. From 1961 to 1964 she attended the University of Ghana at Legon, where she was an active participant in the school of drama and the writer's workshop. Between 1964 and 1966 Aidoo was a junior research fellow at the Institute of African Studies at the university, which influenced her writing by strengthening her commitment to the use of African oral traditions in her work. She was also affected by the pan-Africanist and socialist ideas that were prevalent in the 1950s and 1960s in the period leading up to and immediately after the independence of Ghana in 1957.*

Aidoo has written one other play, Anowa *(1970), two novels,* Our Sister Killjoy *(1979) and* Changes: a love story *(1991), a collection of short stories,* No Sweetness Here *(1970), and two collections of poetry as well as numerous essays on African literature, gender, race and the status of women in African society. As a writer and critic she has been one of the formative influences on women's writing in Africa. At the same time, she has also pursued a career in education, teaching and lecturing in various parts of Africa and the United States. She has always been an activist, involving herself in Ghanaian politics, and was the minister of education in the early 1980s. This interview took place in 2002 during one of Aidoo's visits to London with Dr Nana Wilson-Tagoe, a distinguished critic of African and Caribbean literature.*

Nana Wilson-Tagoe I want to begin by taking you back to a point you made, which everybody thought was so central to our attempts to examine conceptualizations of gender in the twenty-first century. You talked of a generational gap in the understanding of gender and feminism. And you asked, 'Where did we go wrong?' Can you elaborate a little on the social and global dynamics which have created this gap?

Ama Ata Aidoo Some of the dynamics that have helped the growth of this gap are outside the Academy, outside humanity. We are talking about a world where fundamentalisms of all sorts have arisen. Certainly from this side of the world, from Europe, it is almost as though the only fundamentalism in the world is Islamic fundamentalism. But we know very well that we are coping with Christian and other fundamentalism. None of these fundamentalisms differ in how women are regarded. I think the female, both as a physical being and as a force – psychological, mental, etc. – is the most contested element outside the male. Since men have been the majority in organizing society, of course we have inevitably fallen into the role of the 'other'. So it is almost as though, outside their prescribed traditional spaces, women are looked upon as some kind of threat to society. As far as I am concerned, it is almost as if our very existence as the other human being is regarded as something that has to be watched and possibly organized outside of ourselves. It is a very complex issue. So we are looking at economics. We are looking at religious fundamentalisms. Look at something like hair dye. For me it is one of the most interesting areas to watch: the universal rush of the woman to want lighter hair colour, the blonde thing. Everybody is wanting something else other than what they have. If it is true that the ideal figure for a model is six inches all round – smaller than it used to be – then where are we going? The pressure on younger women to take grooming seriously as if we never came out of the 1920s. The fact is that whatever the feminist movement gave to the younger generation was not enough for them to withstand some of these pressures.

I want to take you back to gender and your work as a whole. From the short stories to _Anowa_, _Our Sister Killjoy_, to _Changes_, you have always located a discourse on gender in the context of change. In _Anowa_ it was the late nineteenth-century changes in society, trade and politics at the coast, which made it possible to reimagine marriage in terms of shared relationships, shared works, shared ideas, shared pain, shared anxieties. I notice that this conception of marriage has in fact run through your work, right through to _Changes_, where it is located not in Esi's relationships, but in Fusena's relationship with Ali. Now what kind of understanding of gender in Akan society influenced this confidence about transformation? Let me explain, what I find so excellent about this play, and all your other work is that there seems to be no rigid polarities between men's roles and women's roles, but rather a dialectic which sets up several perspectives within which transformation may take place. So was there anything about your understanding of gender in Akan society which made you envisage this view of fluidity?

Really, shame on you! As an Akan yourself you shouldn't be asking me this question! I mean this is the background against which we all grew up. Akan society is matrilineal and that is a major departure. I mean I didn't say matriarchal because that is very different and people mistake the two. Matrilineal as in the simple business of the inheritance of material wealth and who matters: your grandfather or your grandmother; and within the Akan society it's your grandmother. And it is unbelievable. I have known women who have had up to four sons and who still consider themselves 'infertile' because they didn't have a daughter. I grew up in my father's house but I also knew everyone who passed through our house, like wandering minstrels and prophets. So I got this incredible birds-eye view of what happens in that society and I definitely knew that being a woman is enormously important in Akan society. People say to me, 'Your women characters seem to be stronger than we are used to when thinking about African women.' As far as I am concerned these are the African women among whom I was brought up. In terms of women standing on their own feet, within or outside marriage, mostly from inside marriage, living life on their own terms. Literally everybody was like that. People might quarrel as rivals over a man, and men in exasperation might tell their wives that they are to do this and do that, but we know perfectly well that there are certain things that are taken for granted in other societies which no Akan male can take for granted. You can beat your wife but you will be counted. People will come and literally not say good morning to you and take her out, whether she likes it or not. We know that in all societies there are women for whom it is some sort of affection to be pulped by their husband. Among the Akan it is completely unacceptable.

This is how I grew up. Of course the head of the family is still a man and we are taught that men are ruling in proxy for women in Akan society. So that is why I am very careful not to say that Akan society is matriarchal because women are supposed to have the authority but not the power to rule. For me the past few years in Ghana have been an eye-opener because that matrilineal thing has not gone away anywhere. There are women who are still apologizing for not having girl children. It is incredible. The child in Akan society has something of a double inheritance, the father's and the mother's. You belong to your father's paramilitary organization but then you belong to your mother's clan.

You create a central character who at least struggles, as you say in one interview, to negotiate the traditional and the modern, and Esi attempts to create a space in which she will be both a career woman who enjoys and luxuriates in the body and sexuality, and at the same time keeps the relationship and the career. I find that this kind of feminist subjectivity is rendered questionable throughout and in fact is also continually undermined throughout this text. What is the meaning of this? Esi is central and yet in fact she too can be seen as a devourer of people. She too can be seen as someone who commits emotional violence.

I don't think it is an aspect of my feminism that a woman should be an angel. Esi is a devourer because there are the Esis of this world who can be as voracious as anybody. My contention as a writer and a feminist is that such women also have a right to be. It may undermine my feminist aims. Feminism for me is not about women being victims all the time. Life is a complete and moving dynamic, including eating and getting eaten. You know, people have told me, 'But Esi is a cold fish.' And I say, 'So what?' Or people say, 'Esi is not a very likeable character.' And I say, 'I don't like her myself.' I don't have to like her. But the fact that I don't like her doesn't mean that she has no right to her existence.

It sort of comes after characters like Sissie and Anowa. Sissie who is rather ambiguous about love and in fact feels that love must exist in a setting and context of politics.

I know Esi is not a very warm or pleasant character, but I was also interested in a woman who is selfish, who is cold. I like Esi's friend better, Opokuya. In fact in the course of writing the novel I could feel Opokuya trying to take centre stage and I literally had to shunt her aside because it was not her story. It is Esi's story, it is her life. To me this is important to my own views on humanity and womanness. If we are going to envisage a world where women have the right to exist then it is not just going to be revolutionaries, the nice women, the warm women, but it is all women.

I remember a scene at the hotel when Opokuya's husband comes in and she is immediately ready to go and very apologetic. Whereas, in fact it was not her fault in the first place that she finds herself at the hotel. In a sense, despite her own outspokenness and her desire to maintain a career, she also exhibits certain traits that would make her susceptible to that kind of vulnerability that Esi is attempting to escape from.

We are struggling and it is going to take some time. It has been several thousand years since the beginning of societal organizations and in all societies it has been the same. A woman's place has long been associated with the domestic so it is not going to take just half a century for us to overcome all of these things or nearly all of them.

It is probably the only novel in which the attraction of a man and a woman is explicitly stated in terms of romantic love. The whole scene in which they meet is seen very much in terms of what you might call romantic novels.

I thought I was going to write a potboiler that was going to make me lots of money so that is the genesis of *Changes*, originally it was a radio play. I accepted a commission to write a play for the Zimbabwe radio corporation because I was so poor and a German organization was giving money to the Zimbabwe radio organization to help them develop their drama department. In fact it won an award as a play. Then the characters stuck around as though they didn't want to go away, so one day I thought maybe I'll do a novel with these characters so they will leave me be. I write a novel like *Our Sister Killjoy*, and people tell me they think it is experimental and I am not making any money from it. Although it was successful and it is still in print. So I was going to write a romantic tale that people will pick up. That people would read at airports. Well, it didn't work out like that. You know how in these romantic stories the woman has to be thin and tall and pretty and the man has to be tall, craggy and rough. In the long run everything has to fall into place.

I read one interview in which you had said that in *Our Sister Killjoy* you were dealing with hard issues of public politics. You were saying this in relation to *Changes*. I think in a sense *Changes* also deals with issues of politics and one ought not to see it only in terms of relationships and marriage because there are so many asides central to the concerns over Esi's problem. For instance, looking at their presence in the hotel. There is a very interesting reference to the fisherman. I thought that bringing this in in a context in which we are looking at how somebody has fallen in love is itself an enlargement of the public issues surrounding relationships and love.

Because there are public issues surrounding love.

It is a very political novel.

I cannot dispute that. It goes back to a politicized imagination on that level. Therefore, I would have to admit that I haven't written a single novel, play or poem that is not political. It is not something that I work very hard at. When I sit down to write, I don't know how it happens. I find my imagination throwing these things at me. I became aware of it a long time ago. Not to write in this way would be to commit violence to my own imagination. You can't say, 'OK, I want to do a love story. Please, politics stay out.' How do I do that? I probably could and maybe one of these days I shall rechallenge myself to do a completely unpolitical love story.

That would be impossible.

Even a fairly innocuous story like Esi's love affairs. I didn't make references to fishermen, it is just that it came in from her own immediate
mind and universe. Of course, you always have a choice of cutting them
out but I have always known that I had better not do that because that
would be terrifying. It would be like acting as the chief censor on my
own imagination. If I am scared of censorship applied from outside,
how much more for auto-censorship. That is even more dangerous for
a writer.

**You started writing at a very, very young age. You won a competition
for a short story when you were eighteen years old. I want to get a
sense of this whole nurturing. Which people did you read? I mean,
how did you become a writer? How did you come to write a short
story at that age?**

Without mystifying or glorifying, I think I was born a writer, I believe
that talent is transferable. I may have been, I don't know, a singer – I
don't have the voice, but definitely a performer of sorts. I got hold of
the pen and therefore I wrote. I knew I wanted to be a writer when I
was fifteen years old. When I came across those things I wrote two or
three years ago, I said, 'My goodness, look at what I was writing!' What
were the environmental factors that led to my writing? I think it was
where I grew up. My mother, I think they would call her an insomniac.
My mother is the kind of person who is up at three o'clock in the
morning and most mornings she doesn't sleep again until daylight, of
course. When we were kids, unlike most people who would tell stories
in the evening, my mother would tell her stories early in the morning;
you woke up to her voice and she was always telling these stories. Some
true, some fictional. And *Anowa* was inspired by these stories, although
it doesn't resemble in any way a story that my mother told me. When I
was growing up in the village we had this man who was recognized as a
storyteller. We used to go and listen to his stories. We were lucky when
the primary school was established and we were going to school, there
were these incredible teachers who really just encouraged us to tell

stories in the afternoon. So all of that started me. And then at Wesley
Girls I came across Shakespeare, so it was like, 'Ah, this is the other
side.' And then of course I had Miss Bowman my literature teacher. She
encouraged me greatly by giving me an old-style Olivetti typewriter
from her family. An incredible machine. Then of course a good school
library. I just read everything in sight. I remember when I was in form 4
I always had a story book under my desk, which I would read during
maths classes until Miss Jacobs discovered it. Coming across what
clearly was fantastic literature and reading a whole lot, I didn't know
that I was reading to prepare myself for writing. I just loved reading.
One day I opened a chest of drawers in my uncle's room. And guess
what I found? Bram Stoker's *Dracula*, Lord Alfred Tennyson's collected
poems, stuff like that. Crazy things which I picked up and started
reading, in about 1958. It was almost like everything around me was
conspiring to get me writing.

26

Maggie Gee
with
Maya Jaggi

Maggie Gee's The White Family *is a condition-of-England novel set in Hillesden Rise, a fictitious part of London. Through Alfred White, the keeper of Albion Park, his wife May, and their children Darren, Shirley and Dirk, the novel explores themes from racist violence and interracial relationships to black homophobia and friction between African and West Indian, amid urban decline and gentrification. A horrific murder in the park creates a dilemma between protecting family and upholding values of justice and fair play.*

Born in Poole, Dorset, in 1948, Gee studied English at Oxford and has a Ph.D. in the twentieth-century novel. She was chosen as one of Granta's *Best of Young British Novelists in 1983, and is a Fellow and current Chair of the Royal Society of Literature.* The White Family *(2002) is her eighth novel and was shortlisted for the Orange Prize. Her previous books include* Dying, In Other Words *(1981),* The Burning Book *(1983),* Light Years *(1985),* Grace *(1988),* Where are the Snows? *(1991) and* The Ice People *(1998). Her latest book,* The Flood, *appeared in 2004. This is an edited version of the interview which took place at the author's home in Kensal Rise.*

Maya Jaggi *The White Family* explores issues of race and racism in present-day Britain, in London. What was the impulse behind it?

Maggie Gee Living where I do, the subject was on my mind. But the crunch was the Stephen Lawrence murder [in April 1993] – being upset by it, and ashamed, and thinking I must use my writing to express that. I thought, 'I have to try and understand why white people every now and then kill black people in London', and perhaps, like Shirley, I felt quite naively, 'I want them to know all white people aren't like that.' So it was trying to understand and even trying to expiate.

Were you also aware of a gap in British fiction?

It wasn't really a literary thing. All the same, the more I thought about it the more I thought that, at the moment, this book doesn't exist in Britain. Of course, you don't write books because there's a gap, but I do think there was a gap in the discourse, in the way people talked publicly then – though I don't think it's so true now. Living here for fifteen years since 1987 – I got to know more black people. It takes time to make friends. So things that had previously been theoretical to me were actual.

You've said you started writing *The White Family* in 1993. What was the road to its publication?

Very rocky, very stony, very hard. It was the second book in an 80,000 pound two-book contract, which was pretty good at the time; it's the only contract I've had like that. But this book, the second, was turned down, which was devastating. I thought somebody else would take it, but they didn't. This was extraordinarily difficult, because you feel ashamed. You start by feeling indignant, but if enough people turn a book down it's quite hard to maintain your sense that the book is all right. So I wrote another book, *The Ice People*, which saved me from despair. It dealt with a bi-racial child, but in a very different, light way. I felt I mustn't go deep into emotion, because if you write a book with a lot of emotion and it gets turned down you do feel naked. That book got very good reviews but I hadn't forgotten *The White Family*. I was advised by my agent to give up on it, which I did not feel able to do because I had put so much of myself into it. I went to Mike Phillips, who was writer-in-residence at the Royal Festival Hall, and asked him to read it. He encouraged me. But I thought, 'Books can always be made better', so I did a lot of cutting. I wanted it to go out again completely defended, if it ever could be. I finished it maybe eighteen months ago and, with a different agent, sent it to four good publishers, and again they turned it down.

Did anyone tell you why?

Well, there was this repetitive use of the word 'dark' and I did wonder if unconsciously it was because I was writing about black people, and they weren't sure whether I was writing correctly about black people. The English way of dealing with issues about colour is often to say nothing at all and hope it goes away.

Would it have occurred to any of the publishers to find a black reader?

I would love to know who read it. One editor, a poet, wanted the book but she was overruled by the editorial board. Then I showed it to Saqi and they loved it. The interesting thing is that the main people at Saqi come from the Lebanon so in that sense they are outside mainstream British culture. It was interesting and horrifying (and wonderful!) to find that after all that struggle, and being uniformly turned down, the book has sold well, got mostly very good reviews, and was shortlisted for the Orange Prize.

The perspective of the novel shifts between members of the White family and their friends and acquaintances, but the voices are predominantly of white characters – other than Winston, who is black and gay. You portray life in black churches, but on the whole, the black characters are not the main ones. Was it a deliberate strategy to stay with the voices of the white characters?

Yes, but it was a stratagem that came late. I was always writing about the White family – that's why it has that title. But Elroy, Shirley's black lover, began as quite a main character. I just lost confidence. I lost my nerve when the book had problems and I wondered if that was what the publishers were worrying about, that I shouldn't be doing this voice. I thought it would be valid artistically to restrict the book to the white characters, because then I would be talking about whiteness in a society where it is on the whole taken as the invisible norm. To pick it out and look at it from the other side seemed interesting to me. But the truth is I got to the point where I would have tried anything.

What were your black readers' reactions?

Positive. I got encouragement from my black friends when things got tough, like Hanna Sakyi, to whom the book is dedicated, and from black writers, and did specifically ask them about the language. Writers in general encouraged me, black and white – chief among them the poet E. J. Scovell, a very dear and old friend of mine. She died two years ago in her early nineties, but her belief in this book was very strong. I am quite a determined character but maybe without that encourage-ment I would have given up.

What would you say to those who might criticize you for 'appropriat-ing' the voice of black characters?

My initial, instinctive response would be, 'Sod off. I'll write about what I want to.' A more intelligent response would be to acknowledge that if people feel their voice is not represented enough, the last thing they want is for somebody else to nick it; that seems to me quite logical. I think a challenge like this might well have come from black writers who felt under-appreciated or suppressed, and I would respect that. But in fact it didn't. I do think in the end imagining is all about trying to live other lives and create other selves who are superficially unlike us but at a deep level just like us. If white liberals were to tell me I shouldn't be writing through black characters I wouldn't take much notice, whereas I would have taken notice if I had got that reaction from my black readers.

On imagining lives across gender, is it right that you were one of two women on the Booker judging panel in 1989 who didn't want Martin Amis's *London Fields* to be shortlisted?

Kind of right. My reactions were probably based upon the fact that I am a woman and found particularly distasteful the portrayal of the woman who wants to be murdered – she's a fantasy figure, not a real figure. How many women want to get murdered? Nevertheless, the arguments were literary: it's a very long novel, and nowhere near Martin Amis's best book although the comic character is very funny. So many books by well-known authors tend to just float through on to prize longlists and shortlists because people are embarrassed not to include them, but they have no divine right to be there. I would have felt irked in a personal way if *London Fields* had been shortlisted, but that doesn't mean the arguments I used were as crude as the media portrayed.

Was it a challenge to create the uncensored voice of a BNP [British National Party] or sub-BNP racist in the character of Dirk, and were there any dangers in that?

Yes, for me that was the most difficult thing, both in terms of what people might think, saying where does this come from? And also in terms of my attitude to this boy, because nearly everything he thinks is forbidden: it mustn't be expressed. In a sense, for a writer, transgression is always fun. But while I felt I did all the characters from inside, I dealt with Dirk by trying to distance him through comedy. I make him ignorant. He is not a stupid boy: he has a level of intelligence; he is very good at maths. I think the bitterest and angriest people are those whose gifts have never been noticed. But he is linguistically and personally stupid; he understands nothing. Every speech or thought of his is satirized. I wouldn't have minded if people laughed at Dirk. But I think people feel anxious because what he expresses is so bad. They don't realize that I actually did mean it to be funny. It is a very fine line to tread. I worried that people might find the comedy unacceptable. The character is obviously very frightening and terrible, though, so in fact most people didn't see the comedy at all.

Some writers say they have to sympathize with all their characters when they're writing.

I think Dirk was a bridge too far. I had a theoretical sympathy; he is not loved. But I find it hard to see him as pathetic, whereas I did sympathize with Alfred. It's not that I don't see where Dirk is coming from; that blind rage that comes from having nothing. However to some extent I must have been using forbidden and censored parts of myself in Dirk and Alfred. I think all human horrors are in all of us somewhere, though I'm not clear how this works. All my characters are in a way myself, but I'm not sure if the author directly mines their unconscious or whether it's more active and exploratory. Once you start thinking of a character you start projecting yourself into them and, like an actor, becoming them. You may, though, be using similar, rather than absolutely identical, parts of yourself. Thus all griefs and losses, I truly believe, are interchangeable, or bleed into each other, and link people. Maybe all fears and hatreds and rages do the same.

On the source of Dirk's voice, there are phrases you capture – 'no opportunities for the native English'. Did you do any research into the far right?

Not a lot. I read some magazines; I read a lot of rhetoric. Some of it you just get from listening to people. I always talk to people because I'm interested in what everyone's got to say. For example we had a workman come the other day, a complete racist. I would only ask questions, in the hope of sowing some doubts, because there is no point in flatly contradicting; they can't hear what you say. It is exhausting. I wrote a novel called *Grace* in 1988 about the murder of Hilda Murrell, the Greenham Common anti-nuclear protester. Again, it was something that really upset me, a murder that was never solved. It seemed she was murdered by a guy who was sexually abusing his daughters. I thought, I cannot invent this character from inside. So I changed it; I made him sexually confused, which is a different thing. As an author, I would like to be able to do everything, to invent anything in human life, however wonderful or terrible, but I don't think I can, because some horrors might become part of you, and I need to keep some of my head free, so I can be myself.

I thought there'd be a danger with many of these characters of being condescending, or parading the author's disapproval – neither of which you do.

Yes, I hope I wasn't condescending. Every day there are so many things that I don't understand myself until later; I say and do the wrong things all the time. Therefore, all the characters I've ever written always have the same kind of misunderstandings; Dirk is just another example. I don't worry about class condescension because, although my parents got to the middle class, they were working-class. Therefore lots of my family were still working-class, and so it's quite familiar.

You also explore middle-class racism. For example, Thomas assumes a documentary on James Baldwin is of 'specialist inter-est'. What was your interest in that more genteel form of prejudice?

It's something I hear, and once you start hearing it, you hear it a lot. It's just blindness. I wanted to put it in quite delicately, so people would either notice it or not. Thomas is quite a sympathetic character but narrow. I think cultural and intellectual life are still incredibly com-partmentalized in Britain. A lot of people still see black writers as people they just don't read. Unconsciously, they are just not interested. And if you are someone who is interested in black artists and multi-cultural politics, the question gets asked why: 'But why wouldn't I be?' However, when I was, as you put it in your [*Guardian*] review, 'skewering' liberal racism, I think I was also thinking of the kind of mistakes I've made myself, and the kind of blindness I've had. I've been interested in these issues for a long time, because I lived in Wolverhampton for five years in the 1970s. Books, though, take a long time to germinate.

You show that unconscious compartmentalizing, and harbouring of assumptions, among the kind of people who might say racism is no longer a problem.

This is fascinating. I am very interested in the idea of 'post-racism' which I'm sure describes a mind-set, like 'post-feminism'. I think some people I know bordered on irritation when I was talking about writing this book; they thought it was out of date in the modern post-prejudice world. I was annoyed by the [*Observer*] review which said *The White Family* was old-fashioned in comparison with Zadie Smith's *White Teeth* [2000]. In a way I see what the reviewer meant: Zadie Smith looks forward and describes – mostly – young people; I look at the fruit of the Second World War and the loss of empire, and my main characters are – mostly – older people. But it isn't fair to say her book is post-racist, as someone said to me, since the 'teeth' are hidden in the middle with that mad old man, and very sharp. I did admire the book. It was full of energy and wit and it is very humane.

Your novel hints at a link between racist violence and 'domestic' violence within the family – with Alfred's wife-beating, and Shirley being pressurized by May to give up an 'illegitimate' baby for adoption. How do you see that link?

I think that what happens inside little houses happens next outside of them. It is re-enacted by people who don't know what they are re-enacting. I don't know what you can do about it, but it seems to me really important not to hit kids, because they will definitely go and hit their own kids if not someone else.

In the end, Dirk is perhaps a real scapegoat who has to be expelled and destroyed in order for the family to carry on?

Yes. What can happen to him except that he must go to prison? I guess that was also partly to do with the Stephen Lawrence case. Of course, the murder is nothing like the Stephen Lawrence murder; it would be most offensive to say that it was. But I do have this feeling that society must have justice, and sometimes that doesn't happen in real life. So perhaps that is something for writers to do, to help those who have lost people.

And you see a role for writers in that space?

Not usually to help the people directly involved. Nothing could help that kind of grief. Though to my surprise my novel *Grace* did comfort the closest surviving relative of the woman, Hilda Murrell. Without doing an investigative book I suggested that the British security services were involved in her murder. In fact that is almost certainly true, though no one has ever been convicted. I was afraid to contact Hilda Murrell's nephew Rob Green in case the book made it worse for him, but in fact he came and found me, and he really liked the book. Books sometimes help by keeping memories alive and getting things out there where they can be discussed. They are a slightly less pressured place where people can sometimes see things more clearly. People are not on the line so much in imaginary spaces – the writers are on the line but their readers are not – so books lift things out of the everyday world where people's ideas are quite fixed into a space where they are free to think again.

In the asylum debate, there are people who think that politicians and a 'politically correct media conspiracy', or some such thing, block resentments from being aired. Is it one of the functions of the novel to air – and perhaps contest – those views openly?

My personal view on asylum is that we are an ageing society and we absolutely have to have newcomers. It would be nice if they were all legal because otherwise they will be exploited. But what do I think about the silencing of people who don't want asylum seekers? I am quite confused here. I don't want asylum seekers and immigrants to have to hear things that are upsetting to them. But on the other hand I don't think it helps just telling people to be quiet. The maddening thing is that it is often middle-class people who don't live in those areas who are shutting up working-class people who do, and that is angering. There are people of the older generation around my area who I can understand and sympathize with in a way, though it still makes me wince to hear what they say. Their area has changed completely. These are people who loved it, who had allotment gardens. They know every-thing about local history, and as they age and start feeling frailer, they get anxious about change, and associate that change with skin colour. In *The White Family* I have tried to show where fear and prejudice like that come from, and understand that there are sometimes sympathetic people underneath the prejudiced remarks. They are probably like my character Alfred the park keeper, in that if they were put in his situation in the novel, where he has to choose between loyalty to his racist son and justice for an innocent individual, they would make a decision that was for the individual and for justice. It's just that they have not been able to keep up with the rate of change all round them.

Alfred is one of the surprises of the novel. He is portrayed in such a way that you feel you know him, then he surprises you.

I rarely let Alfred be seen from the inside for at least half of the novel; he is the patriarch and very racist, always seen from the outside as an oppressor. Then halfway through I started wilting from his viewpoint, and seeing Alfred from a position of weakness – he is dying, in fact. He feels time is running out for him and his world. I found myself much more sympathetic to him then than I thought I would be. Alfred became a more likeable character as I wrote him, though this didn't necessarily mean he would make a decision for justice. I didn't know what would happen until the end in this novel. I didn't know if either parent would make a decision for justice and I certainly didn't know which one.

Alfred's wife May appears more liberal, but ends by wanting to protect her family, regardless of justice.

She is a coward as well. Just as in a war you don't know who is going to be a coward, you don't know what will happen in these situations. Alfred is quite brave and has an absolute sense of right and wrong, which he has failed to apply in his own behaviour, but can apply to his son. Sometimes, as a relativist, I think absolutes are useful. I also think there is always hope; people can get better, and Alfred does. It was more truthful for Alfred to have made that decision, not May, who doesn't like a fuss. Like a lot of women who compromise and fit around people, she is a fitter-in, and Alfred is a sticker-out. But maybe part of her would have been relieved that Alfred did make that better choice, the choice she should have made herself. In marriages sometimes people carve out roles. Maybe May shouldn't be judged too harshly.

Sex and sexuality are important in the novel, both in terms of Shirley's inter-racial relationships, and the way they subvert or surmount racial barriers, and in Dirk's repressed homoerotic desire.

Prejudices project sexuality on to others, on to differentness: fear of the other and desire of the other. This is not a new idea. There is a fear of genetically different people who will somehow take over from our genes – though it's all a dreadful misunderstanding. Recent research has shown that there is no correlation between currently perceived racial groupings and real genetic difference. Skin colour is decided by a tiny number of genes in each person's total of forty thousand or so. There is a fear that 'other people's genes' will take over, and that somehow takes the form of a terror that they might be sexier, more potent. It is terribly banal and unconscious, but I think it is there – though less so all the time, because there are so many mixed-race relationships around here and all over a modern city like London. In Dirk's case of repressed homosexual desire, he really wants to kill himself and instead he tries to kill Winston. He wants to kill or fuck somebody, and the fact that it's Winston who is there waiting for him is unbearable. In a way the penetration by the knife could have been penetration sexually. With the death in the park, which was ghastly to write, I was trying to say, rather sex than death. And I do think Dirk wouldn't have been so murderous if he had had someone who loved him.

The novel has a hopeful ending. Shirley, who 'crosses the river', becomes central to a new family, in place of the defunct White family. There is almost a fantastic element in the black and white twins she is carrying. Did you see it as a departure from realism?

Curiously, I found in a women's magazine a woman who had one black and one white twin, so it is possible. It was an image. I also gave Thomas a black great-grandmother from Barbados; the English, and the British, are always changing. But the end does move away from literal realism: the boys in Shirley's womb are metaphorical. I didn't think 'melting pot' or 'rainbows' or anything so simple, but by making new people there will be new situations. The future takes physical form, and our ideas and prejudices will die. It is our minds that are so poisonous; there's nothing more frightening than a mind without a body. So I did mean the ending to be hopeful. The great thing about human beings is that we are not different species, whatever terrible apartheid fantasies people dream up. People will always integrate. I intended the texture of life in the book to thin and become dream-like after May confesses to Alfred about Dirk. Only biblical language, heightened poetic language, will do for the scale of the tragedy, and also for the possibility of reconciliation: 'He has created both darkness and light.' At the opposite pole there is blind, warm life moving inside Shirley, oblivious.

People in the novel are characterized by what they read. May is a voracious reader, but the novel goes against the idea that the more you read the more enlightened you become?

I don't think I consciously characterized people like that, but because I am very interested in literature it's always going to come in. As for May, yes: she is very proud of having read Baldwin and Martin Luther King, and she thinks she is much more modern than poor old Alfred. She rather despises and looks down on Alfred, although she adores him. But although I personally believe in reading and education, I don't think it's entirely the answer. I don't think a liberal education or liberal culture is predictive of liberal, tolerant actions. We all know about Nazis listening to Mozart.

Thomas is a librarian, writing a boring tome on 'the death of meaning'.

Thomas loves books in the defeated way that librarians often seem to. What I try to do through Thomas is a skit on academic theory. I get very irritated by complicated formulations in theory because I think the ideas in structuralist and post-structuralist theory are very interesting but the language is so elitist it's a form of seizing power; a power discourse that excludes and includes. I was trying to set it against the clarity of someone like Baldwin – the way his ideas and language come together.

This novel seems deliberately accessible, readable. Do you see it as a departure from your more experimental early fiction?

I only really wrote two experimental novels, and I don't think even they were very difficult. But it's true that something happens when you write through characters, when you use voices. You don't use overt literary language then. The literariness of *The White Family* comes from the structure and the fact that most of the novel is in verse, if you listen: a basic four-stress line, in tetrameter, which I think is the commonest in English poetry. It's like the beating of a heart. But it's supposed to be concealed so people don't need to notice. My ideal is what May says, that 'books were meant for everybody'. It is quite hard to gauge the accessibility of your own work, but I believe it's possible to make complex ideas and feelings accessible; it's just a great technical challenge. My ideal would be maximum richness of thought and feeling and reference, and of internal formal connection, under the surface, with a completely clear and lucid surface. So people can skate across it if they want to, and not feel the author is trying to drag them down by their feet.

27

Nadine Gordimer
with
Hermione Lee

The following discussion originally took place at the University of London's Centre for African and Asian Literatures and focuses on Nadine Gordimer's new collection of short stories, Loot *(2003). Born in 1923, Gordimer has consistently condemned the apartheid regime in South Africa. Unlike many others of her generation, she not only chose to remain in South Africa during this difficult period, but became centrally involved with the activities of the African National Congress and the struggle for freedom. In this interview she discusses the South African world in which she lived both during the apartheid years and since apartheid was formally lifted in 1994.*

Gordimer's first novel, Lying Days, *appeared in 1953. Other works include* The Late Bourgeois World *(1966),* Burgher's Daughter *(1979),* A Sport of Nature *(1987),* My Son's Story *(1990) and* The Pickup *(2002). As well as being a distinguished writer of fiction, Gordimer is also a well-known essayist and delivered the prestigious Charles Eliot Norton lectures at Harvard University in 1995 – a collection of essays which appeared in book form as* Writing and Being *(1995). She was awarded the Nobel Prize for Literature for her life's work in 1991.*

Hermione Lee In the last ten years you have published three novels: *None to Accompany Me* [1994], *The House Gun* [1998] and

The Pickup. These are all novels of cultural transition, reflecting power shifts in the private and the public domain. There has been a volume of short stories, *Jump* [1991], whose topical themes include war refugees and terrorism, and several collections of illuminating essays on literature and politics, and the responsibilities of the writer. You have also been working as a UN goodwill ambassador. One of the essays in a recent volume, *Writing and Being*, is called 'Adam's Rib'; it talks about the fallacy of the idea that writers draw their ideas directly from life. In this essay you argue that 'The morality of fiction is being questioned by those who accuse the writer of looting the characters of living personages. Fictional creatures are brought into the synthesis of being by the writer's imagination alone, which is a different kind of looting.' It is this idea of the writer as looter that I imagine lies behind the title of this collection published today. It is very different from your last, a very fascinating combination of social realism, satire, fable, and it has many different voices. Do you see *Loot* as a moral fable, a political allegory or a writer's fantasy? If you were forced to define it, how would you describe it?

Nadine Gordimer I suppose it is a little bit of each. Maybe it is more of a political fable, about material things and possessions, the loss of possession as well as the desire for things. It's one of the very few stories of about two hundred or more I have written that was set off by a particular site and a particular occasion. I mean 'site', as well as 'sight' in the sense of looking at something. I was in Chile a couple of years ago and went to the area where an earthquake took place. It was the biggest earthquake ever measured on the Richter scale and it had the extraordinary effect of changing the landscape forever. Even the rivers changed. When people told me that there was this extraordinary event, that the sea drew back, and there was all this stuff there, I was absolutely fascinated. I hadn't seen any photographs or drawings. And so out of that came this imagining.

But it turns into a kind of political allegory for regime change – to use that now-awful phrase – whereby those who haven't had power take possession of it, but they in turn may be taken over by the next great wave. So in a way it has a kind of historical determinism.

Yes, I suppose so and also of course the reference towards the end, which was really a reference to the people in that part of the world, especially Argentina, where political opponents were thrown into the sea. That sort of illumination of people from my own background in South Africa keeps coming to mind in different contexts.

Has that been one of the challenges for you in recent years, a period in which, as it were, the world turned upside down? I recognize that in your recent novels, where those who have been in control – in power or in possession – suddenly find themselves dependent in a way that they haven't been before. There is a wonderful story in here called 'Mission Statement', where a white woman working for a development agency in an African country has an affair with a black political figure. I would love you to talk about it. The analogy between the way that relationship works and the transition period in this country is very subtly pursued in this story.

Well, it is interesting that you connect it with *Loot* because that wouldn't have occurred to me. But as with all writers I am always approaching certain themes from different angles, quite sub-consciously, so perhaps that was there. I hadn't thought that they were aligned in any way to each other. 'Mission Statement' and I think, 'Karma' (the longest in the collection), are the most recently written. The other stories were written over a period of six or seven years.

I think critics always look for links and novelists always resist them. One of the things I am very struck by, certainly in the recent work, but also in early novels, like *July's People* [1981], is the way that the turnaround of power, or the battle for power in a political context, is very often acted out in work and personal relations. It also happens here in the comic but rather upsetting story about a father of a family, who after forty-two years has left his wife and gone off with a young girl, who of course in turn leaves him. It is from the children's point of view, and they are completely appalled and thrown by this power shift in the relationship.

What intrigued me when writing that story is evident from the title, 'Generation Gap'. The generation gap is always regarded as that between parents and the children and what the children do appals the parents. I think in every generation we have done that with our parents. But here it was reversed, because it was the father's behaviour that is being judged by his adult children. So that is very much a tongue-in-cheek story. But it is also about the reversal of power that you have been talking about.

Would it be simplistic to say that in your work there is no such thing as a private life? That these very private emotions of parents and children and mothers have necessarily to always be played out in a political context or have a political meaning?

Not always. It depends where you live. If you grow up and your emotions mature, so to speak, within a conflict situation, then your private emotions do tend to be influenced and coloured somewhat by this, because it is a kind of a cage that you live in. The morals of your society, whether it is here or in America, or in the divided Germany, or in the divided South Africa, wherever it is, these things subconsciously impinge upon you; this is something central to my thinking. We all know that when you are born, in the process of coming down the birth canal, the bones of your head are pushed together. You come out with your head formed but I think the society we live in completes that process in a way. The pressures of that society also pressurize you this way and that and impinge upon you and make you partly what you are. Part of it is inside, part of it is hereditary. There is no such thing as an apolitical being in the sense that they are totally unaffected by the values, morals and manners of the society in which they live.

There is a very interesting tension between individual, private, anarchic free choice and the constraints that are placed upon people, certainly even now, in your country. For instance, in 'Karma', which is about an abandoned white baby who is adopted by coloured parents. Eventually it turns out that she is not permitted to marry white boys.

That was in the 'informal' settlement part of town and was absolutely what happened.

It is interesting reading it now in this collection, because it still seems to have a very powerful resonance – although the context of it has, thankfully, passed – in terms of how you see the individual and individual choices: that they are always played out in a very confined way.

There are people who have gone through that kind of experience. I mean it doesn't just blow away. It is with you for the rest of your life. Of course there is a tendency, especially among young writers, to write about the past rather than the present. This worries me a little bit because the present is so interesting. It is a new way in which we are all living. And so far it is not even a decade. There are not many works, whether poetry, stories or novels, that deal with the present. I suppose it is a repression of the past where you couldn't say this, or didn't think you could get away with it, but people tend to write more and more about what happened in the apartheid past than in the post-apartheid present.

Do you think that's because it lends itself in all its appalling consequences to drama and intensity, a tragedy of a kind that is perhaps not available to contemporary South Africa?

Probably. Then people forget. A close friend of mine, the poet Mongane Wally Serote, has been through everything. When I first got to know him, he was seventeen or eighteen years old and he had just been in detention as one of the African National Congress (ANC) youth. He has always been a very talented writer but he has also been very much absorbed in the liberation struggle and in the building up afterwards. Coming back from the army he became an MP. I've known his children, who have been dragged around all over the world. I was once with him, and the son who I think was about fifteen suddenly heard us talking about the past – as we do – and said, 'Dad, you know I can't understand. You mean you really went around with that pass in your pocket? How feeble. Why didn't you just throw it *away*?' So you can see the enormous change in the psyche that has happened.

For the writer there is also a need to remember the past, so that people won't forget that past.

But I see this among my friends, especially among my black friends, because theirs are the lives that have changed the most physically. Many of them have moved out of the ghettos but there are all sorts of new situations that come up for them. Not many of them have begun to write about it. This is something that I await with great eagerness.

But in your stories – in *Jump* and in this volume and in *The House Gun* too – there is a tremendous amount of darkness, violence, catastrophe, tragedy, death and loss and there is also, at least in one of these stories, a certain amount of corruption. In one of the 'Karma' stories there is a woman who is exposed as having been involved in corrupt dealings, having previously been involved in the fight for liberation. Does this reflect any kind of cynicism on your part about the new South Africa?

No, it reflects the reality. I often compare the two circumstances. When the Berlin Wall came down we all saw these marvellous visions on television and in newspaper photographs. The wall came down, everyone was pouring across and hugging each other, breaking champagne bottles, and it was all brothers and sisters and great partying and rejoicing. We had the same reaction when the apartheid walls came down. Then comes the morning after. Then comes the hangover. Realities, which during any kind of political struggle you don't really have time to think about. So I have found in Germany that the Easterners had lived such a different life that the Westerners hadn't realized that the Easterners didn't even know what a cheque book was. Nobody had a cheque book, the kind of things we take for granted in our way of life. The whole idea of having a new wave of competition for work, for housing, for all the things that had been exclusive to the Westerners and in our case had been exclusive to whites. These realities I don't think we had given much thought to, or indeed in some cases any thought at all, the idea of what would happen the morning after. That of course is what we are dealing with now. It includes other things which are psychological and not so surprising. But people have been very deprived and once they are leading normal lives – it seems that once you have something – you seem to want more and more and this leads to corruption. It amazes me that someone who is in parliament in South Africa and is so respected because of their past as freedom fighters, that they should be tempted by bribery. Whether it is for some defence equipment or for any other form of development of the country. What is corruption? Corruption comes from wanting more. From having material ambitions that maybe before were a way out of your mind. You couldn't ever think that you would aspire to such things.

It is the image of 'loot' again.

The image of 'loot', yes.

Having lived through and come out of a period of censorship, do you feel any kind of inhibitions now in your role as a writer? I mean do

you feel it incumbent upon you to give a positive picture of the new South Africa, or do you feel entirely free in what you can write?

Entirely free. In *None to Accompany Me* there was a reflection of the phenomenon of people coming back from exile as well as people who had been carrying on the struggle at home and had been imprisoned. When you come into power and there are powerful positions to be handed out, who is going to get them? Is it going to be the one who has been in exile, a freedom fighter in battle, or is it the one who has been underground working at home? Some of the characters in that book are living that particular drama. I am a member of the ANC and I did not get any rap over the knuckles for exposing the external conflicts that came up.

To me that is an example of freedom of expression. To move away from my own case, there is an enormous amount of social criticism in the theatre. There are three plays on at the Market Theatre Complex in Johannesburg and all three contain, in very different ways, criticism of some of the things that we are doing in South Africa now, including one absolutely uproarious satire on a wedding. We have had *Monsoon Wedding* and then there was *My Big Fat Greek Wedding*, now this is the South African new-black-empowerment-class wedding. People who have now made money and make big decisions, and it is their wedding. The stage is circular and the audience sits around it as the wedding guests. It is a marvellous send-up of bourgeois conventions. It is very funny but it is very sharp. I think this shows that you really can say what you like. I suppose if you are directly in politics you run into trouble for not being politically correct, but as writers and people in the theatre we are really wonderfully free.

But you are a writer who has a public role around the world as well as in your own country. I am very fascinated by how you stay free, how you keep the imaginative domain that is just anarchic and free. That is not as the Nobel Prize winner or the UN ambassador. How do you shut the windows against your public role?

Well, I think I started doing that when it was much more difficult, during the apartheid time. I had to make up my mind, 'Am I going to become a propagandist for the cause that I passionately believe in or am I going to act one way in my person as a citizen, a human being, a South African, and keep that separate from what I write?' In other words, was I going to create my characters from the society around me and show them warts and all? I made that decision long, long ago and stuck to it. I don't think I would have been a very good propagandist anyway and I don't think that you serve your society well in that way. I think that real loyalty to anything you believe in is keeping the right to criticize it when you think that it has gone wrong. Then of course living in South Africa I have learnt so much from other people. From good friends, including some who are sitting here tonight. My education as a human being has come out of others, many of whom did far more than I in the struggle for justice in South Africa.

I was listening to the novelist Don De Lillo on the radio yesterday, who was being interviewed on the *Today* programme. He was asked, 'Your work is very dark. What solutions do you pose to the problems which you raise?' And he replied, quite politely, 'I don't really think in terms of solutions and problems, I just see how an idea will develop.' I thought this was a wonderfully typical exchange between an author and a journalist. You have said in a fairly recent interview, 'Fiction is open-ended. The story continues outside the reader. There is no final page.' I thought, particularly in this volume, that a lot of the stories seemed to be purposely inconclusive. Not solving problems. Not even telling us sometimes whether a character in a story is dead or alive, is a memory or a reality. Is this something that interests you increasingly or is it something that has always been very central to your work? This sense of fiction's inconclusiveness, its reluctance to resolve issues and problems.

Well this has come to me from other people's work. If you are going to write something that is totally conclusive you have to start in the good old Victorian way that so and so was born and then you have to kill this person off. And even that is not conclusive because sometimes that death produces consequences. So all of us as writers are telling part of the human story. There is no conclusion. I think all that we write is merely pieced together. Nobody can explain all that was happening in their society or in their age. Whether we go to Tolstoy or Dostoevsky or Proust, or any of the greats. All you can do is to contribute your little bit of insight. You pick up a life and then when you have created it, watched it, seen it move this way and that, you put it down there but it doesn't end there.

You actually show that process in your work and you put that process into the narrative. You say, 'Let's call that person X, but they might be someone else. Or perhaps the person I am writing about is still out there alive.' There is a kind of narrative voice that is not very personal. I never feel that it is an objective voice but it is kind of authorial, almost a technician's voice, saying, 'Try this, or how about this?'

I think it is interesting that you have brought that up because I have always kept myself right out of the story. But in the little story 'Loot' I said, 'Now the writer is going to tell you something else.' As Graham Greene said, we see things happen in people's lives or we catch a glimpse and then we see an alternate life for them.

One of the things you do, particularly in these stories, is to inhabit quite alien voices. For instance, there is a political assassin who tells one of the stories. You inhabit that voice, which could not be, I presume, more alien to you. Is that a challenge you set yourself, to go as far away from yourself as you can?

But I don't do it consciously. It just happens. I don't know what to call writers. Androgynous? We are all sorts of strange things. Funnily enough yesterday I was talking to someone and they wanted to know about early things I wrote. Because I wrote kid stories and then when I was fifteen my first adult story was published in a journal [*aside*] . . . quite an intellectual journal. It was an enormous thrill when I first saw that in print, a thrill that has never been surpassed by anything since. It was wonderful. But in that story the central character was an old man, who for some reason or other had to go and stay with his son, a young man and his daughter-in-law. And he has no kind of relationship with his son, which is rather strange, but this girl – whom he felt nervous about having any contact with at all – there is some sort of rapport between them. So why I at fifteen found myself with this old man I really don't know.

So where does it come from? For instance, this political assassin who tells one of the stories. He is going back to the grave of his victim. Would that be something you had read about, or a story that someone might have told you, or is it just something that comes into your head? Where does it come from?

That comes from my being in Sweden, and seeing that in the middle of Stockholm there was a little garden and in it is the grave of Olaf Palme, who was murdered. It is diagonally opposite outside of the tube station where he was murdered. The man who did it has never been discovered. Indeed, enquiries still pop up now and again, and there may even have been a South African involvement. Because Sweden was so anti-apartheid and he was the leader of the movement he may have been murdered by some people from the apartheid regime. But somewhere in the world the man who killed Olaf Palme is still walking around and he might be in this room now for all we know. This fascinated me. So that's where that came from.

I want to ask you about reincarnation, the idea that somewhere in the world a person still exists. There is an extraordinary series of stories at the end of the volume. It seems to me that in these stories there is a kind of moving voice that inhabits a whole series of different lives, which in themselves expose power relationships

turned upside down. I wasn't completely sure whether 'Karma' for example was a story about reincarnation, or whether it was a story about the afterlife. In the end I decided it was probably a story about the writer's imagination and how the writer's imagination works to inhabit a whole series of different lives.

No, you have it right. I am someone without any religion. I am an atheist. I don't believe in the afterlife at all. But I became interested in Buddhism and adapted the whole theory of karma to my own purpose. In one story a white couple's house is then inhabited by a black couple. The white couple are full of material ambitions to make a home that is up to their standards. The wife, as a woman, has a new kind of position that she would never have had under the apartheid system. Apartheid parliaments had about two women. For the white couple, the woman becomes caught up in corruption and so they have to leave that house, and then you get a new wave of people with ambitions coming in. The black family moves in. So it fascinated me to show how class now seems to be so important. There are divisions now between people who were all one. They were all oppressed South Africans but now there is a rift. Some have taken the opportunities that have come to them and have socially and economically moved up.

I want to take you back to the idea of the voice of the author which goes through all these fragmentary narratives. You say you have no religion and you don't believe in an afterlife or in reincarnation. Is there some sense of a unified collective unconscious here, a vision that the writer is not an isolated imagination but taps into stories which are somehow out there?

I think so. What is a writer? To be a writer, what is the essential quality? Unusual perception and observation; a lot of it comes from childhood. Having your ears open to hear what people say. Looking at people and really seeing what they say and how they move and sensing also what they haven't said. That is your training.

28

Ngugi wa Thiong'o
with
Harish Trivedi

Ngugi wa Thiong'o was born in 1938 in Limuru, Kenya and educated in Uganda and the University of Leeds. His early novels Weep Not, Child *(1964),* The River Between *(1965) and* A Grain of Wheat *(1967) explored traditional Kenyan society and the impact of colonialism on it, while with* Petals of Blood *(1977) he began to show a more explicit political concern with neo-colonialism. As a teacher in the Department of English at the University of Nairobi, he called in 1968 for the abolition of that department as a step towards cultural decolonization, a theme he has developed in essays collected in* Decolonising the Mind *(1986) and* Moving the Centre *(1993). In 1977 he was detained for a year without trial in a maximum security prison, where he began to write his next novel in his native language Gikuyu,* Devil on the Cross *(published in Gikuyu 1980, in English 1982). On a visit to Britain in 1982 to promote this novel, Ngugi went into exile. All copies of his next novel,* Matigari *(published in Gikuyu 1987, in English 1989 and translated by Wangui wa Goro, who was also present during this interview) were seized in Kenya and an attempt was even made to arrest its fictional hero.*

For many years now Ngugi wa Thiong'o has argued that African literature should be written in African languages. He has been professor at Yale University and at New York University and is now director of the International Centre for Writing and Translation at the University of

California at Irvine. In this interview, conducted at a conference on cross-cultural translation held at the University of London, Ngugi talked to Professor Harish Trivedi, a distinguished critic.

Harish Trivedi You have probably been the most radical of all the Third World, postcolonial writers that we have read in English. You have constantly advocated a trenchant agenda on decolonization, conducted a campaign against neo-colonialism and even against what you call 'self-colonization', and you've been a tremendous model and influence. I would like you to talk specifically about the role of language, bilingualism and translation. You have had a career in two parts: the first, when you were writing as James Ngugi, in English, what you called the 'Afro-Saxon novel', and the second, when you began writing as Ngugi wa Thiong'o and wrote in Gikuyu what you call the 'African novel'. What caused the move from one to the other?

Ngugi wa Thiong'o I wrote *Weep Not, Child, A River Between* and *A Grain of Wheat* and published the three novels under the name James Ngugi. James is the name which I acquired when I was baptized into Christianity in primary school, but later I came to reject the name because I saw it as part of the colonial naming system when Africans were taken as slaves to America and given the names of the plantation owners. When a slave was bought by Smith, that slave was renamed Smith; the same thing was later transferred to the colony. It meant that if an African was baptized, as evidence of his new self or the new identity he was given an English name. Not just a biblical, but a biblical and *English* name. It was a symbolic replacing of one identity with another. When I realized that, I began to reject the name James and to reconnect myself to my African name which was given at birth, and that's Ngugi wa Thiong'o, meaning Ngugi, son of Thiong.

Does the word Ngugi mean anything?

It means work, hard work.

Was the move from one identity to another connected with the controversy regarding *Petals of Blood* and your imprisonment after that?

No, I rejected the name in 1979 and whenever my books were reissued I asked the publishers to use the name Ngugi wa Thiong'o. Now you could argue that this was in some ways the beginning of my questioning of the whole naming system – including language – because language after all is a naming system. We use language to name our environment and to name reality and so, from being called James to using English as a way of naming my own world was really the same thing.

In the Book of Genesis, at the beginning of Creation, Adam names each object and that's what it becomes.

Exactly. I had been questioning this, and after the publication of *Petals of Blood* in July 1977 the question of language came up in a big way for by that time something important had happened to me. I started working in a village called Kamiriithu, in a centre which later was called the Kamiriithu Community Education and Cultural Centre. And because I was working in this community, the question of language became no longer an abstraction – something you just think about mentally – but something which now demanded a practical response. The work we did in the village obviously had to be done in an African language, in this case the Gikuyu language. And then we did a play together in Gikuyu, *Ngaahika Ndeenda*, or *I'll Marry When I Want*. And it was really a turning point when the play was closed down by top government officials – the Moi regime, the Kenyatta-Moi regime – on 16 November 1977 and I was imprisoned from 31 December 1977 to 12 December 1978 – for a year. And it was when I was in prison that I made one of the most important decisions in my life, that I would continue writing in the very language which had been the reason for my incarceration.

You have worked with the community and chosen to use the language of the community but you began as a student and then as a teacher of English literature. Did you find that you experienced, initially, some kind of distance, some kind of alienation – because of your colonial education – from your own community when you went back to it?

There are two things: first of all, let's face it, English literature is a great literature and the English language carries many important critical and intellectual traditions. So to come into contact with English is to come into contact with something both negative and positive, and the positive has as much to offer as any product of any other language. There are many great English writers – Conrad, Jane Austen, Shakespeare, Dickens, George Eliot – and that tradition is very important. But nevertheless, important as it is, it does not really reflect the human condition as expressed in the actualities of my history, and of my environment. It was really when I came into contact with the novels written by African writers – Peter Abrahams, Chinua Achebe – and most importantly the Caribbean novel – I'm thinking of the work of George Lamming – that I felt that he was reflecting a world which was familiar to me. He was talking about a colonial world and the colonial world was really my world. This recognition was very, very important to me.

In linguistics there is a theory that any language reflects the world-view of its speakers; that what they can say – what they can even think of – is determined and delimited by the language. Would you say that there are things in Gikuyu that you could never have said in English, or are now saying very differently?

I'd say it's a case of saying them differently. Each language has its own capacity, its own possibilities. As I said, English is a great language but so is the Gikuyu language, so is Hindi, so is Gujarati, so is Yoruba, so is Igbo – they are all great languages. What colonialism did was to make us think of English as somehow *the* language and make us think less of our own languages. In other words, it was colonialism which gave us this hierarchical arrangement of languages where some languages seemed higher than the others. Every language carries a memory bank of the experiences, the feelings, the history of a given community and culture. As an African when I'm writing in the English language, I'm actually – ironically – also drawing on that experience of my language equally. And what I'm doing in reality is taking away from the Gikuyu language to enrich English. So when I'm writing in Gikuyu, I'm really exploiting the possibilities of that language and I have found it very, very liberating for me in expressing my environment.

In that connection there is a particular strand in postcolonial theory that argues that postcolonial writing by its very nature is translation because when postcolonial writers write in English, they are mentally, subconsciously always translating from their own native language. Do you think that that is properly to be called 'translation'?

It is definitely translation. When I wrote *The River Between*, which is about a Kenyan community's initial encounter with colonialism, that community speaks the Gikuyu language, and what they are thinking about – their land, the effect of colonialism – they are really thinking in the Gikuyu language. So when I write about the impact of colonialism on characters who are the products of their culture and I make them speak in English to capture their lives and thoughts, I must be translating – doing a mental translation. It is very true of all writers who are writing about one community, or about characters who are the product of one culture, in another language. I would say that my novels – *The River Between*, *Weep Not, Child* – are mental translations. What happens in that process is that there is an original text which should have been there but which is lost. But when you have a true translation, you do actually have two texts. Now in the case of *Weep Not, Child*, *The River Between* and *A Grain of Wheat*, that original text is not there.

Have your early novels been translated back into Gikuyu?

No, not yet. I am involved in the work of the International Centre of Writing and Translation where we are talking about restoration concerning the whole of Africa. Some of the best products of the intellectuals and artists from the communities who have been trained in English draw their strength, their stamina if you like, from their languages. But what's happening is that the original text is now lost to English. English gains, the language from which they draw loses. So we are saying that we are not interfering with those texts as they are, but we are asking: 'Why don't we try to focus on restoration?' For example, in the case of Wole Soyinka, who writes in English, why shouldn't his texts be available in other languages – in Gikuyu, Zulu, Igbo, in all those other African languages. When I talk about the original I don't mean that the writer, for example Wole Soyinka, should write in Yoruba – he writes in English and that was his choice. But what I'm saying is that through translation we can actually restore languages.

Speaking of this kind of restoration, Vikram Seth in his preface to the Hindi translation of *A Suitable Boy* says two wonderful things: one, that his novel would now be available in the language that he heard resonate in his own ears as he was writing it in English, and two, that now, even some of the characters in the novel would be able to read it.

Exactly! That actually sums up the whole situation very well! So, it is not just me; all over the world we can focus on promoting this idea and it can become a programme, rather than just one writer here and there.

I was struck by your formulation in a recent lecture of yours that translation should be seen as a 'conversation' rather than as 'dictation' by one language to another. But as you have just implied, translation as conversation rests on an assumption of equality between the two languages. Now, given the dire asymmetry in all

kinds of relations between the West and the rest, is such an assumption well founded?

It isn't now, but our assumption expresses this idea and also puts an accent on translation not as dictation, not one-way traffic if you like. We're grouping languages into what we call dominant languages, which obviously are mostly located in Europe, English for example, and marginalized languages, which are *marginalized* but not *marginal*, and we envisage focusing on a model where there is conversation among marginal languages. Let me give you the example of Gujarati, Yoruba, Zulu, Igbo. Where is that kind of conversation among them? But we also want conversation between marginalized languages as a whole and dominant languages, such as English. So it becomes a multi-lateral or a multi-sided kind of conversation. In this case, given that asymmetry you were talking about, and given the fact that for historical reasons there may not be any two people who can simultaneously converse in say Yoruba, Igbo and Gujarati, we must pose a different question in order to challenge English, so that the dominant languages *enable* and do not *disable* the marginalized languages. If you look at the past, it is true that English enabled intellectuals to express their own genius and culture. But by enabling it also disabled because these intellectuals and artists from the Third World did not have a platform where they could express their languages and their cultures. When we say enabling without disabling, what we mean is that we now can use English to enable a conversation between Yoruba and Zulu – using English as a meeting point between two languages and then translating them into each other.

But do you think that as English becomes increasingly a global and dominant language, it will enable our own local languages more or actually disable them?

If you don't ask the right questions you will disable them even more. When we say that we challenge a dominant language to enable without disabling, translation in that multisided sense is definitely one of the answers.

I'm not sure I get this. Yoruba and Gujarati translated into each other will enrich and enable both Yoruba and Gujarati. But if Yoruba translated into English is translated into Gujarati then I think both may be serving the cause of English rather better and becoming subservient all over again.

We can't wait until we have scholars who know both Gujarati and Yoruba.

I thought every shopkeeper in Nairobi would know both Gujarati and Gikuyu?

No, no. The idea is obviously for people to be able to talk to each other directly, and there is no substitute for that. But I'm saying that where that is not possible, then you can use English as a meeting point. In that case you are using it to enable rather than disable, because what it is doing is enabling a conversation between Zulu and Yoruba. You might have a combination of a Gikuyu scholar and a Hindi scholar coming together and using English as a medium through which to talk to each other.

May I ask you about your own practice as a translator? You are a busy man and are yourself a creative writer, so why did you decide to translate your own work, to write it twice over?

I have gone through three kinds of experiences here. One was of translating my own work, auto-translation, and another of having it translated by someone else. I translated *Devil on the Cross* into English myself, but *Matigari* was translated by Wangui wa Goro. And then finally, with my new novel, *Wizard of the Crow*, I've done my own translation. First of all, because of the debate going on about African languages and English, it was very important to me to ensure that there was not only an original text in the case of *Devil on the Cross* but also an English text, to prove and to show that when one writes in an African language, one is not invisible to other communities such as the English-speaking communities. So it was very important for me to have that text available in English even if it meant writing it twice over, first originally and then in translation. I found translating it very interesting and as I said, even when writing *The River Between* and *Weep Not, Child*, there was a kind of mental translation going on anyway. My new novel *Wizard of the Crow* is a huge work which I have been writing every single day since May 1997 – about two thousand pages in double space. I have attempted among other things many innovations in language in that novel and I was working so closely with a translator that I thought I might as well do it myself! But the ideal for me is to write in Gikuyu and have my works translated by somebody else.

Are there any texts of yours which are only in the Gikuyu language?

Not just now, but there is a journal which I edit called *Mutiiri* and it is entirely in Gikuyu and we have now had seven issues of it. This means that now we have a platform which has seen the emergence of many Gikuyu-language writers. I'm hoping that what is being done with the Gikuyu language can be done with other African languages.

Are there any other Gikuyu writers who are translated into English and have international visibility?

Not translated, but there are other Gikuyu writers.

Were there any major Gikuyu novelists before you?

Not in the Gikuyu language. It was my decision to write in Gikuyu.

So, you were the founder of the Gikuyu novel!

[*Laughs*] What I would seriously say is that my decision was very important in creating that possibility, but even more important has been the journal *Mutiiri*, which has functioned in the same way that journals have functioned internationally. We now have more women writers in Gikuyu and we have writers who were previously writing in English but are now writing in Gikuyu. I am thinking of someone like Gitahi Gititi, who found his voice as a poet in the Gikuyu language and does really incredible things; he is brilliant. I think of writers like Waithera Mbuthia, who has now blossomed in the Gikuyu language.

I remember I was quite thrilled when I first read about your intention to stop writing in English and to write in Gikuyu – and then I found that your first novel in Gikuyu, *Caitaani Mutharaba-ini* [*Devil on the Cross*] was published in Nairobi by Heinemann! So Heinemann publishes you in English and Heinemann also publishes you in Gikuyu. You seem to be between the devil and the deep blue sea, for your Gikuyu publisher is still a metropolitan Western publisher!

No, actually in this case, although it was the same publisher, they had a branch in Nairobi, Heinemann Kenya, who published me. It was very important that these metropolitan publishers did publish in African languages.

But Heinemann in Nairobi publish mostly in English, don't they?

Yes, they do and they publish very little in Gikuyu, but the venture of publishing in Gikuyu language has continued, and they have continued to publish in African languages although publishing in English is still the dominant trend. I think they have shown how a publishing house can publish in the African languages.

Are there other publishers in Nairobi publishing only or mainly in Gikuyu?

No, not so far. What's missing is publishers who are willing to publish in Gikuyu and other African languages.

May I ask you to comment on an aspect of your life and career which in postcolonial studies has been called 'translation'? For example, Rushdie says, 'We are translated men', meaning not only translation between languages, but using the etymological sense of 'translation', of travelling across from his home country to a Western country – and in that sense he says he is a translated man. This kind of 'translation' is often used to mean exile, being forced to live outside one's country. But again, isn't there a difference between a writer like Rushdie who lives abroad by choice and someone like you who had to leave home for reasons of personal safety? Do you think of yourself as a 'translated' man in exile?

No, I don't think of myself as a translated man. . . . I think of myself more as a *transported* man [*laughter*]. What is the meaning of living in exile? There is of course willing exile and forced exile. But there is another sense in which writers who live in the Third World live in exile – by writing in English or French. And as I argue in *Moving the Centre*, they have an exiled or alienated relationship with their culture and language, and that is a much deeper exile than a physical one. The problem of exile is being forced away from the location of inspiration. A writer feeds on what he encounters – in a market place, in public transport, in a religious centre. So for me it is very hard that I have been taken away from the Gikuyu-language environment. I have been deprived of that and I need that contact. But there are also some positives. I have always tried to reconnect and the result of that continuous attempt is the journal *Mutiiri*, which has had an effect on writing within Kenya and on my own writing of *Wizard of the Crow*.

Finally, looking back, you started writing with a strikingly radical agenda some forty years ago, which caused excitement and hope in people who read literature all over the Third World. Now,

forced out of your country, reconnected with Gikuyu but deprived of a Gikuyu-speaking community, and generally looking at the way the world is going – globalization, neo-colonization, the emergence of America as an even greater superpower than ever before – what do you think is the extent to which that agenda or vision you had has been fulfilled or is likely to be fulfilled?

With globalization, as with every phenomenon in history, there are always negatives and positives. The globalization of technology, the global reach, also brings possibilities for ordinary working people to contact each other across national lines. Now intellectuals from Asia and Africa can communicate about the problems of the South much more easily than ever before. So it is not all negative.

Is there an element of paradox here that such hope is being nurtured through institutional location and support in what we regarded as the greatest neo-colonial power? You are after all based at the University of California at Irvine.

Everything has its own contradictions and it's just a case of what aspect of the contradiction you want to highlight. It was always there. The leaders of the anti-colonial movement – where were they educated? Gandhi for instance was called to the bar at Gray's Inn in London. Jomo Kenyatta, Kwame Nkrumah – they were all educated in colleges founded by the colonial authority in Africa and some were educated in colleges abroad. What is important is the connection between phenomena. Wherever I am I look for connections. I don't say to myself, 'Now I am in America and there is no connection between America and Kenya.'

Have the political circumstances and other factors improved enough in Kenya for you to think of going back?

Yes. I wish to state this categorically: as from December 2002, I am no longer in exile. We have a new government and the old Moi regime is no longer there; the conditions that forced me into exile are no longer there.

Are you contemplating going back to Kenya at any stage?

Yes, next year; I'm going there next year.

But not to live there?

Not permanently. I have a job at the University in California unless something crops up in Kenya.

29

Monica Ali
with
Diran Adebayo

Diran Adebayo talks with Monica Ali, who was hailed by the press as the 'new Zadie Smith' when her first novel, Brick Lane, *was published in 2003. In this interview Monica Ali discusses the experience of writing her first novel. Adebayo and Ali were students together at Oxford; however, their views on the craft of writing as well as the position of the mixed-race or black writer in Britain differ considerably. Adebayo began his career as a journalist for the* Voice *newspaper before writing* Some Kind of Black *(which won the Saga Prize) in 1996. His second novel,* My Once Upon A Time, *appeared in 2000. Ali is currently working on a new novel; Adebayo is writing a screenplay,* Burnt, *for Film Four and a novel,* The Ballad of Dizzy and Miss P.*

Diran Adebayo Did you always want to write?

Monica Ali No. It started after I had my first child, who's now coming up to five. I began to write when he was about a year old. You know that Cyril Connolly dictum about the pram in the hallway being the enemy of creativity? I don't know if it had any meaning for other writers but it certainly wasn't the case for me. I think there's some kind of correlation for me between creating and physically creating. . . . I had this sense of wonder that if I could do it, it would make me feel my strength. In a way, I found it quite liberating. Another point: babies are so over-whelming, or I found them to be so, that I felt the need to carve out a mental space of my own. Writing was one way of doing that. When I had children I just became so busy – every second of the day was filled up – when I did have a spare minute I made the most of the time and worked more productively. I also felt the need to preserve stories for the kids, some of the stories that my father handed down to me. I think I wanted to keep them for the next generation, so in a mixture of ways children had a bearing.

It still seems like a strange thing to embark upon, a long novel when you've only got an hour here or there to spare.

Well, I didn't start on the novel until I had my second child. I had a toddler, a two-year-old, and I was nursing a baby, so yeah, it did seem a bit mad.

You didn't think about writing short stories or . . .

I started out writing short stories but I decided short stories weren't my thing. I wanted to do something else.

Internet sites for writers – do you want to talk about those at all?

That's how I started. There are lots of sites for would-be writers and they range from basic (basically e-mail lists), to really quite grand multimedia, all-singing-all-dancing sites like the one Francis Ford Coppola put his name to. So I found some groups. But what was good about a couple of them is that you could submit a short story anonym-ously; you could critique other people's stories and they could critique yours. What I found useful was not so much getting critique for my work as critiquing others because if something doesn't work you're forced to think about why it doesn't work. It's a kind of rough and ready training in craft.

I wondered what you found most useful to you as a writer. From the age of twelve or thirteen I knew I wanted to be a writer and I kept my first writer's notebook to jot down little phrases or even just note good lines from other books or whatever. Already from twelve I had this self-conscious thing about being a writer so I began reading books from the point of view of writing them. Neither of us did English at university but when I was at school if I found a style I liked, I felt I could mimic that style quite easily. Do you find that?

I don't think I've tried. It would be interesting to see. I think I'm a good reader. I don't understand how people can hope to be good writers without being good readers.

Do you think that's one of the key things in writing?

Well, if it were that simple [*laughs*]. I think it's one prerequisite but knowing how to read doesn't mean you can write. And if people knew what that extra ingredient was you could make a fortune.

You did Politics, Philosophy and Economics at university, I did law, but before that and I'm sure during that time, we both carried on reading. Speaking for myself, there were an awful lot of main-stream people like P. G. Wodehouse, Beckett, Sartre, Ian Fleming I read as well as a number of other books by black and Asian authors. Was it the same for you? What did you read in your younger years?

Well, I went through phases. I had Russian periods, I liked Tolstoy and I read Dostoevsky. I have just started reading *Anna Karenina* again, a translation done a couple of years ago – a very good one. Then I went through a French phase and read Flaubert, and Zola. I reread Zola two or three years ago and I could see how as an adolescent girl I'd been so into those books. There's a passionate climax on virtually every page! And it's so melodramatic, I was so bowled over by them, I remember being totally taken out of myself. And then . . . a Jane Austen fetish and a Thomas Hardy fetish. I had all sorts of manias for different people.

Were there any other authors outside that 'Western canon' if you like whose books you read?

R. K. Narayan. He was my father's favourite. He introduced him to me when I was young, and he is still comfort reading for me. So I can pick up R. K. Narayan's *The English Teacher* [1945] or *Swami and Friends* [1935] any time. I really love those books, that kind of audacious simplicity which I'd love to be able to do. I know you were asking earlier, can you mimic, can you emulate? Well, I could on the surface but I'd know that it was not me, it was somebody else's style.

Do you read your own book *Brick Lane*?

Well, I don't really read it. I have two bits I read out when I have to do readings. There's nothing better to make you hate your own work than to have to read it out!

Who do you feel is in there in terms of other writers who have gone before?

I don't know, probably each and every one of them in some way. I don't really give any thought to it. I've heard some writers say that they can't read any fiction while they're writing for fear that they're going to be influenced by its style and I don't understand that reasoning. If you're going to be influenced by a style it will happen whether you read it three months or three years ago. It's not like I've forgotten every book that I've ever read when I start writing. It's not as though I could deliberately try and copy or deliberately try and remove each and every influence. You are what you are at the time that you're writing.

When I'm writing a book, I like to read books in the style I'm writing in, the style I'm trying to hit. With the book I'm doing now, *The Ballad of Dizzy and Miss P*, I'm trying to hit quite a 'quick' style. It's partly a girl's diary and I'm trying to move in quick sections between this girl's perspective and the other main character so I've been reading quite a few books like Charles Bukowski's *Post Office* [1971]. Somehow I want to be in the modern age, you know, quick, quick, quick! I would say *Brick Lane* feels in some ways like a relatively traditional novel. I mean like a nineteenth-century or eighteenth-century book, you know a big family story of birth, marriage, death . . .

Yes, it's a good old-fashioned narrative.

Ballard has been saying for some time that the age of the novel in terms of the eighteenth- or nineteenth-century tradition is almost done. He's been saying that for a while, in terms of the short time that people have these days. In an ever swiftly moving universe, do they not want quicker books?

Well that doesn't seem to be borne out by . . .

. . . the sales! [*laughs*]

There's not much need to construct an academic argument because people vote with their feet in the bookshops. It doesn't mean there's a trend towards big books either. I saw an article not long ago in one of the broadsheets that asked what is it about all these big fat books people have suddenly started writing? It showed a picture of all these books stacked up. I thought, 'What the hell are they on about? Have they never read any Tolstoy or Dickens?' The problem with any of these theories is that it's usually much more messy and complicated a picture. It depends who is writing and in what way and what appeals to whom. I don't see any straight lines on the grass. I see messy Venn diagrams.

You were saying before that you could perhaps see many different writers in your book *Brick Lane* but no one whose particular influence stands out?

I think the reader thinks lots of different things. People have pointed to all kinds of different writers ranging from Flaubert, to Dickens, to Naipaul, even Austen you know. It's all fine and flattering but I don't think that it's valuable for me to spend time thinking about it really. The books that I really loved when I was turned on to reading in early adolescence, the books which I used to hang off the end of my bed reading with the blood rushing to my head . . . I think if I have any intention it's to create something similar in terms of a reading experience. I mean you write the books you want to read yourself. That's what I want to do. And I write from character as well. I have no investment in my presence on the page.

Because it's other characters you're talking about and it's mainly about exploring those other people?

Right. But at the same time, because all authors have egos of course, it does take an enormous amount of discipline not to indulge oneself.

Knowing you as I do, I could get very little sense of what you're about from *Brick Lane*, which is a tribute to you because it means you've made all your characters three-dimensional and see everything from their point of view. There's often a satiric vibe but that still doesn't necessarily tell you where Monica is coming from. Do you think that's fair?

Well, I would hope that that's the case because I want to let the characters speak and breathe for themselves. And if I'm having a good day, then ideally I'm not in the room when I'm writing. I'm not there. I don't know how that process really works for others and I'd like to explore that, how *you* actually go about writing. When I was writing

Brick Lane, I was writing in a state of such tiredness that I think I almost lost some rational abilities in making sure the plot didn't fall down and so on . . . but not the actual creative stream. I found it quite helpful in a way, maybe in the way other writers write drunk or high, I wrote sort of completely fatigued [*laughs*]. How do you go about it?

There are usually things on my mind. You want to explore things that are bugging you.

To come back to what you were saying before about my own presence in the book. Yes certainly, I was writing about things I'd thought about for a long time. I was drawing on my own childhood, not in a way that was particularly autobiographical in any straightforward way, but it was there.

Yes, there are always issues with which one struggles. For me maybe it's issues around identity. I'm sure you have similar things. You know, children of immigrants; where do I fit in? Who should I look to for my values, the values of the old country and my parents, the values of this mainly white British society, the values of those who look like me in this society . . . these are things I struggle with emotionally. So one's almost looking for characters to illustrate that. I find that the business of constructing a novel is often a bit more like puzzle solving, more mathematical than it is artistic.

Do you articulate those things to yourself before you start writing?

I do, yes. I could write down eight or ten words for the way I want a book to be. Maybe a bit naughty, kind of tragicomic, intense . . . I know I want the book to inhabit a kind of mood.

I could never articulate that to myself when I was writing *Brick Lane* and I can't now that I'm planning the next book because I'm terrified that it will fix things in aspic.

But for me that wouldn't fix things in aspic – it just helps to know when you're on track. Otherwise you don't know what to leave in and what to take out. When you know the vibe of the book, the themes you want to explore, you know what to talk about in a situation.

It's interesting that you're able to be so ordered about it.

I know what's going to happen in every chapter of the book before I start. There's almost a thesis and the book is all about the development or the contradiction of that thesis. Maybe 'thesis' is the wrong word. There are just themes you want to explore.

I guess it's just a question of gradation really. I know what I want to write about in the next book but I run scared from articulating those themes to myself. I run away if somebody asks me. I know what they are but I would never put them into a sentence because I'm appalled at the thought that I'm going to marshal everything from those ideas and not from the characters.

But you make up the characters!

This next book – some days I think I've got the whole thing in my head and the next day I wake up and I think that it is just a mirage. You want to build a cathedral but you've only ever seen a mud hut in your entire life. How do you ever get to that conception and hold the whole thing in your head at once? They're two different things, chapter planning and holding the whole thing in its entirety.

When I think I've got the book, I have an idea of the themes and the characters who are going to explore them but I mainly start with the story. But for me it's more about voice. To be honest, what I mainly like about writing is hitting a certain voice. The plot, the story is almost just something you have to do. When I know I've got the book

is when I have a few sentences in my head that capture the style that I want for the book. It's the same way I love listening to music. I hear the rhythms, I hear the kind of line that I want and am inspired. Often it's music that gives me the rhythm that makes me think I've got the voice and that gets me to the page. Is it like that for you?

I don't know because I've only written one book [*laughs*]. I certainly don't do the same thing with music. I suppose I know I've got a character when I start hearing the voices in my head – when I can sort of feel them in that way as if they're in the room. Otherwise, if it's more mechanistic then I know I've got to think again.

Are you at all worried at the moment in terms of the second book? Is the creative process the same as for the first book and is that something that gives you comfort?

The honest answer is I don't know whether the creative process is the same or not. I've just done a short story for a short-story collection and now I'm trying to get into the next book. Getting back to writing is the prize, the big prize at the end of all this other stuff I've had to do. And that's what's gratifying; to sit in a room and stare at a blank wall for some part of the day is my definition of the 'good life'.

I mean that given that you have just done something that's worked for you in one book, are you at all worried that it might not work for the second novel?

Ask me again when I'm closer to the writing of it. I'm sure it won't work in the same way. I doubt if two books could be written in the same way and this already doesn't feel like quite the same experience.

The last three or four years have seen a rise in the profile of South Asian cultural works, both on television with the success of *Goodness Gracious Me*, *The Kumars at No. 42*, figures like Meera Syal,

and of course your own work. Do you think that things are much better in Britain now in terms of works by non-white writers which are picked up in the mainstream? Is this significant or is it a fashion? How do you see your own work within that wider context?

There are fashions in everything, including in publishing. So for example when Helen Fielding came out with *Bridget Jones's Diary* [1996] there seemed to be a slew of 'chick lit' and people following on the coat-tails of that. It's partly something to do with the Zeitgeist. It's probably to do with changing social climes. It's partly to do with publishers deciding, 'OK, let's try to cash in on this, there's money to be made.' And I don't know, I haven't read any of those books but I presume some of them are better than others, some of them would have made it on their own terms and others wouldn't have. So, sadly, there are trends in publishing like everything else. I do think though that there's something more interesting going on in terms of British Asian or black writing which is perhaps a reflection of a reality, that as the second or third generation, we're getting into our stride.

Coming of age?

We're gaining more confidence. We have a different perspective, we have stories to tell, personal stories about migration and displacement, sometimes with an immigrant narrative but which have enough wider resonance. I know, for example, that *Brick Lane* sold in Czech, Lithuanian, all sorts of different languages where there are no Bangladeshi immigrant populations because new works breathe new life into what are essential human questions about the way we exist and the way we find our place in the world. The truth is that we're here to stay and we're not about to go away whether other people like it or not. There's also the fact that a lot of the energy in contemporary writing today has not just come from black and Asian writers in Britain but from people outside, like Coetzee. That's an interesting dynamic too.

One of the things I have felt – I don't know if you did when we were at Oxford University – is that there were a lot of people there who could write because they'd read a lot of books. They'd had a good education and so on. But I also felt that a lot of our white contemporaries were struggling to find something to write about, something different. When I was younger and wondered 'Will I ever get published?' I used to think that in a way I was in a good position because, like everyone else I'd read Latin, P. G. Wodehouse, Shakespeare and all that stuff . . . but there were also things from my own background, stories that hadn't been told before. There's always been that kind of double-consciousness thing in British society where we have to understand the world through white people's eyes but we've also got another point of view. I always felt that was a huge advantage to me as a writer. Sometimes I think a number of our white contemporaries struggle with that issue and to some degree they retreat into games, into postmodernism, the sorts of things that basically cover up a lack of things to write about. Your book wasn't postmodern, it was traditional, in that sense it was modern. It has all the ingredients of realist fiction, from centuries back. In the West they say that 'history' has ended, in the sense there is only one story to tell, but often I feel that, actually, many histories are still in the making for other people. I wondered if you felt that this was an advantage for you? That there have been lots and lots of stories but maybe it's possible now to tell universal truths from a different angle that's been less explored?

There is something in what you're saying. However I'm also interested in how people have received this book given some of the examples which you cited earlier – you know the idea of something like *Bombay Dreams* and aren't we all living in a lovely multicultural melting pot now. Well, that isn't the picture I paint in the book and that's not how I see it happening. That's not a reality, at least not for the people about whom I'm writing. What's interesting to me is that people are prepared to see this other side of Britain and recognize that it is a world apart but it's part of what makes England now. I think it's also interesting that people are sort of surprised at what's actually on their doorstep and that they can relate it back to their own feelings about family. For instance, there are many people I've talked to who are not from that background who have said, 'So and so is just like my father.'

It seems from what you're saying and the way that people have received your book that readers have been prepared to learn universal lessons from your writing. This has always seemed to me to be one of the most difficult struggles for black and Asian writers – to get people to take universal lessons in love or whatever from black or Asian products. *Brick Lane* is full of Asian characters and my second book was entirely black. I was trying to say, 'Look, if I create an all-black universe, will you take universal lessons from this?' I wonder how you feel about that, whether you feel that the success of your book is that people will take universal lessons from it or whether they will only if it's written in a particular way?

That's interesting. I read London journalists saying, 'It opened up a whole new world that I didn't know about that was so fascinating', and I think, 'Well, if you were so interested, it was always there on your doorstep and there have been other things written about it.' I don't actually think that's why they enjoyed the book. I think the fact that people will be reading it in Polish and all those other languages does say something about the real reason why some people relate to it. I wrote it simply to tell those stories.

30

Abdulrazak Gurnah

with

Susheila Nasta

Since his migration to Britain in 1968, Abdulrazak Gurnah has become known both as an important writer of fiction and as a critic and reviewer of African literature. Born in Zanzibar in 1948, Gurnah's arrival coincided with the heyday of Sergeant Pepper *and was only months before Enoch Powell was to deliver his now notoriously xenophobic 'Rivers of Blood' speeches. From the publication of his first novel in 1987, Gurnah explored the theme of the migrant's displacement, asking what happens 'to people who are in every respect part of a place, but who neither feel part of a place, nor are regarded as being part of a place'. In his early novels –* Memory of Departure *(1987),* Pilgrim's Way *(1988) and* Dottie *(1990) – the focus was primarily on questions of the unhomeliness of place as well as the political and social changes which have caused such huge demographic shifts in the late twentieth-century world.* Paradise, *his fourth novel, was shortlisted for the Booker Prize in 1994 and is set in East Africa in the decade before the outbreak of the First World War. It presents the reader with a number of different and competing stories which not only interrogate standard European versions of history but also complicate the strategic nationalisms of some earlier fictions by African writers.*

Whereas Gurnah's early novels are more explicitly concerned with the physical realities of displacement and the negotiation of questions of race and identity in Britain, his later novels – Admiring Silence *(1996) and* By the Sea *(2001)* – *dwell more on figures who carry their worlds 'within' in an interior landscape built from stories, memories and the unreliability of imagined recollections. By the Sea, his latest novel, juxtaposes the story of an asylum seeker with that of a migrant intellectual. In exposing the discontinuities between two very different narratives of modern displacement, positions which are so often conflated in easy celebrations of the migrant as twentieth-century Everyman, Gurnah seems to be moving into an area explored more extensively in films like Stephen Frears's* Dirty Pretty Things *(2002) as he disturbs the apparently seamless voyeurism of that controversial form, the 'postcolonial exotic'.*

Susheila Nasta In the past twenty years you've published six novels which deal with questions of history, migrancy and survival. These are books which cross between many cultural worlds and frequently shift locations – whether set in Britain, East Africa or both. You left Zanzibar in 1968 – yet it seems that you are still drawing on the stories and voices of that past, reconstructing memories within the realities of the present. Would you start by saying something about your obvious fascination with storytelling and the recreation of voices from history?

Abdulrazak Gurnah It didn't begin like that. I suppose it began from a sense of being loose or adrift. Though in the process of wanting to write about that you go back to things you remember. It's memory that becomes the source and your subject, or should I say, *things* that you remember. You don't always remember accurately and you begin to recall things you didn't even know you remembered. Sometimes such gaps are filled in so convincingly that they become something 'real' as opposed to something constructed. In that way the stories take on a life of their own; they develop their own logic and coherence. At first it might seem like this is a bit of a lie; in reality what you are doing is reconstructing yourself in the light of things that you remember.

In fact your first novel, *Memory of Departure*, suggests just this. I want to go back to the beginning of your writing career, to that journey you made from one world to another, and ask you whether such memories of departure and your experience of arrival in Britain – a place you've elsewhere called 'a strange land' – prompted the writing of that first novel. Were you already writing before you left 'home' or did the experience of Britain in the 1960s jolt you into the writing of fiction?

It was definitely the experience of England that did it, which is not to say I wasn't writing before, but it wasn't *writing*. In other words, I wasn't thinking of it as writing. It was just a thing I did. I didn't immediately think I would write. It was just the reality of being in England and finding that I had begun to write. I think of *Memory of Departure* very much as the novel where I learnt the important difference between writing things down and *writing*, the process of constructing ideas in fiction.

That's interesting because that book resonates for me with much of your later work: the germs of things which come up later even in a book like *Paradise*, your fourth novel. Do you see any links between these works? *Paradise* clearly deals with a different time – set in East Africa between 1890 and 1914 whereas *Memory of Departure* is much later in the 1960s – but there seem to be correspondences in mood. Was there anything that carried over between these two books?

Writers always have a pretty small patch of ground on which they do their work. They just cover it again and again from slightly different positions. They don't do this out of choice. It's simply that the things which engage us, worry us, keep recurring. Even if you think you can suppress them, these concerns resurface. They represent the ways in which the writer thinks and sometimes even form one. So there is always this unfinished business carrying on from one book to another.

I think Jean Rhys said when talking of her novels that 'four rooms and an attic are like life itself'. I am not saying her experience of displacement as a white Creole woman from Dominica adrift in London and Paris in the 1930s and 1940s is in any sense the same as yours, but is there a sense in which all writers create specific rooms or an imaginative space within their fictions that they remain preoccupied with?

Yes, sure. Specifically, in this case, the things that interested me in *Memory of Departure* were grown-up things, if you know what I mean. I wasn't just writing out of personal experience. I was thinking about the place, the society, the experience of living there. It's not surprising that those ideas should continue, whereas if you're writing primarily out of autobiographical experience, it's possible that the material becomes something you want to leave behind rather than something you want to continue with.

Your time in Britain has spanned a significant period of cultural and political history in that the late 1960s coincided with the period of Enoch Powell and his notoriously xenophobic 'Rivers of Blood' speeches. Now, the focus is on issues of asylum and refugees, a subject dealt with in *By the Sea*. Having been a part of this history written about some of these things from the perspective of the 'outsider' in *Pilgrim's Way* and *Dottie*, would you say that things have changed? Or are politicians today still talking about the same issues – race, immigration or a misplaced patriotism – but couched in different words, disguised with different labels?

Things have changed but that doesn't necessarily mean that things have got better, by which I don't mean that whatever 'nastiness' used to take place in the street still takes place in the same way today. But everybody has changed. Some things have become clearer, some things have become harder too. As far as non-European people are concerned, the public has become more 'civilized': whatever they think, they've learned not to just blurt it out and be explicitly abusive or whatever. There is a real sense now of being able to live in a society where people have rights, a right to courtesy as well as legal rights. So in that respect, things have changed. But in the sense of what the world is today, I'm not so sure. Otherwise things like the current imperialisms that are taking place in the Middle East would be harder to do.

And do the same stereotypes keep coming up?

Yes. In this respect it seems to me that empire has certainly not finished. It is still a reassuring and self-comforting view of the world. It still amazes me that the way people think and talk about Britain is somehow separated from the way they deal with the rest of the world.

Some of your early novels which were set mainly in Britain explicitly address issues of race and immigration and attempt to break down reductive stereotypes, rather like Sam Selvon was doing in the 1950s with his classic novel *The Lonely Londoners* [1956]. In *Dottie* you focus on the positive elements of mixed race and in *Pilgrim's Way* the central character, Daud, is an 'alien' attempting to negotiate modes of survival in a strange land. You haven't really addressed that kind of theme in quite the same way in your later works *Admiring Silence* or *By the Sea*. Do you feel you've said enough about that kind of experience, or was it something that preoccupied you at the time?

It's a flattering comparison ... Sam Selvon. It's not that I'm finished with it. In all the books that I've written, I've always been interested in the issue of people negotiating their 'identities'. I suppose at one point I thought this was intensified for people dislocated from their place of origin. I've always been interested in exploring the idea that people remake themselves, reshape themselves. In the first books this seemed to be what I was most interested in. That people come from so far away, to a place like Europe, and have to change or transform. They have no choice; you can't continue as you are.

And then several years later I went on a trip . . . I hadn't been back for a long time, because of all the political restrictions and problems and so on. I think it was out of going back after such a long time that my attention shifted. It didn't do so immediately. The first time I had gone back 'home' was in 1984 and I hadn't published anything at all. So it wasn't that immediately after my return I thought, 'Oh my god, I must think again', but by the time I wrote *Paradise* – something like six or so years later – I went back again and travelled around for longer. When I came back from that trip, I wrote *Paradise*. I suppose from that moment onwards I have been interested in the condition of the migrant in a different way. Whereas before England was the foreground – at least, in *Pilgrim's Way* and *Dottie* – in the works following, the foreground is altered. It becomes an interior landscape where it doesn't matter quite as much where you are for the negotiations go on inside. The outside world is not irrelevant, but it is not quite so central. So it's that sense of people carrying their worlds *within* them that I became interested in. It's not so much that I thought, 'OK, that earlier subject is over', but the lens shifted – although, as you know, in both *Admiring Silence* and *By the Sea* you still have characters who are constantly shuttling back and forth in terms of the ways in which their stories travel.

One of the characters in *Admiring Silence* talks about England as 'disappointed love'. That phrase has always struck me as enormously evocative of the migrant condition.

Yes, and it is an idea which keeps recurring – at least in the later books. I keep thinking that the feeling at the base of this sense of dislocation is disappointment. Disappointed love describes it because it's not simply a question of a disillusionment with England. It's also disappointment with the self, disappointment with how the displaced person has been able to cope with the experience. It's disappointed desires as much as a sense of disappointed realities.

You implied earlier that stories of migrancy or displacement are one of the major stories of our times. I want to ask you if you think this particular story, which has been a preoccupation with many others at the end of the twentieth and early twenty-first centuries, is really any more the 'story of our times' now than it was at any other time? Don't you think narratives and stories have always travelled, always crossed worlds even if people just didn't recognize the potentiality of such crossings?

The sum of the movement in the world in the last century has completely shifted weight and direction. And if you look over the century preceding that, the sum total is that millions of people leave Europe to go somewhere else. They go to understand other worlds and bring back news of the world. Of course they do this through empire and imperialism. What the colonial cultures and people think about those accounts of them is not important because the focus, the emphasis has been in Europe, in the West. So what's known by the West constitutes knowledge, it doesn't matter what those 'others' think they know. Yet, when I say 'the story of our times', I am referring to a reversal of this movement. There is a much more visible movement now, from 'out there' into Europe. This has brought the need to listen to the stories of these people. Whereas before stories would be told *about them*, now their own stories have to be heard. *They* are *here*; they're your neighbours, they're doing drugs in your streets or working in your hospitals. So 'the story of our times' can no longer be sealed in a controllable kind of narrative. The narrative has slipped out of the hands of those who had control of it before. These new stories unsettle previous understandings.

Many other writers today are trying to write across these 'controlled' worlds as you have called them, which have always been dominated by rather myopic or narrow systems of judgement. In the past books were often produced and written in one place, whereas now they seem to derive from many places, from many different influences and cultures – though that plurality was there, if not acknowledged, in earlier centuries too.

Sure. It is an ongoing process. One of the remarkable things about it, however, is that we constantly realize how little we know and how much more there is to know. It also makes us realize how accessible other knowledges are. Whereas without those kinds of raised voices coming from other directions, things often seem unreachable, impossible to understand, or at least to understand in any kind of subtle or complex way. Then you read things by others which give you access – even if one's understanding is slight – to different ways of thinking and understanding. In that sense the world actually becomes a smaller place where we can make connections and which is more and more understandable.

Apart from being a successful writer of fiction you are well known as a literary critic, particularly as a commentator on writing from Africa. In some of your critical essays on figures such as Chinua Achebe or Ngugi, you've talked about an earlier phase in 'African' literature which preceded your work, a phase which focused on questions of nationalism and decolonization and was concerned with the representation of an unsullied pre-colonial world. I am over-simplifying highly complex issues here, but why have you critiqued that kind of position?

I don't really mean to be critical in taking up a position that says there was something crude about representing pre-colonial society as only troubled in minor ways but largely working fine. You can understand why that representation happened – just before or just after independence – in the face of a colonial onslaught which lasted for centuries; in the aftermath of that onslaught of ridicule, of contempt. Independence however was crucial to this too. There was a desire for a progressive ethos that says, 'This is how we unify', 'This is how we come together to respect ourselves.' And after come these rather powerful but

nonetheless crude, it seems to me, fictions. Crude, because they sim-
plify the true complexity and difficulties of the negotiations that had to
take place for what were, in many cases, unstable societies to live alongside each other. And you couldn't get anything much more complicated
than the coast of East Africa where I grew up. So I thought, 'This is just
not true.' On the other hand the idea of a pre-colonial homogeneity
comes in very useful politically – to new nationalist or to new African
governments which say, 'Everyone who is not like me or like us is a
stranger, is marginal to the real political, authentic citizen.' Many
African societies have used this as a way of expelling and tormenting, in
Uganda for example, with Idi Amin, and in Zanzibar. So the idea of
who belongs then becomes one that is made into an essentialist
question. One is made into a certain kind of 'African' so when you ask
the question 'What is an African?' an African becomes somebody 'who
looks like me'. Not someone who has some kind of citizen rights to the
place. So these two things made me uncomfortable with some of these
fictions.

**Because of the way crude divisions continued to be set up between
people?**

Yes. Making it seem that a citizen could be described in terms of their
appearance or in terms of their claimed or, in some cases, foisted ancestry. Even if you didn't claim this ancestry, you were given it whether
you wanted it or not. I felt it was necessary in books like *Paradise* to
perhaps complicate the vision. I thought it was necessary to try and
write and see how it might have worked if you portrayed a society that
was actually fragmented. Fragmented doesn't mean that it doesn't
work. It just means that it worked in a different way. So I wanted to
write about a world that had always been fragmented but manages still
to have something approaching civic and social life.

**In *Paradise* you portray ways in which the mixed racial groups living
within that society create their own racial stereotypes of others. So**

you're opening up both from within and without the reductive oppositions which occur between white, black, colonizer, colonized, Muslim, Christian and all those kind of stark and often reductive ways of distinguishing people.

Yes. By saying this I am not trying to suggest that what was there before was admirable. It was simply that it worked. In fact, if anything in *Paradise*, I tried to suggest that such a complicated balancing act between different societies – the very reason that the coastal regions are so vulnerable when European imperialism comes – is because the society is already at full stretch. All sorts of cruelties existed within it which it can't account for even to itself. Cruelties against women, cruelties against children, cruelties against those people that you see as weak, as every society does. This is not to be too harsh on any one group. I didn't simply want to say, 'Look, it worked before the European colonial encounter' but instead, 'Look how hard it had to try to work and look at the kind of things it had to do to make itself work.'

So you basically wanted to open up the contradictory legacies of the whole historical context of coastal East Africa?

Correct. If you don't show the complexity of what precedes then you're not going to be in any position to understand the complexity of today.

As a writer and a critic you've obviously read and been influenced by a number of writers. Was there anyone especially you read at a formative time that influenced you? Derek Walcott seems to be one. The essay you wrote recently for *Moving Worlds*, 'An Idea of the Past', draws on a similar sense of history to Walcott, the idea of a truly revolutionary literature not being the literature of 'recrimination or despair'. Do you want to say something about the role of literature as politics or the function of literature in a modern 'postcolonial' context?

It's so easy for writing to become some kind of an axe, a tool that can be wielded rather brutally at times to silence this one or to make that one speak. Whenever people ask me to speak on this matter, I say I only represent myself. I don't speak for anybody else. But it's very easy for writing to be made to speak for other people and this is especially so if people feel they have a grievance, that there's something to address and that there's a way it should be addressed. I think writing performs the opposite function. It should actually say there isn't a simple way of dealing with this. It should be about what cannot be easily said. Walcott is a very challenging writer for he shows us this. More importantly, he makes it clear that you cannot reduce people's humanity by simply putting them on this side or that, white or black or somewhere in between. I like very much the sense of his being a 'world writer', a writer who sees himself as belonging to a wider world. He is not alone; he follows a great tradition of others; these things are not new. In the past, there was always a kind of a hierarchy, so what was meant by 'world' was 'Europe'. Now we know that this is not the case. The 'world' that Walcott is talking about, or the 'world' that I'm thinking of, or even people like Salman Rushdie or Caryl Phillips and others are thinking about, is not that 'world'. T. S. Eliot's world of 'tradition' as Eliot meant it at the time – and he was *of his time*, to be fair to him – was a world of European tradition. Now we have writers who come from a wider world. I am part of that.

Well, as the Indian writer Mulk Raj Anand once said, and Salman Rushdie takes up a similar idea in his collection *Haroun and the Sea of Stories* [1990], the great stories of the world have always been drawn from a large reservoir, 'an ocean of stories'. These stories have always circulated and moved across different worlds, creating links and correspondences.

Absolutely.

One final question which is to do with the reception of your work. You were shortlisted for the Booker Prize in 1994 with *Paradise*. There's quite an interesting division between critics who have taken up the novel in a kind of voyeuristic way as a form of 'postcolonial exotic' and those who have read it more carefully. If one looks at reviews of your work before the Booker, many of your novels got slotted into certain kinds of other predictable categories. I wondered whether you think the prize-winning culture in the literary world today has had a significant impact on reading habits or whether it is simply because people are just reading more openly?

I think that prizes do make a difference. The first difference is that your book is reviewed more. It's reviewed more widely but it's also reviewed differently. It's not reviewed as genre writing of some kind. Then you find new readers and that is what counts. I don't say that to be 'right on'. Seriously, it counts because once you find new readers the work is read by different reviewers; it's spoken about differently.

And that, if I may say, is why magazines such as *Wasafiri* are so important – that a lot of writers don't get seen or reviewed seriously until they make that break and get taken seriously in that wider literary world. Maybe some of these writers aren't very good and that's just the way things are. That's always been the case.

What you say is completely true. There are still many writers who don't receive the attention they deserve. To be honest I think every writer probably feels this at some point and to some degree. The answer is just to stick it out; you can't write and worry about these things.

31

Marina Warner

with

Robert Fraser

Marina Warner is among Britain's most distinguished novelists and imaginatively eclectic critics of culture and literature. Daughter of an Italian Roman Catholic mother and of a bookseller father whose antecedents included several imperial servants in the Caribbean, she read French and Italian at Oxford, and her essays include studies of Les Liaisons Dangereuses, Manon Lescaut and Shakespeare. In her Clarendon Lectures and Reith Lectures, and in books such as From the Beast to the Blonde (1994), she has challenged the ways in which we read, write and think about narrative, and her own fiction comprises five novels and two volumes of short stories. She has also recently collected her fugitive critical pieces into a volume entitled Signs and Wonders: essays on literature and culture (2003).

    I met Warner in January 2004, shortly after her return from a three-month stint as a research fellow at the Italian Academy in Columbia on the recommendation of the late Edward W. Said. Making my way past her discarded Christmas tree, I was greeted at her house in Kentish Town with anecdotes and Assam tea. I wanted to find out more about the use of particular historical sources in her novels, and so I began by taking her back to the composition a decade ago of Indigo (1992), a reworking of the plot of Shakespeare's The Tempest set in the seventeenth and twentieth centuries, and in the Caribbean, Paris and London.

Robert Fraser I'd like to start by talking about a couple of documents. The first is your great-uncle Aucher's history of the Warner family, which features the seventeenth-century Sir Thomas Warner, the first British governor of the West Indies. I notice that in Aucher's narrative there's a member of the family called 'Indian' Warner, son of Thomas by a Carib woman, though he's not in the pedigree provided at the front of the book. It's as if, genealogically speaking, he doesn't exist.

Marina Warner His grave, of course, is not known either. He was actually named Thomas, but because his father was Thomas Warner he was distinguished by being called 'Indian' Warner. But the story is extraordinary, and also much less predictable than the later phase of colonialism and imperialism, because Indian Warner became the British-appointed governor of Dominica, and his half-brother Philip, by Thomas Warner's English wife who had come out to the Caribbean, governor of Barbados. So the two half-brothers, one half-Carib and the other English, actually governed these two islands at the same time. And they got involved in the conflict with the French, and found themselves on opposite sides. The British settlers in Barbados complained that Thomas 'Indian' Warner was allowing Caribs on Dominica to raid their island, carry off women and burn houses. There was a battle, and afterwards a parley on Philip Warner's boat under a flag of truce, and 'Indian' Warner was massacred with his embassy. Anybody who knows the buccaneering history of the early empire will recognize features of this bloody conflict. But what is unexpected from our point of view is that Philip was taken to London and tried for murder, on the grounds of having killed his brother under a flag of truce. There was a huge petition mounted – of the kind that one saw later in the eighteenth century – by the colonists of Barbados to get their governor off this charge of murder.

And he was let off the hook?

He was found guilty, but he wasn't hanged, just deprived of office and disgraced. It was a capital charge but he wasn't executed. But the interesting point is that 'Indian' Warner was considered to be the legitimate governor of his island, whereas in the later period when slavery had taken root and really established itself, you would never have had a Carib governor of any island, even if he'd been the natural son of a governor. He would not have been appointed; that didn't happen under slavery. And people were not shipped back to England to be tried for the murder of somebody who was considered a 'native'. Something had changed. I wrote about this in one of the essays in *Signs and Wonders* called 'Siren/Hyphen; or "The Maid Beguiled"'. There's a gender implication in it, but I was very gripped by how one mustn't think of the prejudices and oppressions within slavery as being anything other than produced by precise historical circumstances. They were not given factors in the least. One can't say that enough because people sometimes feel that racism is biologically given and that people will oppress others whom they see as belonging to a different group. They will do so in certain social and political and economic circumstances. We must resist those.

Presumably you read all this history up when you were researching *Indigo*, but were these facts generally known in the Warner family? Or had they been suppressed or conveniently reinterpreted?

Well, the whole connection to the Caribbean was only really conducted to us through cricket, which was a total distortion. My grandfather, Sir Pelham or 'Plum' Warner, was the captain of the England team and then became the president of the MCC [Marylebone Cricket Club], so he was a grand and much-loved figure in English cricket after the war. My father was quite old when I was born, and his father was quite old when he was born, so the age gaps are very long. So I have a grandfather who played cricket in the nineteenth century, quite unusual in some ways. So history came through the skewed lens of the cricketing connection: the empire and cricket combined. One of the first places I went so as to look at this history more closely was C. L. R. James, whose work and thinking in *Beyond a Boundary* [1962] lies behind my attempts at replacing cricket within the history of imperial relations in *Indigo*, where I turn it into another game called 'Flinders' after a line in Ted Hughes, another cricket enthusiast: 'my bat all to flinders'. It's a word that means splinters, and somehow that fitted too. I altered the game because I wanted to make it an allegory of the original battle that had conquered the emblematic island in my book. I also wanted to show that the game ritualizes and orchestrates the old relations of power and conquest. But a lot of people wanted it to be real cricket.

There's another document I'd like to mention: the charter given by Charles I to Thomas Warner in around 1620 as governor of what we'd now call the Leeward Islands. A copy of it was in the family during your childhood. I think you say it was hanging above the fireplace?

Yes, we had a copy. It's a rather remarkable piece of painting by Dutch artists who worked at the College of Arms in the seventeenth century here in London. It's really very beautiful, and it has wonderful, wonderful sea monsters on it; beautiful curly-tusked sort of white whales and things, and so I used all those as imagery.

Presumably the imperial connection – and the charter – were regarded by your father as matters of legitimate pride.

Well, yes. My father was born in 1907 and he had the mindset and the attitudes of a very traditional English gentleman, though he was very cosmopolitan in his tastes and reading, and had lived abroad a lot and spoke several languages. I sometimes see people like him in St James's still. For him it wasn't something that you questioned or challenged, this connection to colonialism. I was deeply upset by this. I mean, in the 1960s I used to be a great rebel against him, and I was and am very much at odds with my background. There are difficulties on both sides of a family of this sort. I would love to be the child of post-war radicals [*laughs*].

But in that case you wouldn't be a radical yourself. You'd probably have become a reactionary, wouldn't you?

No, I think not. I met some impressive second-generation radicals in America recently. Some of the radicals themselves have become renegades of course, but when they haven't they're the only people left in America who are really trying to keep a civic society going, as I see it. Anyway, I was dealt a very interesting hand by fate, one fraught with all kinds of problems. It has been, I suppose, my writing life to try and look at those. But I don't think I could have expected my father to be different really, given that he was the child of a cricketer [*laughs*]. I was deeply distressed when I began looking deeper into this history to find the kind of things the Warners had been involved with in the past, which was just straightforward Caribbean planter history, nothing particularly special, but nevertheless difficult to deal with.

It's surely almost impossible to write the history of any English family without hitting that bedrock sooner or later. How do you look at it now?

Indigo was more involved with the idea of reparation and examination of conscience than I am ten years later. Nowadays I'm much more interested – and I think *Wasafiri* is much more interested – in giving an account rather than expiation. To think of the past as of some kind of transgression which must be expiated in a classic manner isn't really very helpful and also, as you probably gathered from my Amnesty lecture 'Who's Sorry Now?' [the coda to *Signs and Wonders*], I think there's some seeking of virtue in breast-beating, which I also reject. Because I struggle with Catholicism I'm also keenly aware of the uses of guilt. But I am interested in giving a richer account of what took place, and the form that that takes for me nowadays is how we evolved in symbiosis – not in the model of a dialectical oppression of colonized and colonizer, oppressed and oppressor, but how the kinds of society we now live in were made together. How much was taken on both sides, and how much was bonded. Not so much the history of oppression and power relations which have been discussed very well by many people, but this particular cultural enrichment which took place and which is, I think, visible and at the same time invisible, and needs to be explored further.

In your own case, how is the expedition proceeding?

Well, I've tried to push back the dates and to start thinking about what happened at the very end of the fifteenth century, the first encounter with the new world. One of the things I did a very short piece on was how native pharmacopoeia altered the relationships with drugs, states of trance and narcotics. There's an essay in *Signs and Wonders* on Shakespeare's *Cymbeline*, and I got very caught up in the imagery of trance and other states, created in *Cymbeline* through smells. There are tremendous, extended metaphors about changing minds, dream-states caused by smelling things. *Cymbeline* was written very soon after *The Tempest*, and there's no reason to imagine that Shakespeare read a set of books for *The Tempest* and then forgot all about them; they could easily have been at the back of his mind. Early material on the New World and on the Caribbean contains lots of stuff on medical and healing rituals that take place with drugs and with local plants, particularly with infusions taken by nose, not a practice in Europe at the time. Tobacco is a kind of narcotic that had immeasurable influence on the psyche, and that again hasn't been investigated as well as it might.

Another aspect of this symbiosis is myth: mythic borrowing, parallels and affinities. Since nineteenth-century anthropologists started looking at the problem comparatively, we have all come to recognize an international treasure house of mythology: the same stories keep recurring, in the Caribbean, in Africa, in India, in Latin

America. Myth seems to play an important role in all your writing.
Do you regard it as a healing element?

I'm not very keen on myth as healing because it has very dangerous
effects too. Myth itself is morally neutral. It's the way myth is applied. It
can have a healing effect, but I think it's a little bit like saying, 'Does
literature have a healing effect?' – I mean, roughly speaking, literature
has a healing effect because without literature we would be much
depleted. But myth has power. That's why it's important. Myth has the
power to influence and structure our fantasy, and in my view we live via
this very complicated faculty, the faculty we loosely call imagination. I
believe strongly that we do not learn empirically except through what
we already know through imagination. When we experience something
we experience it through the language, through the metaphors, through
the images and through the stories that we already know. It is very
difficult to go out into the street, perceive and understand the street,
except through the narrative structures that we already have. The
materials you interpret, the people you see, the gestures they make, the
facial expressions they have, the way they look, even the shapes of the
trees, and the colours of . . . birds and flowers, somehow need to pass
through the grid of what has already been known. From childhood on,
much of our experience is happening only in our heads. And it's in our
heads that these things take place, these images, these metaphors, and
not just stories, I think stories provide important structures. At the
moment we're completely caught in the combat of good and evil myth.
We've lost myths of transformation and restoration, and we're into
myths of conflict. *The Lord of the Rings* and many of the dominant
stories currently contain this apocalyptic encounter between good and
evil. It comes up in the language of politics, in the language of the
current Iraqi war and other conflicts, and in the whole idea of a war on
terrorism.

There's an essay in *Signs and Wonders* about the role of the *conteuse* as opposed to the *conteur*, and of course you have a *conteuse*

character in *Indigo*. Is it part of your position that women tell different kinds of stories from men, or tell stories in different ways?

I think storytellers tell stories according to their circumstances. And it's still the case that women occupy different roles in society linked to different needs, and they are much more associated, all over the world, with children. I was talking earlier of how children learn structures, and how the imagination is formed; that has been very closely connected to women's work. Not so much now, that link has rather been severed. I'm not particularly mourning it, but it was a feature of storytelling that was aimed at children of both sexes by women thinking about survival, resources. In *From the Beast to the Blonde* and *No Go the Bogeyman* [1998], my books about fear and survival, I show that a lot of these stories are not just about healing as self-protecting, but that self-protecting can sometimes be totally interpenetrated with hostility. In *No Go the Bogeyman* there's a lot about how people structure strangers to ward them off, to expel them.

And men tell different kinds of stories? Stories of celebration, perpetuation and power?

For equivalent reasons, men tell different stories. You have Homeric epic on the one hand, and lyric Sappho on the other. So I think the tripartite anthropological structure is quite useful: sovereignty, priesthood and fertility as the three dominant zones of society that must be cared for and prolonged. On the whole, sovereignty and priesthood have been more in the power of men in Western society, though not so much in societies outside of Western society, where priesthood, in particular, has been female, in Africa and Asia, in Greece to some extent too. But fertility, the future of children, has been women's chief source of authority in society. These are very complicated issues but stories of sovereignty comprise military authority and priesthood, the priestly controlling of sacred texts: the Koran and the

Bible. 'Let women keep silence in the churches' – St Paul's stricture – is a very good example of the priesthood at work.

Though, as you yourself concede, the nuns in the convent where you were educated were anything but docile. Or silent.

Yes, indeed, that's true.

Have Caribbean writers helped you to reinterpret your history? When you were writing *Indigo*, for instance, did you learn from Caribbean literature?

Well I tried to read quite a lot of it. Certainly Derek Walcott was a great influence on me, the way he tangles with his personal history and the history of the islands, and how he deals with British culture and Western culture, how he makes it his own. That's a very exemplary move to make, not so much through retaliation or dialectic as metamorphosis. I did love *Omeros* [1990], and I've loved a lot of his other work too. I just saw his early play *Dream on Monkey Mountain* [1970] in New York. It was on at 141st Street in a small studio theatre in Harlem, put on by the Classical Theater of Harlem. By pure chance I came across Derek Walcott himself at the opening of Isaac Julien's film *Baltimore* [2003]. So we went together and it was a marvellous production, with fantastic zest and power in the acting, especially André de Shields as the hero – the prophetic old man Makak – as well as terrific percussion and music. I thought the play had these wonderful layers in it. It was obviously written at a moment of black power politics, very modulated, already very nuanced, so it was like seeing Aimé Césaire's *Une tempête* [1968], but seeing it with hindsight, in America at a new time of crisis. So it was like looking backwards, so it had extraordinary complex emotions attached to it, of hope, and sorrow, and a heroic moment passed. I was delighted to see it.

You talked to me a while back about *The Leto Bundle* [2001] and your attempts to write colour blind. Could you expand on that a bit?

I am quite taken up by the idea that race was a category invented by slave owners in the eighteenth century pretty much, and that we continue to deploy these categories at our peril. In a sense I would prefer to return to the colour-blind world of Hellenistic literature. Whether you read a Greek romance like Apuleuis's *The Golden Ass*, which takes place in North Africa in the second century CE, or whether you read Augustine's *Confessions*, people are not described in racial terms. Those were simply not the qualities of a person that writers of the period were interested in evoking. They were interested in whether they were villainous or virtuous, male or female.

I agree about St Augustine, who was presumably a Berber, but we're no longer in Hellenistic times. Isn't it a wee bit utopian to think you can recapture that innocence now?

Well, I was interested in this exercise, and I heard that Toni Morrison had written an early short story and had posted it on the web. It's a technique she also uses in *Paradise* [1998]. In her case she does it because she's writing black history for black readers. She's written, of course, in *Playing in the Dark* [1992], that so much black presence in literature is posted there for the benefit of the white reader, and she doesn't like these categories being made visible for the benefit of whites feeling better about themselves. As very many black writers have pointed out, why should black writers have to signal their characters as black when no white writer signals their characters as white? Anyway, that's one starting point. So Morrison creates situations of great complexity and perplexity that challenge the reader. In the beginning of *Paradise*, when the posse goes in to the convent and shoots the women, one of them is white, we are told, but you never learn which. This creates a feeling of dislocation and an unsettled rhythm throughout the novel. You're made to think about it; you're challenged, your presuppositions are kept in check because she isn't letting you off the hook. In a sense that's what I wanted to do. I wanted to engage my readers too. They're having to see how their own structures of othering are working.

Presumably you can't abolish colour-consciousness from the point of view of your characters, though you can obviate it in your own perspective as narrator.

Yes. In a sentence like 'He came into the room and saw this beautiful black woman in the corner', it's the narrator speaking, bringing in his (or her) baggage of preconceptions. I leave all such ascriptions to my characters, and Leto for example keeps changing in their eyes as a result because at different times different features become salient and significant. So it is the author who's colour blind. I'm not using that range of description myself, not making them available to myself. Caz Phillips has also worked in this vein. Even in the eighteenth century you don't get descriptions of physical appearance either. The famous example is *Manon Lescaut* [1731], which is all about her beauty and her effect on men, and we never learn what she looks like at all. The colour of her eyes is never described, nor the colour of her hair. It sounds so strange to us, but obviously the Abbé Prévoste thought he could write a novel about somebody without describing her physically in that way.

And do you think you can get back that state of consciousness? How do you approach the problem, say, in *The Leto Bundle*, where you take a fugitive and her children through many times and places?

That book's about the ways in which people are seen as strangers, the modes of exclusion we use to keep them out, how barriers are drawn up. At different times they operate in different ways. One of the means by which we exclude people now is through race, and I thought it would be interesting to abolish that category and see what happens. To give you an example of how I handle it in the book, when Leto has stowed away on the ship, she's discovered and brought above to meet the collector of antiquarian valuables who sees her as this dreadful, smelly, feral, stinking creature. He sees her as a figure of dirt; she is seen only through his eyes.

What are you writing now?

I'm writing a study of spirits and technology. And it begins with wax-works and ends with ectoplasm. There is an element which is very important and which is interconnected with the mercantile system and the expansion of Western influence. It's about the way, as I remarked just now, that we were 'made together'. Roger Luckhurst in his book *The Invention of Telepathy* [2002] also says this, and you say something about it in your book on Sir James Frazer. Long-range communications made this imperial adventure possible, and also emphasized the curiosity or desire to find spiritual explanations. In the encounter with so many cultures that were settled, either by the British or by other empires, different belief systems were discovered. A book like *The Golden Bough* [1890–1915] is a product of that, of becoming interested in different worlds of magic and the supernatural. So many home-grown quests for spirits and spiritual activity, so many Victorian explorations of these themes, are profoundly tinged by animism, or by Hindu beliefs in reincarnation: African, Indian and Caribbean influences.

Among the Contributors

Diran Adebayo was a journalist on the *Voice* newspaper and worked in television as a researcher and producer before his book *Some Kind of Black* (winner of the Saga Prize and the Betty Trask Award) was published in 1996. His second novel, *My Once Upon A Time*, appeared in 2000. He is currently working on a screenplay, *Burnt*, for Film Four and a novel, *The Ballard of Dizzy and Miss P*. Adebayo lives in north London.

Maggie Ann Bowers is a lecturer at the University of Portsmouth, where she teaches postcolonial and American literature. She previously taught at the University of Antwerp, Belgium, where she co-edited a collection of essays, *Convergences and Interferences*. Her forthcoming book is on magic(al) realism.

Fred D'Aguiar trained as a psychiatric nurse before reading African and Caribbean literature at the University of Kent. His first collection of poems, *Mama Dot*, was published in 1985 and he was awarded the Guyana National Poetry Prize for *Airy Hall* (1989). His first novel, *The Longest Memory* (1994), won the David Higham and Whitbread First Novel Award. D'Aguiar's work has been adapted for television and performed in theatres in London. He is currently professor of creative writing at the University of Miami. He published his fourth novel, *Bethany Bettany*, in 2003.

Denise deCaires Narain is a senior lecturer in the School of Humanities at the University of Sussex. She has published widely on Caribbean women's writing and her book, *Contemporary Caribbean Women's Writing: making style*, was published in 2001. Following a Leverhulme Research Fellowship in 2002, she is working on a study of contemporary postcolonial women's writing. She was judge of the Guyana Fiction Prize in 2003 and is a member of the advisory board of *Wasafiri*.

Richard Dyer is Managing Editor of *Wasafiri*, London correspondent for *Contemporary* magazine and assistant editor of *Third Text*. He is a widely published art critic, reviewer, poet and writer. He has authored, with Peter Woller, a book on the artist Jason Brooks and on the performance and video artist Tina Kean titled *Electronic Shadows: the art of Tina Kean* (2004).

Robert Fraser is the author of several monographs, including studies of Sir James Frazer, Proust, Victorian quest literature and postcolonial fiction. His critical portrait of Ben Okri, *Towards the Invisible City* (2002), was described in *Wasafiri* as 'poetic psychobiography' and *The Chameleon Poet* (2002), his life of George Barker, became a *Spectator* book of the year. He is currently a senior research fellow at the Open University and is working on a history of the biographical form. He is one of the contributing editors to *Wasafiri*.

Fernando Galván is Professor of English literature at the University of Alcalá, Madrid, Spain. He co-edited *Mary Wollstonecraft and Her World* (1998), and his recent publications include the following editions: *On Writing (and) Race in Contemporary Britain* (1999) and *(Mis)Representations: intersections of culture and power* (2003). He has also translated and edited Samuel Richardson's *Pamela* (1999), Daniel Defoe's *Robinson Crusoe* (2000) and Milton's *Paradise Lost* (2003).

Gretchen Holbrook Gerzina is author of *Carrington: A Life* (1989) and *Black London* (1996), and is editor of *Black Victorians/Black Victoriana* (1999). She hosts the nationally syndicated US radio programme *The Book Show* which interviews authors on their recent books. She is

Professor of English and Director of Pan-African Studies at Barnard College, Columbia University, and in 2004, two more of her books will appear: *Frances Hodgson Burnett: the unexpected life of the author of* The Secret Garden and *Bijah and Lucy: love in the time of colonial slavery.*

Aamer Hussein was born in Pakistan and moved to Britain in the 1960s. His first collection of short stories, *A Mirror to the Sun,* was published in 1993. Since then he has produced several other collections of stories: *This Other Salt* (1999), *Cactus Town and Other Stories* (2002) and *Turquoise* (2002). He is a well-known reviewer and literary critic and a member of the *Wasafiri* editorial board. Hussein has also published translations of Urdu poetry and fiction in English and was one of the judges in 2002 of the Independent Foreign Fiction Prize. In 2000 he co-edited *Hoops of Fire: fifty years of fiction by Pakistani women* (2000). Currently the Royal Literary Fund writing fellow at Imperial College and Fellow of the Royal Society of Literature, he is working on his fourth collection of short stories.

Maya Jaggi, formerly Literary Editor of *Third World Quarterly,* is feature writer and lead reviewer on international literature for the *Guardian* newspaper. She has twice been named national newspaper writer of the year in the Race in the Media Awards (1996 and 1998) and feature writer of the year in the EMMA awards (1998 and 1999). Some of her literary profiles appear in *Lives and Works* (2002). Judge of several literary prizes, most recently the Commonwealth Writers Prize, 2004, she is one of the members of *Wasafiri*'s advisory board.

Hermione Lee is Goldsmiths Professor of English Literature at Oxford University and a fellow of New College. She is the author of numerous biographical and critical studies, editions and introductions, including books on Elizabeth Bowen, Willa Cather and Philip Roth, and an acclaimed biography of Virginia Woolf. She is currently working on a life of Edith Wharton and a collection of essays on life-writing. Well known as a reviewer, broadcaster and interviewer, she was one of the judges for the Booker Prize in 1981 and presented Channel 4's first book programme, *Book Four*, between 1982 and 1984. She continues to broadcast for BBC radio and reviews regularly for the *Observer* and the *Times Literary Supplement.* She was awarded a CBE in 2003.

Susheila Nasta is a critic, teacher, editor and broadcaster. Currently a reader in literature at the Open University, she has also taught at the universities of London and Cambridge. She has published and lectured widely in the field of contemporary twentieth-century literatures, particularly on Caribbean literature, women's writing and the fictions of the black and South Asian diasporas. As founding editor of the literary magazine *Wasafiri*, she has produced over forty issues of the magazine since 1984. She has acted as judge for a number of literary awards and is currently a member of the advisory committee for the Commonwealth Writer's Prize. Her most recent book is *Home Truths: fictions of the South Asian diaspora in Britain* (2002). Her study of Jamaica Kincaid, entitled *Writing a Life*, is due to appear in 2005.

Alastair Niven is Principal of Cumberland Lodge, Windsor, and president of English PEN. He was former director of literature at the Arts Council of Great Britain (latterly the Arts Council of England) and the British Council. Currently chair of the Commonwealth Writer's Prize Advisory Committee, he was one of the judges of the Booker in 1994. He has written several critical books, including two on D. H. Lawrence and two on Indian fiction. For thirteen years he was editor of the *Journal of Commonwealth Literature* and has been a member since 2001 of *Wasafiri*'s editorial board.

Caryl Phillips was born in St Kitts and brought up in Leeds. He now divides his time between London and New York. He is a prolific novelist, dramatist, critic and screenplay writer. As author of seven novels and three works of non-fiction, he has won many awards and accreditations for his work. His first novel, *The Final Passage* (1985), won the Malcolm X Prize for Fiction and *Crossing the River* won the James Tait Black Memorial Prize as well as being shortlisted for the

Booker in 1993. His latest novel, *A Distant Shore*, was published in 2003. Phillips is Fellow of the Royal Society of Literature and professor at Barnard College, Columbia University, New York. He is a member of the *Wasafiri* editorial board.

Minoli Salgado teaches English at the University of Sussex. She has a special interest in literature from the South Asian diaspora and has published widely in the field. Her recent essays include contributions to *British Culture of the Post-War* (2000), *A Reader's Companion to the Short Story in English* (2001) and a study of the relationship between complexity theory and diasporic literature in *Diaspora and Multi-Culturalism* (2003). She is currently working on a study of Sri Lankan literature with the support of a Leverhulme Fellowship, as well as an anthology of short stories.

Chris Searle was formerly a lecturer in educational studies at Gold-smiths College, University of London, and is a well-known educational campaigner. In 1973 he won the Martin Luther King Prize for his book *The Forsaken Lover: white words and black people*. He is author of *None But Our Words* (1998) and *Living Community, Living School* (1997).

Sudeep Sen is a poet and critic. His writing has been published in a number of international journals. His book *Postmarked India: new and selected poems* was awarded the Hawthornden Fellowship (UK) and nominated for the Pushcart Prize (USA). He has been international poet-in-residence at the Scottish Poetry Library in Edinburgh and visiting scholar at Harvard University. His most recent work, *Distracted Geographies: an archipelego of intent*, came out in 2003. He lives and works in London and New Delhi.

Mark Stein is Junior Professor for Theories of Non-European Literatures and Cultures at the University of Potsdam in Germany and Reviews Editor for *Wasafiri*. He has co-edited *Postcolonial Passages: migration and its metaphors* and *Zeitschrift für Anglistik und Amerikanistik* 49, 3 (2001), and currently has two works in preparation: *Jackie Kay* for the British Council 'Writers and their Work' series and *Black*

British Literature: novels of transformation forthcoming with University of Ohio Press.

Harish Trivedi is Professor of English at the University of Delhi and has held visiting professorships at the University of Chicago and SOAS in London. He is the author of *Colonial Transactions: English literature and India* (1993) and is co-editor of *Interrogating Postcolonialism* with Meenakshi Mukherjee (1996), *Postcolonial Translation: theory and practice* with Susan Bassnett (1999) and *Literature and Nation: Britain and India 1800–1990* (2000). He translates between Hindi and English, and was the guest editor for the translation issue of *Wasafiri* in 2003.

Nana Wilson-Tagoe is Senior Lecturer at SOAS, University of London. She has also taught in universities in Africa, the West Indies and the United States. She has received the Rockerfeller, Fulbright, Chapman and Cadbury awards for research and has published several articles and books on African literature, including *A Reader's Guide to West Indian and Black British Literature* (1988), edited with David Dabydeen, and more recently *Historical Thought and Literary Representation in West Indian Literature* (1998).